{ Coding for Kids }

Learn JavaScript

Build the

Room Adventure Game

Written by

Stephen J. Wolf, PhD

Table of Contents

To my beloved mom, who passed away while I was writing this book, thank you for all the love and support you gave me through my entire life. You taught me that I can do everything I set my mind to. You are part of all that I do, in every way. Forever, you are in my heart.

Chapter 1

Getting Started

There is a lot of information in this book. My purpose in this chapter is to introduce who I am, to discuss the flow of this book, and to explain the project we will be working on together.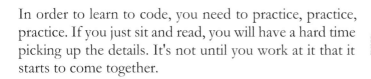

In order to learn to code, you need to practice, practice, practice. If you just sit and read, you will have a hard time picking up the details. It's not until you work at it that it starts to come together.

If you can't be at a computer when you're reading, all is not lost. You can still read through and do your best to picture the concepts and how they flow together. But, as soon as you can, put those ideas into practice. I explain a lot, so it can be wordy, but it's all meant to teach you.

Feel free to jump to the JavaScript Crash Course in Chapter 8 as a reference for whatever you need. If you just want to work on the game, go right ahead.

Happy coding!
—Dr. Wolf

1.1 About the Author

 Dr. Stephen J. Wolf has been a New York middle school science teacher since 2001. In 2006, he earned his PhD in Science Education, specializing in inquiry-based laboratory activities from Curtin University, Perth, Australia. Dr. Wolf currently teaches chemistry and physics to seventh-grade students.

All his life, Dr. Wolf showed an interest in the sciences, video games, writing, and computers. He has written several fantasy novels, including his *Red Jade* series, and he enjoys role-playing games such as *Final Fantasy* and *Dragon Quest*.

In the 1980s, he was introduced to the Commodore 64 and he learned to program in BASIC. He created projects for school and for fun, using this new technology to track bowling scores and to animate the process of metamorphosis of a caterpillar into a butterfly.

While completing his BS in Chemistry at Long Island University: C.W. Post, he took an advanced honors class in Fractals. During this class, Dr. Wolf created a program in QBasic that demonstrated aspects of the Mandelbrot Set, random walks, and bifurcating curves by having the computer draw a snow scene with these techniques.

Without a formal background in computer science, Dr. Wolf has trained himself on most concepts of programming, with the help and support of his husband, Kevin, a career software engineer who had been a principle engineer at Microsoft before creating his own consulting company, Huntington Phoenix, and releasing apps for iOS.

Dr. Wolf learned HTML in order to create a website for his students, which contains a set of class notes, organized by category. Over the years, he has improved upon the website and added better visuals and explanations to various pages. But he wasn't finished yet.

To assist his honors classes, Dr. Wolf wanted to make a program that would allow students to practice calculating heat equations. He had the logic in place and he picked up some books on C#, notably *Head First: C#* by Andrew Stellman and Jennifer Greene, and, with guidance from his husband, he was able to make a successful applet. Getting it onto the website was another matter.

Webpages can easily run JavaScript, but the applet was written in C#. Dr. Wolf then wanted to learn JavaScript so he could create applets for his website that would integrate without add-ons or conversions.

During this process in 2017, Dr. Wolf proposed a new course for his middle school students: Intro to Coding JavaScript. This meant he needed to master the concepts and create lessons for his students, so he could help them build their own learning.

This entire process, as well as many steps left out of the telling, led to the current document. This book will explain the basics of JavaScript and some HTML. We will also touch briefly upon CSS. This is not meant to be a complete compendium of JavaScript, but beginners should be able to learn enough concepts to begin their coding journey.

Dr. Wolf takes great pride in his work and he has sought to adhere to standard coding practices and conventions. But as this book is intended for newer programmers, it will not cover certain advanced concepts, such as classes, data structures, and recursive algorithms.

You will have a playable text adventure game after completing Chapter 2 and Chapter 3, but further chapters will add more features.

1.2 Acknowledgements

I would like to thank my husband, Kevin, for all his help and support as I worked through this project. From encouraging me to dive into coding again to the advice with the book, I couldn't have done this without you.

Thank you, Rochelle Deans, for all the advice with the wording and structure. Thank you also for coding the game as you edited the book, making sure everything worked and looked correct. Thank you also for the added features you suggested, which have become helpful additions for the website.

Matt Caulkins, thank you for the artwork. You took my theme from *A Shocking Journey* and adapted it for this book, bringing the characters to life once more. As I saw each character, I knew exactly where each would go.

To my students, I thank you so much for challenging me to constantly update and improve what I do every day. You inspired me to create a coding class and to develop this game in order to teach the course in an organized, cohesive way. You are my inspiration.

1.3 About this Book

This first chapter is here to help get you started. It explains where to write your code and, if needed, how to set up new files.

From there, you will do some exercises and start creating an adventure game where you walk around a house trying to fix things. The focus of this book is on building aspects of the game piece by piece in JavaScript.

Once the main game is complete, the focus will shift to improving the game experience. Additional features will be added. Changes will be made to the main code to allow for better experiences for the player.

We will also adapt the game for webpages using HTML so the final creation can be played more easily.

HTML, CSS, and JavaScript are three different languages that work together to create the web that we know today. HTML lays out the page. CSS styles it. JavaScript gives it behaviors. Our focus is on the behaviors and, later on, we will move toward the presentation pieces.

Throughout the book, I use a `specific font style` to refer to typed code, variable names, and so on. Often, these will relate to things you'll be typing in, or things you already typed in.

If you see lines of code that are indented by more than just a few spaces, that means they actually go on one whole line when you type them in.

So this:
```
var somethingRandom =
          "This is totally random!";
```

Should be typed in like this:
```
var somethingRandom = "This is totally random!";
```

All the code for the basic text version of the game is located in Section 9.1: Room Adventure — Version 1 (Text). The final code for the upgraded version of the game is in Section 9.2: Room Adventure — Version 2 (HTML). You can also find all the code on my website.

```
http://coding.stephenjwolf.com
```

The code has been tested many times. However, if you find any issues whatsoever or have suggestions for improvements or features, or if you have any questions, please notify Dr. Wolf.

```
coding@stephenjwolf.com
```

I hope you enjoy your coding adventure!

1.4 Where to Write Your Code — Using repl.it

You need a place to create your programs. There are many online sites where you can do this, but you can also code on your computer without going online. There are IDEs you can download, like JetBrains WebStorm, but these often cost money.

To run your JavaScript, you do need a browser, like Google Chrome, Apple Safari, Mozilla Firefox, or Microsoft Edge, but you don't need to be connected to the internet to test it.

Repl.it. To write code, I prefer the site `http://repl.it`. It has different programming language options and it's a great place to write and test your code. It is free to use as of this writing.

> Good tools make the job easier.

`http://repl.it` saves your work automatically and you can access it anywhere you have a web connection. This means you can write code one place and go somewhere else to continue. You can also share links to your code so others can try it, and so on. It's a great site.

I will assume you are using `http://repl.it` throughout this book, but any IDE will work. An IDE is an *Integrated Development Environment*, which is a fancy way of saying, "where I write my code." Some IDEs help you correct mistakes when you're coding.

7

Using repl.it. Go to `http://repl.it`. You need to log in to the site when you get there. If you have a Google or Facebook account, you can log in with those, or you can create a new username for yourself. Once you are logged in, find the option to create a new repl.

Choosing a language. You need to choose a language. We're coding in JavaScript, but you have two ways to select this.

Option 1. You can choose ***JavaScript*** for your language. The first half of this book focuses only on JavaScript so this option will be a great place to start.

Figure 1. A new repl, JavaScript only.

Option 2. You can choose a web project, ***HTML, CSS, JavaScript***. This gives you access to HTML, which we won't get to until much later in the book. You have to pay attention to where you're coding. You get *three files* with this option. Make sure you're always in the `index.js` file and don't touch the `index.html` file, which already has some code in it. If you accidentally delete the code inside the `index.html` file, your JavaScript won't run. You can add this line to `index.html` to make it work again.

```
<!DOCTYPE html><script src="index.js"></script>
```

We will be displaying information either in popups or in the console window. To get there, select the `console` tab on the right.

*Figure 2. **repl.it** Web Project page with index.js and console tabs selected*

Running a repl. To test your code, you need to run it. In repl.it, you can press `Ctrl-Enter` on your keyboard or click the play button ▶ on the screen.

When you do some of the exercises in this book, you will be typing directly into the console window. You may need to run the repl before the site lets you use the console window.

Console output. When you type code into a console window (in repl.it or in a browser) you often get a result of `undefined`. You can ignore it. It means that whatever you typed in did not send back a value. The `alert()` function shows a popup on the screen when you press enter, but doesn't send any information back. But if you do some math, the console will show the answer.

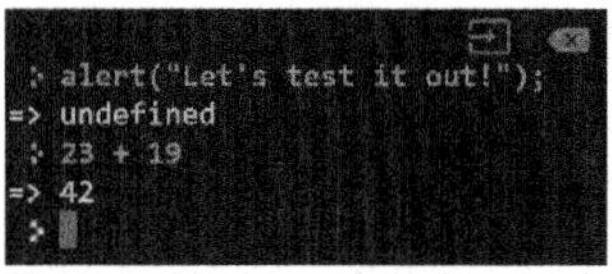

```
> alert("Let's test it out!");
=> undefined
> 23 + 19
=> 42
>
```

Figure 3. Showing undefined in a repl.it console window.

Going forward, we're using repl.it. I will assume you are using a site like **http://repl.it** that does the setup for you. You can skip Section 1.5: Basic File Setup.

Can't use repl.it? If you want to create your own files and run them in the browser, there is some setup you need to do. Check out Section 1.5: Basic File Setup for details.

1.5 Basic File Setup — Without repl.it

If you don't have access to an IDE or a website like `http://repl.it`, you can do all your coding anywhere you are. You need to use a text editor on your computer, like Notepad. There are some things you must do to get started, so here goes:

First, make a folder on your computer where you can store your files. If you're on a PC, this can be as simple as right-clicking the desktop and selecting `New > Folder`. It's the same basic process if you're using Google Drive (click `New`, then `Folder`) or something else like an iMac. Give the folder a meaningful name, like *Room Adventure Game*.

Inside the folder, create three text files. You can use a basic text editor like Notepad or a Google Doc, etc. Save them with the names: `index.html`, `index.js`, and `index.css`. You can actually call them whatever you want, but keep the file extensions (.html, .js, .css).

Set up the HTML file. There's a basic structure needed for HTML. In the HTML document, put the following:

```
<!DOCTYPE html>
<html>
  <head>
    <meta charset="utf-8">
    <meta name="viewport" content="width=device-width">
    <title>The Room Adventure</title>
    <link href="index.css" rel="stylesheet"
        type="text/css" />
  </head>
  <body>
    <script src="index.js"></script>
  </body>
</html>
```

Notice where it has **index.css** and **index.js**? If you used other filenames or paths, then put those names here instead. Watch your spelling, capitalization, and punctuation throughout.

All you need to do to test your JavaScript code is double-click your `index.html` file, which will load in your internet browser.

Test the JavaScript file. Open the `index.js` file in your text editor. Type in the following line and then save it.

```
alert("Testing!");
```

Next, run that `index.html` file and you should get a popup that says `Testing!` If so, then you're all set. You can delete the `alert` line so it doesn't run every time you test your code. If it doesn't work, then your file extensions may not be correct. They may have `.txt` after the name, which could be hidden from you. There's a way to fix it if you know how to change the view to show your file extensions. If you can't figure that part out, your other option is to try changing the filenames in the HTML to `index.js.txt` and `index.css.txt`. If your text editor uses different file extensions, then use those instead.

Remember: All your JavaScript goes into the `index.js` file and is then run with `index.html`.

What's with that index.css file? Why is it blank? Why do we need it? The truth is, until we create some webpage displays, we won't need it. However, it's a good habit to set one up right away and have it already linked to the HTML document so we can easily add to it later.

If you want to test if the CSS is working, you can type this in to the CSS file. It will change the background color of the webpage. Run `index.html` to see if it works.

```
body { background-color: lightsteelblue; }
```

Getting to a console in your browser. For what we are doing, you need access to a console window to test things out. If you're not using repl.it, then you need to use your browser's developer tools. You can find this in the menu, though it may have a slightly different name.

First try using the F12 key on your keyboard. Many browsers have that as a default shortcut key for their developer tools.

Here are some keyboard shortcuts for some of today's browsers.

Browser	Shortcut to Developer Tools
Google Chrome	Ctrl-Shift-J
Mozilla Firefox	Ctrl-Shift-K
Microsoft Edge	Ctrl-Shift-I
Opera	Ctrl-Shift-I
Apple Safari	Option-Cmd-J

Figure 4. Accessing Developer Tools in several internet browsers.

1 . 6 Our Goal — The Game Concept

Let's take a look. We are coding in JavaScript to create a small adventure game, where you travel around a house and fix things that are broken.

Along the way, you will be introduced to fundamental coding concepts and JavaScript syntax.

My goal is to teach you the concepts through example. After the game is complete, you'll have the option of adding game features and tackling some HTML and CSS to add some visual flair to the game.

The best way to learn is to practice. Follow along and type in the code samples. Try your own variations too.

Let's talk about the game itself first and what it's all about.

Game concept. Jumping into a project can be fun, but let's pause first and plan out what we are going to do. Here is our game plan, which we will be working through over the next couple of chapters.

Here's what we're building.

- You will lay out the foundation of a house.
  - Name and describe each room.
  - You don't have to use a house specifically. Any structure will do.
- In each room, there is something broken that needs to be fixed.
  - We'll call it a `brokenThing`.
- For each `brokenThing`, you need something to fix it with.
  - We will call this `fixWith`.
- Each `fixWith` item needs to be placed in a different room.
  - If you need a light bulb for a lamp in one room, you will find it somewhere else.
  - We will call this `itemFound`.
- You also need to set up the navigation. What rooms connect to the room you're in?
  - We will start with exits north, east, south, and west.
- You'll pick up items from each room and use them elsewhere.
  - These actions will happen automatically.
- Add points for each object fixed.
- The player wins when every `brokenThing` is fixed.
- Allow the player to restart the game.

The fun doesn't end!

Extensions. Once the core game is complete, there are many things we can do to improve the gameplay experience. This book will cover the following features in the order listed below. As you work down the list, the coding concepts become more advanced. You should also come up with your own ideas and see if you can implement them once you've learned the basics.

Some features we will add:
- Add alternate text for after you fix something
- Randomize the room the player starts in
- Randomize the locations each item is found in
- Randomize the point values for fixing things
- Track the player's progress through the house
- Have the player get tired and be unable to fix things
- Randomize the broken object in each room
- Increase player interactivity by having them pick up and use items instead of it being automatic
- Change the end goal by letting the player find pieces of a passcode when they fix things and using the completed passcode to escape the house
- Randomize the layout of the house
- Adapt the game for HTML
  - Allow the user to click buttons instead of typing
  - No more popups
  - Add images for rooms
  - Add styling with CSS

I designed this tutorial so most of these features can be added to the game in any order you want. A few of them rely on other features, but I'll let you know the rare times that happens.

The jump to HTML is the largest undertaking, but it breathes life into your game and makes the experience even more enjoyable for you and the player.

Why a house? I chose to use a house for the design here because we all live somewhere. It's an easy place to visualize and to work with. However, this game can easily be converted into something else.

> It's familiar and we can adapt it.

If you want a fantasy world where you find items to complete quests, you can do that. You want your player to be a space captain warping from planet to planet? Sure, why not?

Primarily, your descriptions would be different and you may want to change the wording of some of the in-game text. The rest of the game structure wouldn't change much.

Make the game your own. Use the rooms to build your skills, then adapt the game into what you want it to be.

I included some suggestions for adapting the original Room Adventure for use with a fantasy theme. If you want to see the adaption ideas early, you can check them out in Section 7.2: Change Your Game's Theme.

Chapter 2

Beginning the Adventure

As we move forward, I am going to introduce basic JavaScript concepts we will use to create an adventure game.

The beginning of this chapter includes some non-coding exercises to complete. These will help you plan out the game and/or understand how certain programming concepts work. You should try to do all the exercises.

I will sometimes show you more than one way to do something, since many problems can be solved in more than one way. You need to be flexible when you're coding because one process may not work as well for a different task.

I will walk you through a few of the basic concepts to introduce or refresh your memory of the language and then we will start putting things together. Sometimes you will be rewriting sections of code and throwing away other things altogether. This is common in programming. You should make an effort to try the different ways in order to see what works best.

Without further ado, let's get started.

2.1 Jumping in to Some Code

Let's jump
right in!

You probably want to do some coding right away, so let's do it! Then we will step back, plan the game, and get into our ultimate goal: learning to write programs.

Start a new repl in repl.it or you can run a browser's developer tools. (See Section 1.4 if you need help with these.) In repl.it, you will need to "run" the program first. Then type this into the console window for practice.

Practicing basic syntax. Syntax is how computer statements are structured. If you enter something incorrectly, you'll get an error. Go to a console window. Type in each line and press enter. Type them in the order you see below.

What to type in	What you should see
`2 + 2;`	The console shows 4 and then it says undefined
`alert("Hello there!");`	A popup shows Hello there!
`confirm("Are you ready to code?");`	A popup appears; you can click OK or Cancel
`prompt("What is 19 + 75?");`	A popup appears; you can type an answer
`alert(19 + 75);`	A popup appears and shows 94
`var whatsUp = "What's " + "up?";`	The console says undefined
`console.log(whatsUp);`	The console shows What's up? and then it shows undefined again
`45 * 19;`	The console shows 931

Errors? Did you get any `Reference Errors` or `Syntax Errors`? That means you've got a typo somewhere. Try again and check your spelling, quotes, and parentheses.

Semicolons. There is a semicolon at the end of each line. If you try typing in a line without the semicolon, it still works. JavaScript tries to read commands even if you leave certain semicolons out. However, the best practice is to leave them in and to get used to using them.

No spaces in names. One thing that's very important but easily forgotten when you're starting out: when you name things, you can't use spaces.

Here's something to remember!

Did you see the variable name, `whatsUp`? There's no apostrophe and there's no space. It's important to get this right.

CamelCase. Because we can't use spaces, some names become hard to read, like some hashtags. To link some words together for a variable or function name, keep everything lowercase, but capitalize the first letter of each new word and stick them together without spaces.

No good	Good
first rule of coding, no spaces	firstRuleOfCodingNoSpaces
#no, @punctuation!	noPunctuation
Only _ and $ are ok	Only_And$AreOk
Yay numbers 23	yayNumbers23
12 no numbers at start	no12NumbersAtStart

Figure 5. Some camelCase examples.

19

Safe symbols. The only safe symbols you can use in your variable names are an underscore ⬚ and a dollar sign $. Underscores are often used by programmers to show special variables and functions that should not be altered in the code. Dollar signs are often used by external libraries. It's not a rule, exactly, but it's a common practice. We won't use them in this book.

Practice making errors. You should see what happens if you mess up. Type these in the console window directly, one at a time.

```
aler("Yo");
2 ++ 3;
var favorite food = "pizza";
alert(testing);
myVariable var = 12;
```

You get an error for each one!
1. The first (`aler`) is not a defined function.
2. The second (`2 ++ 3`) is an incorrect way to do math.
3. The third has a variable name with two words (`favorite food`) which can be fixed with camelCase (`favoriteFood`).
4. The fourth one has an undeclared variable (`testing`). To say the word `testing`, it needs quotes: `"testing"`.
5. The last one needs the `var` in the beginning to declare the variable.

Practicing these should help you recognize other errors later. Can you fix all the examples above to make them work? Give it a try.

See what other things you can do to cause errors in the console and then try to fix those too.

When you're ready, let's get to the game!

2.2 Planning the Game

One of the most important steps in programming is *planning*. If you start typing without thinking about what you're creating, it's going to be harder to pull it all together. With planning, the rest comes faster. Let's take a minute and talk about what we're going to create together.

Let's make a plan.

Game concept. A player will go from room to room in a house, finding items and using them to fix things that are broken.

The house. We need a floorplan for the house. Let's start with four rooms. Think about a house. It can be based on your home or an imaginary house. You can make it more complicated later, but start with four rooms for now.

Each room will need the following.

- Name: *"living room"*
- Description: *"A cozy room with a fireplace."*
- Something broken: *"fireplace screen"*
- Item needed to fix the broken thing: *"new wire"*
- Points: *25* — a number that represents how many points the player earns for fixing the thing
- An item that is needed to fix something in a *different* room: *"batteries"* (for a TV remote)
  - Each item should only be needed once
- A list of exits from that room: north: *"dining room"*

Create a floorplan. You can do this on a separate sheet of paper. Take some time to plan it out. Have fun with it. Think about what a player might enjoy.

When figuring out the north, east, south, west, if you can't go in a certain direction, use the word `null`. Put a wall in the house to limit movement. A bathroom, for instance, should probably only have one entrance.

Make sure your rooms are connected to each other somehow. It should also be logical. Let's say you have a living room and you can go north into the dining room. The dining room, then, should have a south exit back to the living room.

Even a rough sketch of your house will do, but trying to plan this in your head and coding it later will be challenging. Take the time you need to set up the floorplan before turning to the code.

You can certainly make more than four rooms right now if you want. You will be adding more later, anyway.

House Blueprint

Room Name: Description (1-2 sentences): Broken thing: Fix broken with: Points for fixing: Item found in room: Exit north ↑: Exit south ↓: Exit east →: Exit west ←:	Room Name: Description (1-2 sentences): Broken thing: Fix broken with: Points for fixing: Item found in room: Exit north ↑: Exit south ↓: Exit east →: Exit west ←:
Room Name: Description (1-2 sentences): Broken thing: Fix broken with: Points for fixing: Item found in room: Exit north ↑: Exit south ↓: Exit east →: Exit west ←:	Room Name: Description (1-2 sentences): Broken thing: Fix broken with: Points for fixing: Item found in room: Exit north ↑: Exit south ↓: Exit east →: Exit west ←:

* Put `null` if there's a wall in the way and you can't exit in that direction. *

2.3 JavaScript Variables

There are many constructs in programming. One of the main ideas is the use of variables. These are pieces of information in the computer's memory that can be used in different places.

Let's say you ask someone to type in their name. The computer can save that name to a variable, like `playerName`. In your program, you put `playerName` wherever you want the computer to use the name, like "Hello, _____!" or "Great job, _____!" The computer would insert the name into the blank each time if you tell it to. (We'll talk about how soon.)

Variables sound important.

Variables. These are key to programming. It's hard, and not very useful, to write a program that doesn't use any variables. Variables work the same way they do in a math or science equation. Each one represents a value that you substitute in where you need it.

If you have a math expression for area like *base x height*, you put different values in for *base* and for *height* depending on what problem you're solving. That's what computers do too. They use the value of your variables to do calculations, to make decisions, and to show words on screen that you can react to.

Declaring variables. Variables must be *declared* so the computer knows you're using one. All declarations have the same basic format.

```
var nameOfVariable = someValue;
```

You always use the `var` keyword to tell the computer you're creating a variable. It's like saying, "Hey, look over here! I'm making a variable!" Then you give the variable a name using camelCase. Beyond that, you can assign a value to it using an equals sign.

It is possible to declare a variable without giving it a value. This gives the variable a value of `undefined`. There are times it makes sense to do this, but if you can give a default value, it's good to do so. We'll see an example of an `undefined` variable a bit later in the book so you have an idea where it's useful, but most of the time we will give them a starting value.

```
var variableWithoutAValue;
```

Strings. These variables define words, like the names of the rooms and the items we need to find or fix. Strings have to be typed in with quotes around them, like `"living room"` or `"batteries"`. Many times, strings are used to communicate with the user (player), but they have other uses, too, like when we need to figure out what room to go to next.

```
var thisIsAString = "Well, hello there!";
```

Numbers. These are numbers. Nothing magical about it. They can be whole numbers, like `42`, or decimals like `3.17`, but no fractions. If you try to put a fraction, like `1/4`, the computer does the math to convert it its decimal form `0.25`.

```
var thisIsANumber = 317;
```

Booleans. These are special "flag" variables that can only be `true` or `false` (no quotes!). These are needed for making decisions. If something is `true`, do *this*, else if it's `false`, do *that*.

```
var thisIsABoolean = true;
```

Booleans are also created as a result of comparisons, like `5 < 3`, which would be `false`. We'll get more into these when we talk about loops and conditional statements.

Arrays. These are lists. They can hold any variable type, including other arrays. We tell the computer it's an array by using square brackets `[]`. Each item in the array is separated by commas.

```
var thisIsAnEmptyArray = [];
var thisIsAListOfNumbers = [2, 7, 1200, 86, 4.5];
```

Objects. These are the heart of JavaScript. They can hold any type of variable, organized into *properties*. We need curly braces `{}` to declare an object and we use colons and commas to set up the properties. Those properties can be easily accessed using the dot operator (a period) or through array notation, which we'll get to shortly. These keep related information close together. For instance, details related to a room! We'll get into details of using objects soon.

```
var thisIsAnEmptyObject = {};
```

Special values. `undefined` means the variable exists but the computer has no idea what kind of variable it is. `null` means it has "no value". Both you and the computer can set values to `undefined`, whether on purpose or by accident.

Only you can set a value to `null` and it must be done on purpose. Use `null` to control your flow and to show that you purposely wanted a variable without a value. We're using `null` in our rooms to show we can't go in a certain direction.

Functions. These are not variables, but they can act like them. Functions are chunks of code that can be used over and over whenever we need them.

Many times, we write sections of code and then come back later to wrap it in a function. When possible, keep your functions small so they only do one major thing.

You can send arguments into a function to be used by the function as parameters. Functions can send back (return) information, allowing them to act like variables.

Functions are declared with the `function` keyword instead of `var`. There's more to functions than this basic sample, but this gives you an idea.

```
function thisIsAFunction()
{
  //code for the function to do stuff
}
```

Throughout our game, we are going to create a bunch of functions. Each one will have a main purpose.

They're not as scary as they sound. The most important thing is to keep each function separate. They can go at the top or the middle or the bottom of your code in any order, sort of like a bunch of magnets on your fridge. Just don't overlap them — the functions, that is. Keep them outside another function's opening and closing brace.

2.4 Practicing Room Variables

We're going to convert one of your rooms into a set of variables. In the next section, we will convert those variables into an object. Code often gets rewritten like this. Try it one way to make sure it works, then turn it into something else more useful.

> Practice makes perfect.

To declare a variable, you need to use the `var` keyword. For each detail you have of a room, you're going to convert it into a variable. Choose one room to start with — any one you want. Follow my lead and turn one room into all variables.

Variable names. Variable names can't have any spaces in them, any special characters (except `_` and `$`), and they can't start with numbers.

Example:
```
var name = "living room";
var points = 25;
var brokenThing = "fireplace screen";
```

Remember to use camelCase, like I did for `brokenThing`.

Variable Word Bank. Choose from these for your variable names.

brokenThing	description	east	fixWith	itemFound
name	north	points	south	west

Now it's your turn. Convert one room into a list of variables:

_____

_____

_____

_____

_____

_____

_____

_____

_____

_____

Test it out. The best way to code is to write small things and test them out. Over and over. You can't have enough testing. If you make sure small changes are working, you'll have a better time fixing bigger problems.

Go to a console window. Refer back to 1.4: Where to Write Your Code — Using repl.it, if you need help knowing where to go. Repl.it may tell you to run your project first; if so, press the Run button on the upper left part of the screen.

Type in your variables one at a time. Press enter at the end of the line to put the variable into memory. Test each one by typing in just the variable name and pressing enter. There's an example on the next page.

Try this.

```
var name = "living room";
name
```

You should see something like this.

```
: var name = "living room";
=> undefined
: name
=> 'living room'
:
```

```
> var name = "living room";
< undefined
> name
< "living room"
>
```

Figure 6. repl.it console (left) versus Google Chrome console (right)

Don't worry about the `undefined` line. That's the console saying you didn't return a value. If you typed in `2 + 5`, it would show `7` instead of `undefined`. (Go ahead, you can try that.)

Do you see how typing in `name` and pressing enter gives you the value of the variable you typed in? For me, it was `"living room"`. Repl.it shows single quotes. I use double quotes instead. They work the same way, but be consistent.

What do I do with a syntax error?

One by one, test all your variables. Make sure they work. You might get something like: `SyntaxError: Unexpected identifier`. This basically means you typed something in wrong. Remember that spelling matters, and so does capitalization. Check my examples above, try again, then look ahead at the next page.

It is important that you get used to typing things in correctly. Don't skip this exercise.

Here's one of my rooms:

```
var name = "living room";
var points = 25;
var brokenThing = "fireplace screen";
var description = "A cozy room with a fireplace.";
var fixWith = "new wire";
var itemFound = "batteries";
var north = "dining room";
var south = null;
var east = "hallway";
var west = null;
```

Look carefully at the formatting.
- Each line starts with var
- Each variable name (after var) is "one" word with no spaces
- There's an equals sign =
- Strings needs quotes "" around them, like dialogue in a book
- Numbers, true, false, null, and undefined do not get quotes
- Put a semicolon ; at the end of each statement

This is how you need to declare your variables. These are all initialized with a value. It's usually a good idea to give a variable a value right away, even if it's null. However, you can also declare a variable like this: var someVariable; This sets memory aside for the variable but it's not defined in any way. Go ahead and try it in your console like the others. It will say it's undefined.

Were you able to get all of your variables to work? If not, you need to go back and try to figure out why. It's really important. Make sure you're not using "smart quotes." Keep them "straight."

Smart quotes aren't smart here.

At this point, you've created a bunch of variables and displayed their values in the console window. You've successfully written some code!

2.5 Coding a Room

Having all those variables is nice, but it's not a good way to do things. Imagine trying to keep track of all those details as we add more rooms. Also, if we have a name for one room and then we add a name for another room, we would end up rewriting the first name! Try this in the console.

```
var name = "living room";
var name = "dining room";
name;
```

It will only say `"dining room"` because the original value no longer exists. We often do want to overwrite variable values, especially if we're computing things, but we want our rooms to stay the way they are!

Declaring an object. We are going to convert each room into an *object*. This is a more complex type of variable that can hold all the other variables (as *properties*). To declare an empty object without anything in it, you could do this.

```
var emptyRoom = {};
```

Do you see how it's the same basic format as the variables we already wrote? We have `var`, a name, an equals sign, some kind of value, and it ends with a semicolon. The difference is with those braces `{}`. Braces tell the computer we're making an object. The format of an object is a little different inside those braces. We have to use colons and commas.

Syntax:

```
var objectName = {
                propertyName1: value,
                propertyName2: value,
                propertyName3: value
              };
```

We can have as many unique properties (*think*: object variables) as we want. They have to be named with the same rules that regular variables are named (with an exception I'll get to soon). We put a colon after the name of the property and then the value. If there's another property coming, then put a comma. After all the properties are added, close the brace and use a semicolon.

Creating an object. Let's take the first room and turn it into an object. Are you ready? **From now on, you're typing in your JavaScript (.js) file** unless I tell you otherwise.

Here are some of the properties for my first room:

```
var name = "living room";
var points = 25;
var brokenThing = "fireplace screen";
```

Here's how to convert that into an object.

```
var livingRoom =
{
   name: "living room",
   points: 25,
   brokenThing: "fireplace screen",
   //put the rest of your properties
       here
};
```

We want to save the code we're creating going forward. Typing it into the console window won't save any of it. Make sure you're using `http://repl.it`, something similar, or a file system as described in Where to Write Your Code — Using repl.it (Section 1.4) and Basic File Setup (Section 1.5).

Notice what's similar and what's different? I'm creating an object called `livingRoom`. It has no spaces in the name and I'm using camelCase so it's easier to read.

The object starts with the opening brace {. Many programmers put that brace on the *first line* with the variable name. It's fine either way. If you use `repl.it`'s Format or `jsfiddle.net`'s Tidy feature, it will move braces there automatically, so it looks like this.

```
var livingRoom = {
  name: "living room",
  //the rest of the properties here
};
```

The variable names we had before, like `name` and `points`, are now *properties*. They're still just variables, but now they belong to the `livingRoom` object. If we made a `diningRoom` object, we could use the same property names without them overwriting each other because they would belong to a different object. It's like how people each have their own name, and naming someone else doesn't change your name.

After you've made two or more rooms, you'll be able to see how they can each have their own `name` property.

```
livingRoom.name;          //shows "living room"
diningRoom.name;          //shows "dining room"
```

Alike but different. Colons versus commas.

Property syntax is different than variable syntax. After the properties, we use *colons,* and at the end of the line, we use *commas.* Technically, the computer sees all of this as one long line of code. We break it down line by line so it's easier for us to read.

Code should always be readable to the programmer and formatted for the computer.

When you type in your last property for your room, don't put the comma. Most browsers today will understand what to do if you keep it, but if you happen across some older browser, it can cause a crash.

Lastly, you need the closing brace }. And because that's the end of the declaration (`var`) statement, you add that semicolon ;.

Type in your object. Take a few minutes and convert your first room into an object. When you're finished, *run* the project and then in the console window, type in the name of your object (like `livingRoom`) and hit enter. It should show you the whole thing. If you get an error, check your syntax.

Syntax error! Notice how repl.it tries to help pinpoint the problem below? There is a red X on line 4 and, sure enough, there's a problem there. Can you see it?

```
1    var livingRoom =
2  · {
3        name: "living room",
4        points: 25;
5        brokenThing: "fireplace screen",
6        description: "A cozy room with a fireplace.",
7        fixWith: "new wire".
```

Figure 7. Entering an object, but with an error!

Properties need to end with *commas*, not semicolons. This is causing an error, which spills out onto lines 5 and 6!

Good news, though: if you fix that one typo, all the errors go away.

Try adding an error to your code on purpose, then fix it.

The lesson here: If you get a bunch of red Xs, start fixing them from the top and work your way down.

Completed room object. Let's look at a completed room. Of course, your room should have its own values for its properties, but it's ok to use mine while you're starting off.

```
1  var livingRoom =
2  {
3    name: "living room",
4    points: 25,
5    brokenThing: "fireplace screen",
6    description: "A cozy room with a fireplace.",
7    fixWith: "new wire",
8    itemFound: "batteries",
9    north: "dining room",
10   south: null,
11   east: "hallway",
12   west: null
13 };
14
```

Figure 8. livingRoom object (left) with console display (right) in repl.it

Testing your object. Before we move on, we should practice accessing those properties. Let's do some exercises to make sure you understand. For this, make sure you run your program first. You'll then be typing into your console window.

Accessing object properties. There are two ways to access object properties in JavaScript, with *dot notation* and with *array notation*.

Dot notation is used when you know the name of the property you want to access *and* the property name is a standard name (we haven't talked about nonstandard names yet).

Array notation is used when you need to access properties through a variable or if the property names are nonstandard. Not all languages have array notation for things like this. It's one place JavaScript is particularly helpful.

Dot notation. In the console window, type in the following and hit enter. Be sure to use whatever name you gave your object and make sure you run your repl first.

```
livingRoom.description;
```

This is my result.

```
"A cozy room with a fireplace."
```

You should see that the console popped out whatever description you had typed in! Try it with some of your other properties, like `north`, `south`, `name`, `points`, and so on.

Comments. I'll show you my results below. When I do, I will put the resulting output on the same line in a comment. A comment is started with a double-slash `//`. The computer ignores anything to the right of this marker on that line. **You don't need to type in these comments.** The won't *do* anything. They're just for you to see.

> If they don't do anything, do we need them?

It's always a good idea to add comments to your code for things that aren't clear, for parts you still need to work on, to explain what's happening, and so on. It's documentation for yourself to help you understand the code later when you look at it, or if someone else does.

Here are my displayed properties.

```
livingRoom.north;          //"dining room"
livingRoom.south;          //null
livingRoom.east;           //"hallway"
livingRoom.west;           //null
livingRoom.points;         //25
livingRoom.brokenThing;    //"fireplace screen"
livingRoom.fixWith;        //"new wire"
livingRoom.itemFound;      //"batteries"
livingRoom.bunnies         //undefined
```

Oh hey, I threw in a property in there that I never created! Yeah, I just wanted to show you what would happen. You get `undefined`.

Adding properties. If, for some reason, we need to add a property to one of our rooms after the object was defined, we can do it easily. Simply assign a value to one, like this.

```
livingRoom.color = "beige";
```

And now there's a new `color` property for the room. That's it!

Array notation. Let's practice using array notation. Either method works fine for most things. Arrays use square brackets `[]` to access their member elements. For an object, we can use those same square brackets to access the properties. It's important to understand that property names are all strings, so they need to be placed in quotes.

```
livingRoom["brokenThing"];      //"fireplace screen"
livingRoom["points"];           //25
```

Now you give it a try. Access your properties in the console window using array notation. Go on, go try it! Getting the hang of it yet?

Just like with dot notation, we can use this to add new properties.

```
livingRoom["temperature"] = 71;
```

And yes, we can access it with `livingRoom.temperature` too.

Why use array notation? This allows us to use variables to access properties. It also allows us to use other strings to create nonstandard property names, such as using two separate words, like `"living room"` or numbers. Property names like these can't be used with dot notation.

Array notation is extremely useful.

First let's try a variable exercise. Continue working in your console window for this. Remember to run your repl first to activate the console if you haven't done so recently.

Create a variable named `prop` and set it equal to one of your room's properties.

```
var prop = "fixWith";
```

Now pass that variable into the square brackets, without quotes: (Remember, my comment // shows what my output is.)

```
livingRoom[prop];           //"wire screen"
```

It's showing you the `fixWith` property, right? Now let's change the value of `prop` to something else.

```
prop = "north";
```

Now that the variable has a different value, type that previous line again and see what it says.

```
livingRoom[prop];           //"dining room"
```

Play around with it a few times until you understand what's happening. The `prop` variable is being used to accessed whatever property it is assigned to. This makes reaching certain object properties a lot easier in some situations.

You can do it! Build that house!

Create the rest. When you're ready, it's time to do more coding. You need to create the rest of your rooms as objects. I'm only going to put one more down here, but the rest will be in the code section at the end of the book. Use your own rooms for this part. Get all your rooms typed in and then test them out like we did for the `livingRoom`. Access the properties and make sure you have no errors. Once you've done all that, go on to the next section.

Each room goes under the room before it. You can even add a space or two between them so they're easier to tell apart.

Don't use copy and paste. I know it's tempting. It may seem easier to copy one room, paste it in, then change the values. Yes, it would help you make sure all your property names are correct, but, especially while you're learning, the more code you type outright, the better your skills will become. Copy/paste can also lead to unexpected bugs in your code if you're not careful.

```
var diningRoom =
{
  name: "dining room",
  description: "A great place to
               enjoy a meal.",
  brokenThing: "chandelier",
  fixWith: "light bulb",
  points: 15,
  itemFound: "new wire",
  north: null,
  south: "living room",
  east: "kitchen",
  west: null
};
    //<--empty space, for readability
var hallway =
{
    //all my hallway properties
};
```

I put an empty space between my `diningRoom` and the `hallway`. This is just for my sake, so it's easier for me to see the code for each room later. The computer doesn't care if that space is in there or if I used a hundred spaces.

You may notice that I rearranged the order of some of the properties to make them more logical. You can (and should) do the same.

For the most part, the order of the properties does not matter. The only time it matters is if you have properties that need other property values. We'll get to this at a much later time.

2.6 Checking Your Code

You have to take a few minutes and check your code. Run through this checklist to make sure you've got all the details you need.

- ✓ Did you spell everything exactly right?
    - o "Spelling" includes capitalization
    - o Property names need to be the same among all your rooms (`name`, `description`, `brokenThing`, etc.)
    - o All room names must be spelled the same in the `name` property and in any direction properties (`east`, etc.)
    - o Do all `fixWith` items have a matching `itemFound`?
- ✓ Do all your rooms connect in a logical way?
    - o For example, my living room exits north into the dining room, so my dining room needs to exit south into the living room.
    - o You can pass through doors in both directions, right?
- ✓ Do you have at least one room that only has one entrance and exit (like a bathroom)?
- ✓ Does each room have a different `fixWith` item?
- ✓ Does each room have a different `itemFound`?
- ✓ Is each `itemFound` needed for a different room than the room it's found in?
    - o My living room needs a wire screen, which is found in the dining room.
- ✓ Did you give different point values for each broken item that gets fixed?

I wanna play the game too, but let's be patient. We're getting there.

We will get to a point where we can test this out by actually playing the game, but it's better to get into the habit of writing the cleanest code you can right up front. Plus, we need to do a number of things before we can really test this out.

2.7 Creating the Rooms Object

Now that you have a set of rooms, lets lump them all together into one larger object, called `rooms`. I suppose we could call it `house`, if you'd rather. The reason I'm choosing `rooms` is because it will be a collection with each room in it. This is one of those design decisions to make.

We have two options for grouping the rooms together. We could add all of them into an array, which is a list of things. That would work. We can also create a new object that holds each room object as a property. Both methods would work but accessing each room we need would have to be done differently.

If we use an array to hold the rooms, each time we want to go to a new room, we have to cycle through the array to find the room we are looking for. This isn't a problem. It's a `for` loop and an `if` statement.

If we use an object, we can use array notation to access the room by name. It's one step.

Either way, we need to bring our rooms together. You're going to need a list of all your room names. Here are my first four rooms. You can see them all in the code at the end of the book. Later, you'll add more rooms to your starting set.

livingRoom	diningRoom	hallway	kitchen

Declaring the rooms object. We are going to create a `rooms` object to hold all the rooms. We will start by creating an empty `rooms` object and adding properties to it afterward through array notation.

This code *has to* go **under** all the rooms you created. The rooms can't be added to the object if they don't exist, right?

```
var rooms = {};      //empty rooms object
rooms[livingRoom.name] = livingRoom;
rooms[diningRoom.name] = diningRoom;
rooms[kitchen.name] = kitchen;
```

> Why is it empty?

Let's take a look, ok? The first line creates an empty `rooms` object with no properties in it at all. We're just telling the computer, "Hey, we need you to set some memory aside for this thing we're making."

The next line looks kind of weird, right? It seems repetitive in a way. Let's break it down.

Sidenote. There are generally several ways to solve each problem in code and this is one of those situations. Another problem that had multiple solutions is how we pointed to rooms with our directions. Right now, our directions point to room names, like
`north: "dining room"`
We could have, instead, pointed them to room objects, like so:
`north: diningRoom`
This would make some things even easier. However, you wouldn't have been able to test your properties earlier and that's important for you to learn how to do. Since we already have our directions pointing to room names, we're going to stick with it.

Remember when you typed `livingRoom.name` in the console when you were testing properties? It showed you the value `"living room"`. And remember when we used the variable name `prop` to test how that works? Well, this puts both of those ideas together. Here's what the line is really saying.

```
rooms["living room"] = livingRoom;
```

This makes a new property called `"living room"` and points it to the `livingRoom` object we created. I know it sounds weird and confusing because we're using the same words over and over. If it helps, try saying them differently in your head so you can see how they're not the same. For example, when it's with quotes, use a Southern accent and when it's not, use a British accent, or whatever you feel like.

44

String properties. Our code is actually creating properties with strings as names, whereas before I said you had to use camelCase. This is a special JavaScript feature. Here's an example of the difference.

With a Regular Property	With a String Property
| ```
var livingRoom =
{
  brokenThing: "chandelier"
}
``` | ```
var livingRoom =
{
  "broken thing": "chandelier"
}
``` |

Add your rooms. Go ahead and make sure you have each room added into your `rooms` object. You should have something that looks like this.

```
var rooms = {};
rooms[livingRoom.name] = livingRoom;
rooms[diningRoom.name] = diningRoom;
rooms[kitchen.name] = kitchen;
rooms[hallway.name] = hallway;
```

Always gotta test it!

Do you know what's coming next? Yep. Test it out. Run the code, make sure it works. Type `rooms` in the console window and see if it shows you all the rooms.

You can try selecting individual rooms by using the properties with dot or array notation, like `rooms.kitchen;` or `rooms["dining room"];`.

Remember, you can't use dot notation for things like `rooms."dining room";` or `rooms.dining room;` They won't work (syntax error), but feel free to try and see for yourself. You won't break anything. Testing is good.

2.8 Wrapping the Rooms in a Function

We have created a whole bunch of rooms and grouped them together in a `rooms` object. We've done a lot and you probably have over 100 lines of code already. We could just continue to our next major game piece, the `player`, but let's take a moment to clean something up.

As the player goes around the room fixing things, we're going to make changes to the rooms by removing things that are broken so we don't fix them twice. If the game ends and we want to play it again, we would have to reload the browser, otherwise nothing would be broken.

Or, we can make it so that we can load up the rooms again any time we want to. This is easier to do than it sounds. We're going to wrap all of our `rooms` code up in a function. Then we will *call the function* to get the information we need and store it in a variable we can use.

At the very top of your code, hit enter a couple times to make some empty space. Then type in this.

```
function getRooms()
{
```

That's all
there is to it.

Now go all the way to the bottom of your code and type this in.

```
    return rooms;
}
```

Refactoring. Poof. You've just wrapped your rooms in a function that we can use over and over any time we need to. Wasn't that ridiculously easy? When we do things like this, it's called *refactoring* the code. We're pulling code out into functions that we can call whenever we need them.

There's one more thing we need to do though. We need to *call* the function from within the program in order to use it. Go back to the tippy top of your program (before `function`) and on line 1, put this.

```
var rooms = getRooms();
```

This code snippet shows the top and bottom parts of the code. It skips in the middle. If you want to see the whole thing, check out Section 9.1: Room Adventure — Version 1 (Text).

```
 1   var rooms = getRooms();
 2   |
 3   function getRooms()
 4 ▾ {
 5
 6       var livingRoom =
 7 ▾       {
 8               name: "living room",
 9               points: 25,
10               brokenThing: "fireplace screen",
11               description: "A cozy room with a fireplace.",
         / / / / / / / / / / / /
145      rooms[bathroom.name] = bathroom;
146      rooms[basement.name] = basement;
147
148      return rooms;
149  }
150
```

Figure 9. rooms object, refactored into a function [code snippet]

Function placement. Going forward, make sure you don't add any code inside that function. You may want to move it down and add some blank space at the top of your program to get it out of the way. Keep line 1 at the top (`var rooms = getRooms();`) and you can shift everything else down by hitting enter.

> Where do functions go? This looks really important.

Your functions can be arranged in any order you want. The computer doesn't care. Come up with an order that makes the most sense to you. Just don't stick one function inside another.

I usually move larger functions to the end, out of the way. I group related functions together. I move critical functions toward the top. It's really up to you, though.

Once you've done that, run it and test it. Type `rooms` in the console and hit enter. It will show the rooms. There's one more thing to test while you're there. Try running the function directly in the console. Type in `getRooms();` and hit enter. What do you see?

This is a quick and easy way to try out your functions to see if they work. You can't always do it, because sometimes there are other parts of the code that need to be running, but for things like this, it's great.

We need to do a few more things before we can see our game in action: we need a player and a way to walk around.

2.9 Creating the Player Object

Who's in this house, anyway? We need someone, don't we? Let's create a `player` object. We always want to name things descriptively and simply. It helps us understand our code. We could be silly and call this object `playerRunningAroundAHouseToFindItemsInOrderToFixStuff`. Yeah... silly. But it would also be silly to call it `spaghettiAndCheese`. It doesn't help you (or anyone else) understand what the object is.

Code challenge. Create an object called `player`. Give the player a certain set of properties. What properties do you think the player needs? Think about it for a moment before you read on. Make a list.

Properties the `player` will need for the game and the values they should start with.

- _____
- _____
- _____
- _____
- _____
- _____

Once you have an idea, go ahead and create the `player` object. Follow the basic format of the room objects we started with.

Put this `player` object below `var rooms = getRooms();` (near line 1 at the top of your code) and above `function getRooms()`.

Go ahead. Get the `player` object up and ready!

Once you have it, run the program and test it out in the console window, like you did for `rooms`. Did you give your player a name? Then type `player.name;` in the console window and see what happens.

Player ready? Now that you've given that `player` object a try on your own, let's discuss it in more detail.

Here's a possible `player` object.

> Is this close to what you were thinking?

```
var player =
{
  name: "Lica",
  score: 0,
  currentRoom: rooms["living room"],
  inventory: [],
  itemsLeftToFix: 4
};
```

The currentRoom property. For this game to work, we need to know what room the `player` is in. A good property name is `currentRoom`. You can start your player anywhere in your house. I'm going with `"living room"` as my starting point.

The inventory property. The player is going to be picking up items along the way. It's important for the player to have a place to carry them, right? Let's give the player an `inventory`. This will be a collection of items, so we need a type of list. Do you know what construct makes a good list? (Spoiler: it's an array.)

Will the player start with any items in his or her inventory? Probably not, but you could lend a helping hand if you want. You could also give the player items at the start in order to debug or troubleshoot your game. Then, later, take those starting items out to play the game as intended. Not sure why the faucet in the kitchen can't be fixed? Well, give the player a `"wrench"` to start off and see if it works. If not, you probably have something wrong in your code.

To start the player with an empty inventory, you need an empty array `[]`. To give the player a wrench, make it `["wrench"]`.

The score property. We want to have a scoring system, so the player can earn points as they fix things. You can even make it so the player earns points for finding things, or lose points for each room he or she enters (so they don't wander aimlessly). Or get really complex and keep track of all the rooms entered already and give points for each new room discovered. (Sounds like you'd need another array for that.) Regardless, we need a way to keep score.

The name property. It's not necessary, but did you want to let the player enter a name? Or did you want to assign a name to a player? If so, you want a `name` property too. You'll need a way to ask for that, though. You could use a JavaScript `prompt` or pull it from a text box on the HTML (website) page. (I'm jumping ahead.)

The itemsLeftToFix property. There's no one right way to make a game. Do you want to keep track of each item that gets fixed? You can give the player another array to track that. I created four rooms, so we'll say the player has `4` items to fix, and we'll reduce it each time something is fixed. If you have six rooms, then put `6`. This isn't the most flexible way to write the code, but it works. And when you're starting off, you want it to work first, then add complexity later.

Did you have other properties in mind? That's great! You may add them and work them into your game, too.

2.10 Wrapping the Player in a Function

It's time to refactor the code a little. Once again, we want the code to be reusable. If the user ends the game and wants to play again, we have to reset the player. The easiest way to do that is to use a function we can call to make a new player.

Do you remember how to wrap code in a function? And then how to call it to make a variable we can use? Try seeing if you can do it on your own first, before checking the code. Look back to Section 2.8: Wrapping the Rooms in a Function to see how we did it before. It'll help you to learn if you challenge yourself to figure these out on your own.

Here's the player object, wrapped in a function, with the function call.

```
var player = getPlayer();

function getPlayer()
{
  var player =
  {
    name: "Lica",
    score: 0,
    currentRoom: rooms["living room"],
    inventory: [],
    itemsLeftToFix: 8
  };
  return player;
}
```

The function call (the first line with `var player = getPlayer();`) needs to go at the top of the code. Put it right under the line `var rooms = getRooms();`. The order is important here because the `player` object is making use of the `rooms` object. Therefore, the rooms have to be created first. If you reverse the order of these lines, you'll get an error when you run it.

```
1    var rooms = getRooms();
2    var player = getPlayer();
3
4    |
5
6
```

Figure 10. Adding whitespace

You can move the `getPlayer()` function down lower and out of the way by hitting enter a few times after the function call.

And yes. Test it out.

The player's properties. Let's discuss these properties.

```
var player =
{
  name: "Lica",
  score: 0,
  currentRoom: rooms["living room"],
  inventory: [],
  itemsLeftToFix: 4
};
```

The `name` is a string with a character name in it. You can make the name anything you want. Do we even need a name? Probably not. We could allow the player to enter a name and then display it on the screen. If we never use it, we could delete it.

The `score` is a number set to zero. This is the score the player starts the game with, and zero seems appropriate. We could set this to something else if we wanted to give the player a different starting point. That's up to you as the designer.

The `currentRoom` property is more complex. This sets a pointer to one of the rooms in the global `rooms` object. In my case, I'm starting in the living room. Remember, though, that each room itself is an object with a name, a description, and directions. We can access the player's `currentRoom` with dot notation like we have before by using `player.currentRoom`.

What if we want to know the room's description? It's easy. We just add another dot to it! This is called *chaining* properties. We can use this for finding which directions are available too using dot or array notation. We're going to need this!

```
player.currentRoom.description;  //"A cozy room..."
player.currentRoom.north;        //"dining room"
player.currentRoom["north"];     //"dining room"
```

Look at that last one. It combines dot and array notation. That's totally fine. You could even do this:

```
player["currentRoom"].north;
```

For this to work, we have to keep the properties in order.

You can think of it as the `player` has a `currentRoom` that can exit to the `north`. As long as you have the set in the right order, it works.

But you can't use `player.north.currentRoom` because we didn't set the objects up that way. The `player` itself does not have a `north` exit. That would be kind of weird.

The `inventory` property is an empty array. We're going to add to that as we pick things up.

The `itemsLeftToFix` property is a number we'll count down from as we fix things. When it's zero, the game is over. Make sure this is equal to the number of rooms you have that have something that needs to be fixed. When you add more rooms to the game, increase this number accordingly.

2.11 Getting Interactive — Text Version

At this point, we have our first set of rooms and a player. It's time to start putting them together and letting a user interact with the game we are building.

For starters, we will keep everything in JavaScript. This means it's all going to be text and popups for now. When we dive into some HTML, we will bring in buttons to click, pictures, and so on. Right now, let's focus on the structure of programming.

To communicate with the player, we need a few preprogrammed JavaScript functions.

Communicating with a user. We have four functions to choose from, depending on our needs.

We need to be able to work with the player.

Using console.log(). Information can be sent directly to the console using `console.log();`. You've already done a lot of typing directly into the console. This method will allow you to print things to the console from within your program. For our game, however, this is more useful for debugging, not for communicating with a player.

```
console.log("Testing is good for you.");
```

Using alert(). An `alert();` will send information to the user in a popup. This is great for telling the user what the game is about and sending information outward only.

```
alert("Don't disable or block your popups!");
```

Using confirm(). A `confirm();` popup works like an alert with an added feature. It provides two buttons the user can press: `OK` and `Cancel`. These return the values `true` or `false`, respectively. By setting `confirm();` to a variable, we can record which button the user pressed and act accordingly. For instance, if the game ends, we can ask if they want to play again. If `OK` (`true`) then we will restart the game.

```
var tryAgain = confirm("Click OK to try again.");
```

Using prompt(). A `prompt();` popup is even more detailed than `confirm();` Instead of just a `true` or `false` response, this allows the user to type in anything they want. The result is returned as a string that we can use.

```
var tellMeAnything = prompt("What's on your mind?");
```

Popups overrule the console. There's one thing to be aware of. If your program uses both popups and the console, you may have a problem. All the popups in your program will run before your console window will display anything. You can't send a question to the console then use a `prompt` to get an answer. The user won't see the question in the console until after they've sent an answer.

If you want to see for yourself, you can put these lines at the top of your program and run it to see what happens. Just make sure you delete them after.

```
console.log("Determine the sum of 200 and 42.");
prompt("What is your answer?");
```

2.12 Building a Text String

When you want to communicate with a user, it is a common practice to build a text string and then send it all at once to a display. It doesn't have to be done this way, but it's very useful, especially when we're using alerts and prompts.

To do this, we start with an empty string. Then we add to it everything we want to have appearing at the same time. We next send it off to be shown to the user.

This looks like something we will use a lot.

Consider this.

```
var text = "";
text += "Hello there. ";
text += "Welcome to the game! ";
alert(text);
```

You can type this in and run it to test it out. (You can do so either in your JavaScript file or in your console window.) You should see a single popup that says, `"Hello there. Welcome to the game! "`.

If we just use alerts on every line, the popups would get really annoying, really fast.

Notice that I added a space to the end of each line before the ending quote mark. That's just so it looks nicer. The computer won't add spaces on its own.

This process will allow us to make good, descriptive text for the user to see. We can do the following.

```
var text = "";
text += "You are in the ";
text += player.currentRoom.name + ". ";
text += player.currentRoom.description;

alert(text);
```

We could use this over and over and whatever room we are in, it will display the text for that room. This sounds like it would be a good function, doesn't it? We're going to wrap it as a function and then call it when we need it. Can you do it on your own? Name the function `textRoomDescription()`.

Where do I put this?

Where does my new function go? Functions can go anywhere in your code file. You can put this near the top, in the middle, or at the very bottom of your file. What really matters is that you don't accidentally put it inside another function's code block `{   }`.

I would suggest for now that you put each new function near the top of the file, right under the couple of `var` statements we have for the `rooms` and `player`. With each new function, just push the other ones lower down by pressing the enter key. If you want to use a different order, go right ahead! It's your code.

Here's the `textRoomDescription()` function.

```
function textRoomDescription()
{
  var text = "";
  text += "You are in the ";
  text += player.currentRoom.name + ". ";
  text += player.currentRoom.description;
  alert(text);
}
```

Global scope player object. This new function will work because our `player` object is a variable in the *global scope*. The function can find and access the `player` without us having to do anything. We declared this player in line 2 of the code, outside of any function. That means all parts of our program can access it. For our game, this will be fine.

Officially speaking, it would be better if we controlled which player gets sent to this function. We only have the one player, though, so for now it doesn't matter.

When we run this function with the call `textRoomDescription();` it will show what we want it to. It accesses the global `player` and shows the room.

If we had a second player, `player2`, however, this function would only show the original player. We could make a simple change to allow this to work for different players. It would require us to "pass in" a player object each time we used this function.

I'm going to leave this out of the code for now. In case you want to know the difference about how to pass in a player, all you'd need to do is this; change the function header to include a `player` parameter. And when you call the function, pass in the current player.

```
function textRoomDescription(player)
```

Call the function using a `currentPlayer` object defined elsewhere.

```
var currentPlayer = player; //or player2, etc.
textRoomDescription(currentPlayer);
```

2.13 Asking for Directions

It's time to ask the player what direction they want to go in. We are going to start very simple and then we will add more detail.

Here's what we need to do.

- We will create a `getDirection()` function.
- We should be nice and tell them what their options are.
- We will have to `prompt()` the user for a direction.
- If we get a valid direction, then send it back using `return` so we can do something with it.
- If we don't get a good direction, we must ask them again.

Let's be extremely basic and give the barest version of this function first. Then we'll add the other things.

```
function getDirection()
{
  var text = "Which way do you want to go? ";
  var direction = prompt(text);
  return direction;
}
```

We can't make assumptions.

If the user knows what direction they can go in and if they typed everything in correctly, then great. This would work. However, that's asking a lot, especially if someone has never played your game before. We need to make this function better.

We will need to make use of the player's `currentRoom` property. This property has directions in it, like `north` and `south`. We can check those to see if there is a room that goes that way. Remember, we put room names there, like I had `"dining room"` in my living room's `north` property. Some of them are `null`, which means we can't go there. Also, a player might type in something like `southwest`, which isn't valid right now.

Before we get to decision-making, let's refresh our memories about array notation and how it can help us figure out if we can get to a certain room.

2.14 Checking for a Valid Room

Let's first assume that the player isn't trying anything funny. The player wants to get from room to room, so they typed in a good direction. We can check `player.currentRoom` to see if it's possible. Does it point to the `"dining room"` or a `"bathroom"`?

We use array notation to check for this. For my living room, the player can go north into the dining room. Remember when we tested those things out?

```
player.currentRoom["north"]              //"dining room"
```

Instead of checking each one of these individually, we can use this.

```
player.currentRoom[direction];
```

This will give us whatever the value is.

If `direction` is `"north"` it would give me `"dining room"`.
If `direction` is `"west"`, it would give me `null`.
If `direction` is `"east"`, it would give me `"hallway"`.
If `direction` is `"itemFound"`, it would give me `"batteries"`.

Um, wait. That last one's not a room.

Again, there are many ways we can fix this. But we have a simple solution here. We have a `rooms` object. What if we take the answer we're given and try to see if there is a room there?

62

We could use array notation again for this. Same process, right? If we have `rooms["hallway"]`, that's a valid room so we can go there. If we tried to find `rooms["batteries"]`, it would be `undefined` (unless we had a room called `"batteries"`).

We need the computer to make decisions based on what is entered and on what's available. It's time to look at *conditional statements*.

2.15 Conditional Statements

We make decisions all the time. We check for a condition and then do something based on what we see.

- If it's cold outside, we put on a jacket.
- If we like a movie, we watch it. Otherwise, we put on something else.
- If there's no heat, we get a blanket.
- If we're hungry, we look for some food.
  - o If there is food, we eat. Otherwise, we go buy some.

These are all conditional statements. Computers do the same thing. We give them a condition to test for and then we tell them what to do if it's `true` and (sometimes) what to do if it's `false`.

Syntax:

```
if (condition)
{
  //do this if it was true
}
else
{
  //do this if it was false
}
```

The condition needs to be a Boolean result of `true` or `false`. If it's `true`, then the computer runs the first code block. If it isn't `true` and if there is an `else` block, then it runs the second block. The `else` block is optional, so you don't have to have one.

We want to know if the direction the player selected is a valid one. There are several ways we can check for this. Because of the way we set up our rooms, this is a little messier than it needs to be. Our exits are all lumped in with all the other room properties. They aren't organized at all.

Here's what we know from our variables: The player has a `currentRoom` property that points to whatever room we are in. The room has some exits that point to the names of other rooms. We use those names to find a room in the `rooms` object.

What happens if the room isn't there? We would get an `undefined` room. We could make use of that, no? If we get an `undefined` room, then we know we can't go that way. Otherwise, we move into the new room.

Maybe we should move all the exits into an `exits` property within each room. It's an idea we will look into later in Section 4.1: Update the Rooms Object with Exits.

Evaluating true and false. JavaScript is a little loose on how it interprets things. All of the following things are treated as `false`.

First, let's see how we could handle things the way they are. It's a good coding exercise.

- False: `false`
- Empty string: `""`
- Number zero: `0`
- Undefined: `undefined`
- Null: `null`
- "Not" operator on a true statement: `!true` or `!(10 > 3)`
- Comparisons that aren't true: `5 < 3` or `"hi" === "bye"`

These are all treated as `true`.

- True: `true`
- Non-empty string: `"hello"`
- Non-zero number: `1`
- Any object: `{}`, `{name: "living room"}`
- Any array: `[]`, `["red", "blue", "green"]`
- "Not" operator on a false statement: `!false` or `!(5 < 3)`
- Comparisons that aren't false: `10 > 3` or `"hi" !== "bye"`

There are more cases you could look at, like comparing `12` to `"12"`. You would get a different `true`/`false` answer depending on whether you compared `12 === "12"` (false) or `12 == "12"` (true). That *third equals sign* means it doesn't just check the value, it also checks the type. A number (`12`) is not the same type as a string (`"12"`). When creating conditional comparisons, you should always use the triple equals to make sure your code is written properly.

Optional: truth testing. If you would like to test these things out, you could create a function like this. *This is an optional exercise.*

```
function testForTrue(condition)
{
  if (condition)
  {
    console.log(condition + " is true.");
  }
  else
  {
    console.log(condition + " is false.");
  }
}
```

Run it by passing things into the function.

```
testForTrue("hello");            //true
testForTrue(undefined);          //false
testForTrue(6 > 10);             //false
testForTrue(["array"]);          //true
testForTrue({});                 //true
```

Let's test our room direction. The player typed in a `direction`. Let's look at the `player.currentRoom` and get the value.

```
var exitTo = player.currentRoom[direction];
```

Now `exitTo` will be equal to something like `"dining room"`, `null`, or `undefined`. If we test the trueness of `exitTo`, it would be `false` for `null` or `undefined` and it would be `true` if it has information like `"dining room"`. We're on the right track.

```
if (exitTo)
{
   //we MAY be able to go this way
}
else
{
   //we definitely cannot go this way
}
```

This isn't everything we need, though. Remember, if a player typed in one of the other property names, like `itemFound`, then we'd get an incorrect `true`, so we need to check for that, too.

We really have to watch for all these things?

We need to see if the `exitTo` room is an actual room. We can do this by checking the *truthiness* of `rooms[exitTo]`. If this evaluates to `true`, then we do have a good direction and we can move the player there. If it's not `true`, we cannot move the player, so we will need to ask again.

```
if (rooms[exitTo])
{
   //we CAN go this way, send back the direction
}
else
{
   //we cannot go this way
}
```

This conditional looks like it will work better than the last one, so we're going to use this. Where is it going? We have a function that is used to `getDirection()`, right? It would make sense to put this in there.

We don't actually need the `else` statement. The `return` command will send back a valid direction and the rest of the function won't run any more. If there is no valid direction, the rest of the function will keep going on its own. There's nothing wrong if we keep the `else` statement; it's just unnecessary, so I'm deleting it.

```
function getDirection()
{
  var text = "Which way do you want to go? ";
  var direction = prompt(text);
  direction = direction.toLowerCase();

  var exitTo = player.currentRoom[direction];

  if (rooms[exitTo])
  {
    //we CAN go this way, send back the exitTo
    return exitTo;
  }
  alert("You can't go that way.");
}
```

Capitalization issue. If you created your room properties with correct camelCase, then your directions are all in lowercase, like `north` and not like `North`. A player, however, may type with an uppercase letter or their autocorrect may do that for them. It can ruin the experience for a player. Luckily, there's an easy fix. We can use a premade method to convert the `direction` text into lowercase for us.

We have this right after the prompt.
```
  direction = direction.toLowerCase();
```

This converts the typed `direction` into all lowercase letters and assigns it back as the `direction`. It gets rid of any uppercase letters. As long as your direction properties are lowercase, this fixes those minor bugs.

One more thing. This still isn't finished, though. This function sends back a direction if the player gets a valid direction on the first try. Otherwise, the function sends back `undefined`. Why? Because that's what all functions send back if you don't `return` a value. We can't use `undefined`. We need to ask the player to select a direction again.

2.16 While Loop

We have a situation where we need to keep repeating code until we get a valid answer. That is, we need to keep looping over the code until the condition changes. It's time to talk about `while` loops.

A `while` loop runs forever until the condition it's testing for is `false`. It's like an `if` statement that keeps running as long as it's a `true` condition. There are a few key parts to a `while` loop. You need an *initializer* (a starting point), a *condition* to test for, a *code block* to run, and a way to *alter the condition* so you can end the loop.

Syntax:

```
//some kind of initializer

while (condition)
{
   //code block where condition can change
   //or exit loop with break or return
}
```

You have to be careful not to enter into an infinite loop accidentally. This is a loop that never ends. Some infinite loops are good. Your browser runs in one, constantly checking for clicks and things to load or do. It only ends when you close the browser. Your computer's operating system (even on your smart phone) does the same thing.

> Infinite loops are useful sometimes, but we should make sure we don't create one accidentally.

But in our case, an infinite loop can be a problem. You need to make sure you always have a way out of the loop. Otherwise, you may have to force-quit your program and possibly lose some of your work. One reason I keep suggesting repl.it is because it saves your code instantly as you type it. If you do have to close your browser because of an infinite loop, when you go back in you should still have all your code. It happens to the best of us, even when we think we have it covered.

Sometimes, you will see suggestions for using a `while(true) {}` loop. It's an infinite loop with a `true` condition that can never change. Honestly, we actually could use that for our code because we exit the function with `return` if we find a good direction. But I don't like it.

Using the while(true) loop. I will show it to you anyway because it's good to see things. Our code will work with this case.

Inside our `getDirection()` function, we need to wrap that code in the `while` loop. You're good at wrapping now, right?

```
function getDirection()
{
  while (true)                         //<-- new
  {                                    //<-- new
    var text = "Which way do you want to go? ";
    var direction = prompt(text);
    direction = direction.toLowerCase();

    var exitTo = player.currentRoom[direction];

    if (rooms[exitTo])
    {
      //we CAN go this way, send back the exitTo
      return exitTo;
    }
    alert("You can't go that way.");
  }                                    //<-- new
}
```

And that's it. It will keep asking for a direction until it gets a valid one. *We don't want to run this yet, though.* I think it's a good idea to have some way of exiting a `while` loop like this so we don't get stuck. Let's use a codeword that will let us `break` out if we have to. How about `"quit"`?

Using break. Let's add this to an `else` block to check if the user typed `"quit"` after we checked on the room exit. We're going to use a loop-controlling keyword inside: `break`. This breaks us out of the loop when it's run.

```
if (rooms[exitTo])
{
  //we CAN go this way, send back the direction
  return exitTo;
}
else if (direction === "quit")        //<-- new
{                                     //<-- new
  break;                              //<-- new
}                                     //<-- new
alert("You can't go that way.");
```

Test it. Run your program and type `getDirection();` in the console.

Not using a while(true) loop. I said earlier that I don't like a `while(true)` loop. Maybe it's a personal preference. We handled it in a way where creating an infinite loop isn't a problem. The loop can exit (`return`) if a good direction is chosen, but we also inserted a backdoor exit (`break`) by sticking that `"quit"` option in there.

You won't use infinite loops too often. I want to show you another process. It's similar in its result here for what we're doing, but it has greater applications for other things.

To do this, we need to declare the initializer (`direction`) before the loop starts. Then we will test to see if there is *not* a good direction (`!direction`). Then we'll prompt for one and do what we did before. At the end, we will set direction to `null`. I also want to reduce the number of popups, so we will change the value of the text string before the loop goes through again.

Here's what all that looks like.

```
function getDirection()
{
  var text = "Which way do you want to go? ";
  var direction;

  while (!direction)
  {
    direction = prompt(text);
    direction = direction.toLowerCase();

    var exitTo = player.currentRoom[direction];

    if (rooms[exitTo])
    {
      //we CAN go this way, send back the exitTo
      return exitTo;
    }
    else if (direction === "quit")
    {
      break;
    }
    text = "You can't go " + direction + ". ";
    text += "Please try again. ";
    text += "Use compass points like north.";
    direction = null;
  }
}
```

You can use either version of the loop you prefer. They both work. But there is one last thing we need to fix before we can connect this to the game directly.

When we set up our rooms, we gave them direction properties: north, south, etc. Here, we're asking the player to give us a direction: north, south, etc. In other words, we are asking the player to type in one of the room's properties. They don't know that, nor should they.

We have a name property, right? And that name is the name of the current room we are in. If the player types in name as a direction, the computer will think it's valid!

```
var exitTo = player.currentRoom["name"]; //"living room"
if (rooms[exitTo])                       //this would be true!
```

Edge case. This is called an *edge case*, where something unexpected has to be controlled for. It's a special case that may not come up until the game is fully tested and run hundreds of times. But we're aware of it now, so we can fix it right away.

Is this why we should test things so much, to find things like this?

Remember how we used `"quit"` to break out of the loop and stop it from working? There's another keyword we can use to say, "Hey, don't process the rest of this loop, but don't quit either. Go back to the top and continue from there." It's called `continue`.

Using continue. Once the player inputs a direction, if they entered `"name"` then let's `continue;` the loop and skip the part where we check for it to be a valid room. What do you think, can you handle that? Oh and you'd want this in either form of the `while` loop, whether you're using the `while(true)` loop or the `while (!direction)` loop.

Put this right after the line with the `prompt` command.

```
direction = prompt(text);            //already there
direction = direction.toLowerCase(); //already there

if (direction === "name")            //<--new
{
   continue;
}
```

Single line code blocks. By the way, when you have a statement that uses a code block (like `if` or `while`), if you *only have* **one** command to process, you don't need braces. You can even put it all on one line. It looks neater, but makes the code look less consistent. it can be harder to find what you're looking for when you have lots of code. *Note*: You cannot do this for functions; functions **require** the braces.

```
if (direction === "name") continue;
```

2.17 Getting Directions

The last thing we're going to do for the `getDirection()` function is let the player know which direction(s) they have available to them. There are many different ways we could handle this. The best way would be to alter our rooms in the code and move all the directions available into an object inside each room object.

Let's help the player out a little!

But I want to keep us focused here for now. We could keep things very simple and just tell the player to type in a direction like north, east, south, or west. Or we could be really nice and tell them what their actual options are. Let's be really nice.

We checked directions before using these lines of code.

```
direction = prompt(text);               //ask
direction = direction.toLowerCase();    //lowercase
var exitTo = player.currentRoom[direction];  //get name
if (rooms[exitTo])                      //check
```

We could do something like this.

```
text += "There are exits: ";

var north = player.currentRoom["north"];
if (rooms[north])
{
  text += " north ";
}

var south = player.currentRoom["south"];
if (rooms[south])
{
  text += " south ";
}
```

And so on. These lines would go right *before* the `prompt` command.

It's messy and it opens us up to lots of fixing if we wanted to change something, like if we wanted the directions to be shown in brackets like `[north][south][east][west]`. We would benefit from a `for...in` loop and an array. We're going to get into those later. For now, we're going to leave the clunkier code.

These individual direction checks make this function bigger than it needs to be. If you went into your rooms and added new directions, like `northeast` or `southwest`, you would need to add more checks for those here too.

Check out our completed function on the next page.

By the way, you could give yourself a code challenge if you wanted to by adding other directions like `northeast` and so on. It's up to you! I'm going to add some in my final code for this project.

Here is our currently complete `getDirection()` function.

```javascript
function getDirection()
{
  var text = "Which way do you want to go? ";
  var direction;
  while (!direction)
  {
    text += "There are exits: ";
    var north = player.currentRoom["north"];
    if (rooms[north])
    {
      text += " north ";
    }
    var south = player.currentRoom["south"];
    if (rooms[south])
    {
      text += " south ";
    }
    var east = player.currentRoom["east"];
    if (rooms[east])
    {
      text += " east ";
    }
    var west = player.currentRoom["west"];
    if (rooms[west])
    {
      text += " west ";
    }

    direction = prompt(text);
    direction = direction.toLowerCase();
    var exitTo = player.currentRoom[direction];

    if (rooms[exitTo])
    {
      //we CAN go this way, send back the exitTo
      return exitTo;
    }
    else if (direction === "quit")
    {
      break;
    }
    text = "You can't go " + direction + ". ";
    text += "Please try again. ";
    direction = null;
  }
}
```

2.18 Getting on the Move

That was a lot of work to set up the `getDirection()` function, wasn't it? In the end, it tells the user which way they can go, asks for a direction, and checks to make sure it's valid. If it's a good direction, then it sends back the name of the room, otherwise it keeps trying in a loop.

But the whole purpose of the `getDirection()` function was just to do that... to get the direction from the user. *We still haven't moved the player!*

Still more to do?

When we add this next function in, we will be able to walk all around the house. Finally. Let's break it down into what we need.

- We need to display the room location and description.
- We need to see if there is an item we can pick up.
- We need to see if there is a broken item in the room.
- We need to see if we have what we need to fix the item.
- We need to see if we won the game.
- We need to ask where the player wants to go to next.

We will start with only the first and last bullets and add the rest later. Are you ready?

Creating the moveToRoom() function. Create a `moveToRoom()` function to start us off. When we're inside this new function, let's display what room the player is in and what it looks like in there.

Hey, wait a minute… didn't we already create a function that displays the room's description?

Let's ask the player which way they want to go. If we get a valid room, we'll change their `currentRoom`. We'll need to use the `rooms` object for that. Lastly, let's call this function again to keep the player moving.

> Let's use that function we made before! That's one great thing about functions, huh?

Our first version of the `moveToRoom()` function.

```
function moveToRoom()
{
  textRoomDescription();
  var direction = getDirection();
  if (direction)
  {
    player.currentRoom = rooms[direction];
    moveToRoom();
  }
}
```

Recursion. This is a *recursive* function because `moveToRoom()` calls itself at the end. It will keep calling itself until there is no valid direction returned. We do this so the player can keep moving from room to room. If we didn't have this in there, the player would move once and the game would stop.

Remember how we gave ourselves a way to `"quit"`? We need to use this now because we're making a text adventure. We need the game to keep playing. When we eventually link in HTML and buttons, we will get rid of this recursion because we won't need it.

You can test this out by running the code, then typing `moveToRoom();` in the console. It will let you walk all around your house! Try it!

By the way, if you quit your game and then want to continue from where you left off, just call `moveToRoom()` from the console.

78

Starting the game. Let's make one more function to start the game so you can run it without having to type in any extra commands.

We should probably let the user know what the game is all about, right? And then start it up. In this function, let's also reset the `rooms` and the `player`. Long-term, that will let us use this function to reset or start the game again if we want to.

The last thing you'll need to do is to call this function near the top of your code. Remember lines 1 and 2 where we create the first set of `rooms` and the `player`? Put this function call right *after* those.

```
1    var rooms = getRooms();
2    var player = getPlayer();
3    startGame();
4    |
5
6    function startGame()
7 ▾  {
```

You can temporarily leave out the `text` string in the next function if you're that excited to get it running. But be sure you add it in at some point for a player!

Figure 11. The function call that starts it all...

Describing the game to a player. You'll notice in the code coming up that I build a lengthy `text` string to explain what the player has to do. I make use of some of the player's properties, too, so they can be changed dynamically later (if we let the player change the name or if we have a different number of things to fix, for instance).

If we didn't use a text string like this, we would have one of two issues. One, we would possibly end up with a really long line of code that would be hard to debug later. Two, if we used an alert for each line, it would be super annoying to a player. The text string allows us to have readable code and a nicer experience for the player.

For display purposes, I added a space at the beginning of the text lines. If not, the words will mash together and be harder to read. Last time I put the spaces at the end. I want you to see that you can do it either way.

Try it out.

Here's our `startGame` function.

```
function startGame()
{
  //reset the global rooms and player objects
  rooms = getRooms();
  player = getPlayer();

  //This explains the game to a new player
  var text = "Welcome to the Room Adventure!";
  text += " You are " + player.name;
  text += " and you are in a house";
  text += " where many things are broken.";
  text += " Go from room to room";
  text += " to find the items you need";
  text += " to fix what's broken.";
  text += " Earn points for fixing things.";
  text += " There are " + player.itemsLeftToFix;
  text += " things that need to be fixed.";
  text += " You start in the ";
  text += player.currentRoom.name + ".";
  text += " Good luck!";
  alert(text);

  //move the player into their current room
  //to display the description and start the game
  moveToRoom();
}
```

A tiny tweak. Now that our `startGame()` function creates its own set of `rooms` and the `player`, let's make a slight tweak to the opening lines of code.

```
1  "use strict";
2  var rooms;
3  var player;
4  startGame();
```

Figure 12. Edit globals

Keep the variable names, but remove the function calls: `= getRooms()` and `= getPlayer()`. This is at the very top of your file, *not* inside `startGame()`. Why create a set of rooms and a player if the starting function is just going to make new ones? I also added the `"use strict";` directive to help make sure our code is clean.

Test it to make the best of it.

Go on! Test it out! It took some time, but you have a working game on your hands now. Run through your house layout. Check it with your blueprint. Do the rooms connect the way you intended? Are there any issues with how the descriptions show up? Do you need to fix any of your text? Make any corrections now.

2.19 Skill Check: Make More Rooms

You have come a long way and you've seen a lot of different types of code. Does your brain feel full yet? I hope not, because there's more to do!

Let's see how far you've come!

Before moving on, it's a good idea to do a little review. Take a break from learning new concepts and go back to where we started, creating rooms.

Right now, you have four rooms in your house. Take some time and double that. *Make four more rooms* and add them in. They will make your game more fun, but this will also check to make sure you remember how.

See if you can do it on your own. If you need a refresher, check the next page.

Here are the steps for adding new rooms.

Step 1:

- Go into the `getRooms()` function
- Find a place above `var rooms = {};`
- Create a new room starting with
  - `var nameOfRoom =`
    ```
    {
        name: "name of room",
    //rest of the object
    ```
- Make sure the new room has the same properties as the other rooms
  - `description`, `brokenThing`, `fixWith`, `itemFound`, etc.
- Make sure you connect the new rooms to the old rooms, at least in one place
  - If you don't, you won't be able to get to them in the game
- Shuffle the new `fixWith` items into other rooms' `itemFound` properties
  - Don't lose any items along the way

Step 2:

- Add the new room to the bigger `rooms` object
- Use array notation like the others
  - `rooms[nameOfRoom.name] = nameOfRoom;`

Step 3:

- Go into the `getPlayer()` function
- Change the `itemsLeftToFix` property so the number matches the new number of things that need to be fixed
  - If you now have eight rooms, make this an `8`
  - `var player =`
    ```
    {
        //other properties
        itemsLeftToFix: 8
    }
    ```

Step 4:

- Test it out!

Chapter 3

Adding to the Basic Game

It's time to start fixing things.

At this point, you have a functioning game you can play, but it's not so much a "game" as it is a floorplan you can move around in. You can type in directions and go from room to room.

We need to add a game aspect to it to make it more fun. We have rooms that have broken things (brokenThing) in them and we have items we can find (itemFound) in those rooms.

We want to be able to fix the broken items if we have what we need to fix them (fixWith). Lastly, we want to reward the player for fixing each thing (points).

And once everything is fixed (itemsLeftToFix is 0), we want to let them know they've won the game and then give them a chance to start anew.

There's still a lot to do to get the basic game done. Let's get started.

3.1 Finding Items

In each room, there is supposed to be an item that can be found, which is needed elsewhere in order to fix something. Each room you created has the `itemFound` property to keep track of this. We are going to use that property in the `currentRoom` and let the `player` pick it up.

> Keep it simple first, get it working, then add more features

At this point, the pickup will happen automatically. With some extra time, we could make it so the player would have to pick it up themselves. But let's get the basics done before adding complications.

Each time the player moves to a new room, we have to check if there is an item to be found. If so, we need to add it to the player's `inventory` and also remove the item from the room—otherwise he or she would be able to pick up unlimited numbers of them. That might sound cool, but it violates the laws of physics.

We *could* put the code for this into the `moveToRoom()` function. However, we want to keep functions small whenever we can. Each function should serve a single main purpose. So we will make a separate function for finding items and have the `moveToRoom()` function call for it to run.

Tasks:
1. See if there is an item in the room to find
2. If so...
   a. Tell the player
   b. Add it to the player's `inventory`
   c. Remove the item from the room
3. If not...
   a. You don't need to do anything, so we don't need an `else` statement

```
function isThereAnItem()
{
  var item = player.currentRoom.itemFound;
  if (item)
  {
    alert("You found the " + item + "!");
    player.inventory.push(item);
    player.currentRoom.itemFound = null;
  }
}
```

To make the code easier to read, I created a helper `item` variable right at the beginning. I then used it to test for an item in the room and, if present, to display it and to add it to the player's `inventory`.

That last line sets the room's `itemFound` property to `null`, which means we take it out of the room. The next time we come to this room, there won't be an item to find.

When you're placing this function, as with the other functions, make sure it's not tucked inside a different function. Also, for readability, don't put it above the first three lines of our code that initialize the `rooms`, the `player`, and start the game. Outside of those restrictions, it really can go anywhere in your file.

Inventory array. A long time ago (Section 2.9: Creating the Player Object), we set up a `player` object and gave it an `inventory` property with an empty array `[]`.

Arrays are lists of things and they have a lot of cool features to them. Our current function makes use of one array method, called `push()`. The `push()` method adds something to the end of the list. It's like if you have a shopping list and you add an item to it at the bottom. Same thing here. We'll get more into array features in a little bit. For now, just understand that `player.inventory.push(item);` adds the name of the item we found to the end of the player's inventory list.

Making the item-finding function work. In order for the `isThereAnItem()` function to work, we have to add a function call to the `moveToRoom()` function. We need a line that says `isThereAnItem();` inside the `moveToRoom()` function.

Look back to the `moveToRoom()` function and try to figure out where it makes the *most sense* to put this call. When should you be checking for items? Take a moment and test yourself. See if you can figure it out before looking on.

We have to think about the order of events.

The flow of events is important.
We want things to happen this way:

1. The player enters a room.
2. The room is described to the player.
3. If there's something the player can pick up, pick it up.
4. See if there's a broken thing to fix.
5. If we have the right item, fix the broken thing.
6. Leave the room.

We're not ready for seeing if something's broken or if we can fix it yet, but the flow is still the same. Therefore, the best place to check for an item is… (Have you figured it out yet?)

```
function moveToRoom()
{
  textRoomDescription();

  isThereAnItem();                    //<--it goes here

  var direction = getDirection();
  if (direction)
  {
    player.currentRoom = rooms[direction];
    moveToRoom();
  }
}
```

Test your code. Once this is all set up, go through your house. Make sure everything works. (Remember, you can type `"quit"` so you don't have to run through your whole house.) In your console window, check the player's `inventory`. Do you know how? Type in `player.inventory;`. It will show you a list of things you've picked up.

What are we going to do with all these items? Carrying around a lot of inventory can be fun (yeah right) but we need to *do* something with these items.

Remember that each room has something broken in it. And those broken items need these inventory items to fix them.

We're going to have to check if the player has the inventory item. If they do, we need them to fix the broken item.

It sounds like a lot, but let's take it one step at a time. Just like we did for finding an item, we are going to create a separate function for fixing things. Think about it. What would the function need to do?

It's got a few steps to it when we really break it down.

Here's what the function needs to do.

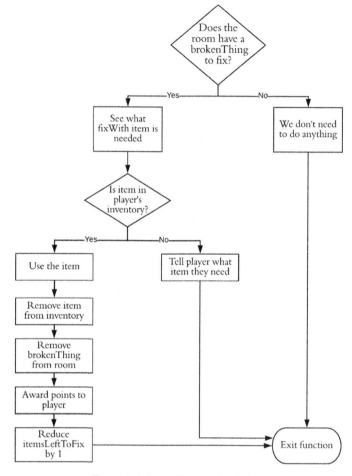

Figure 13. fixBrokenThing function flowchart

Take a moment to think about this and imagine what the function code will look like. It will be pretty similar to the one we wrote for `isThereAnItem()`, so you have a head start if you look back at that. See if you can lay out the function on your own first.

When you're ready, go on.

This flowchart helps me see what has to be done. Now, how would I code it?

3.2 Fixing up the Broken Things

As the player collects items, they need to be used. (Why else have them?) Each room should need one of the items, if you planned it well, and now it's time to use them. The previous page explains what our fix-it function needs to do, so check back there if you've forgotten.

Arrays. An array is a list of items. The items can be strings, numbers, objects, other arrays, and even functions. We are using an array here to keep track of inventory item names, which are strings.

Arrays are indexed from 0. The first item in the array is item 0. If there are five items in an array, they would have indexes 0, 1, 2, 3, 4. This can be confusing at first and it takes time to get used to.

Here's an example using some of my possible inventory items. Let's say I picked them up in this order: batteries, new wire, and wrench. My inventory array would look like this.

```
player.inventory = ["batteries", "new wire", "wrench"];


player.inventory[0];                //"batteries"
player.inventory[1];                //"new wire"
player.inventory[2];                //"wrench"
player.inventory[3];                //undefined
```

If I try to access an index that doesn't have anything, it's undefined.

If I later find a screwdriver, I can **push** that onto the array. It gets added to the end of the array, in this case, index 3.

```
player.inventory.push("screwdriver");
player.inventory[3];                    //"screwdriver"
```

Finding an index in an array. There's a really easy and convenient way of finding out if an array has something we're looking for. We can use an array method called `indexOf()`.

> This is a super helpful method for finding things.

By using the dot operator and putting this at the end of an array name, and by putting information into the parentheses as an argument, you can check to see if the item is in the array. If it is, this will return an index number from `0` up to the end of the array. And if it's not in there, it returns `-1`.

Using the inventory I created above, if I used the following commands, they would return the values shown.

```
player.inventory.indexOf("wrench");        //2
player.inventory.indexOf("batteries");     //0
player.inventory.indexOf("masking tape");  //-1
```

There was no masking tape in my list, so it comes back as `-1`. Do you see how we can use this? Let's say we needed masking tape to fix something in the office, but there is no masking tape in my inventory. Well, I can't fix that thing in the office yet until I find that masking tape.

Let's finally create the function we need to deal with all this stuff. I'm going to create the whole thing and then I'll break it down.

Do you also know where we're going to have to call this from? Think about that, too.

Ready?

Here's our `fixBrokenThing()` function.

```
function fixBrokenThing()
{
  //helper variables to make the code easier to read
  var brokenThing = player.currentRoom.brokenThing;
  var fixWith = player.currentRoom.fixWith;

  //test: Is there a broken thing?
  if (brokenThing)
  {
    //get ready to announce there's a broken thing
    var text = "There is a broken ";
    text += brokenThing + " in this room. ";

    //helper variable
    var index = player.inventory.indexOf(fixWith);

    //test: if fixWith is NOT in inventory
    if (index === -1)
    {
      text += "You need the " + fixWith;
      text += " to fix it.";
    }
    else //the item IS in the inventory
    {
      text += "You fixed the " + brokenThing;
      text += " with the " + fixWith + "!";
      text += " You earn ";
      text += player.currentRoom.points;
      text += " points.";

      player.currentRoom.brokenThing = null;
      player.score += player.currentRoom.points;
      player.itemsLeftToFix--;
    }
    alert (text);
  }                     //this closes if (brokenThing)
}                       //this closes the function
```

The first two lines (with `var`), and `var index` later on, are there to make
the rest of the code easier to read. If we didn't use them, we could have
ended up with a line that looks like this.

```
if (player.inventory.indexOf(player.currentRoom.fixWith) === -1)
```

Kind of a mess, right?

Testing for a brokenThing. We use `if (brokenThing)` to see if there is a `brokenThing` in the room. If so, we run the rest of the code. If you look carefully, you will see there is no `else` statement for this check. That means if there's nothing broken, we don't do anything else and the function exits.

However, we want to tell the player there's a broken thing in the room whether or not we fix something.

Checking the player's inventory. We use the `indexOf` method to see if the player has the item they need to fix the broken thing. This tests to see if they *don't* have it because we check for this being equal to `-1`. I used a helper variable, `index`, to make the code easier to read, but also because we're going to use that `index` again.

```
//This tests for NOT having the item
var index = player.inventory.indexOf(fixWith);
if (index === -1)
```

Clearing the brokenThing. We begin by setting the `player.currentRoom.brokenThing` property to `null`. This removes the `brokenThing` from the room so we don't try to fix it again later.

Adding points to the player. When we created our rooms, we gave point values for fixing certain things. Now that the player fixed something, we increase the `player.score` by adding in those points using the `+=` operator with `player.currentRoom.points`.

Sidenote. We could test for *having the item* instead of *not having it*. For that, we would use not-equal-to: `!== -1`. We would have to flip the code blocks around. It's fine either way. For us, if we don't have the item, we're done, so this code block is over fast. But if we do have the item, we have several things to take care of. I think it helps readability to have the smaller block first.

Reducing the itemsLeftToFix. The last thing we do is reduce the number of items to fix. The `--` reduces the number by 1. When this gets to zero, the game will be over. We still need to check for that, but we'll get there soon.

Checking the number of inventory items. Because the inventory is an array, we could easily check to see how many items the player is carrying at any given time. We attach the `.length` property to the name of the array. It tells us how many elements the array is holding.

```
player.inventory = ["wrench", "light bulb",
                    "batteries", "new wire"];
player.inventory.length;                            //4
```

The `length` property of arrays is used a lot for controlling loops. We'll get to those.

Changing the inventory. There's one thing I left out of the function because it takes a little explanation. We just had the player use an item to fix a broken thing. Is that item still in your inventory if you've used it? No, probably not. We should remove it, don't you think?

I know how to pull something out of a bag, but how do we take it out of an array?

To do this, we are going to use another array method. This one is called `splice()`. Splice is a multifunctional method. It can take things out of an array and it can put other things in.

Syntax: `array.splice(startIndex, numberItems, addTo, addTo…);`

The `startIndex` is the place we want to start at… Oh, that might have been kind of obvious. Let's look at an example, though, to make sure.

Let's say our player has the following items: *wrench, light bulb, batteries,* and *new wire*. The `player.inventory` array would be this.

```
player.inventory = ["wrench", "light bulb",
                    "batteries", "new wire"];
```

The batteries are the third item on the list, so that makes them index 2. Remember that arrays start counting from zero. If we wanted to remove the batteries, we would start the `splice` at index 2. How many items would we want to remove? Just the one. Are we adding any new inventory items at this moment? Nope.

We can use this to remove the batteries in this example.

```
player.inventory.splice(2, 1); //removes index 2
```

This makes our array look like this now.

```
player.inventory = ["wrench", "light bulb",
                    "new wire"];
```

The batteries are gone and `"new wire"` slid down into index 2. The nice part of using splice is that we reduce the chance of having gaps in our array. Gaps can lead to some unexpected results.

Hey, we just talked about `indexOf()` a moment ago.

In our program, we won't know where the batteries are located in the array when the player is playing. They won't always be at index 2. The player could pick the batteries up first, eighth, third, who knows? That's where the `indexOf()` method comes into play. It looks through the array for the batteries and then tells us the first place it finds them.

We created a helper variable, `index`, before checking if the item was in the inventory. This is before the conditional `if (index === -1)`.

```
var index = player.inventory.indexOf(fixWith);
```

We can use that helper `index` now to remove the item from its spot.

```
player.inventory.splice(index, 1);
```

Where should the `splice` go? With these lines:

```
player.currentRoom.brokenThing = null;
player.score += player.currentRoom.points;
player.itemsLeftToFix--;
player.inventory.splice(index, 1);    //<--it goes here
```

Sidenote. Let's take the inventory example from above with the *wrench*, *light bulb*, *batteries*, and *new wire* in it. If we remove the batteries by setting them to `null`, we would get this array.

```
player.inventory = ["wrench", "light bulb", null, "new wire"];
```

It looks fine, with no batteries in it. But if I want to know how many items there are in the array, I can't use the length property.

```
player.inventory.length; //4
```

Four? But there are only three! No, because `null` (and `undefined`) count as elements. They're like placeholders for numbers. They still count. Using splice was a better way to go for what we are doing.

However, setting array elements to `null` and keeping the array the same size isn't always a bad thing. There are situations where this would be better. For example, let's say you wanted the inventory items to appear on screen in a specific spot (ex: screwdriver only in slot 1).

One way you could control that is by `null`ing out the items you don't have. It's also useful if you're using two parallel arrays to keep track of information. Since we're not doing those things here, we'll stick with `splice`.

Connecting our fixBrokenThing function. We went through the whole process of making a function that checks for a `brokenThing`, but we never activated it!

Do you remember what the last step is? We need to *call* the function. It won't work on its own. Think again... Where would be a good place to put this? Think of the order we want things to happen in.

→ *Move to a room* (`moveToRoom`)
→ *Look for an item to pick up* (`isThereAnItem`)
→ *Fix a broken thing* (`fixBrokenThing`)

So where does it go? Immediately after the `isThereAnItem();` function we added to `moveToRoom()`. Add it. Test it!

Here is the current `moveToRoom` function.

```
function moveToRoom()
{
  textRoomDescription();
  isThereAnItem();
  fixBrokenThing();                       //<-- add this here

  var direction = getDirection();
  if (direction)
  {
    player.currentRoom = rooms[direction];
    moveToRoom();
  }
}
```

You can go ahead and test this out and start fixing things in your house. The only drawback now is that you won't see your inventory items or your score. We'll tackle those next.

3.3 Showing the Score

We're walking all around the house and fixing things. We're earning points. But we don't know what our actual score is! We should probably let the player know the score.

Everyone wants to know how well they're doing.

Let's create a separate function for this. It's a small function, but that's good. It keeps the code neat and organized. And if we ever decide to change how we want to display the score (hint, hint) then all we have to do is change this function. No other part of the program ever needs to know anything about this.

```
function showScore()
{
  player.score = Math.max(0, player.score);
  alert("Score: " + player.score);
}
```

The `Math.max()` line makes sure that the score doesn't go below zero. If it does, then zero `0` is the bigger number, so it keeps `0`, otherwise it keeps the player's actual score.

You know what's coming next, right? The function won't run itself. We need to place it in a logical location that will show us the score. What would be a good time to do that?

How about right after you might earn some points?

97

Updating moveToRoom. Take a look back to the `moveToRoom()` function and update it again.

```
function moveToRoom()
{
  textRoomDescription();
  isThereAnItem();
  fixBrokenThing();
  showScore();                        //<-- add this here

  var direction = getDirection();
  if (direction)
  {
    player.currentRoom = rooms[direction];
    moveToRoom();
  }
}
```

3.4 Showing the Inventory

While we are caught up displaying things, let's display the inventory too. You can probably guess what we're going to do next, right? Yep, we're creating a new function to `showInventory`.

> Let's start simple and get it to work. Then let's improve it.

But what should it look like inside? Do we just do the same thing we did before for `player.score`?

```
function showInventory()
{
  alert("Inventory: " + player.inventory);
}
```

And of course, add the function to `moveToRoom()` right below showing the score.

```
function moveToRoom()
{
  textRoomDescription();
  isThereAnItem();
  fixBrokenThing();
  showScore();
  showInventory();          //<-- add this here

  var direction = getDirection();
  if (direction)
  {
    player.currentRoom = rooms[direction];
    moveToRoom();
  }
}
```

Go ahead and give it a try. You will now see that you earn points as you go from room to room and you get to see your score and your inventory.

If you pay close attention, you will see that the inventory items do disappear from your bag as you use them.

What do you think about the inventory display? The array gets automatically converted to a list separated by commas with no extra spaces. It works, but we could make it look better.

3.5 Improving the Inventory Display

JavaScript has a default way of displaying most things. There is a hidden method, `.toString()`, that transforms things into strings that get printed.

JavaScript takes care of some interesting things behind the scenes.

- Numbers get turned into simple strings.
- Arrays get turned into lists with commas.
- Objects and functions aren't as useful.
  o Objects become `[object Object]`
  o Functions become `[Function: functionName]`

Run your program and grab a few items. Then `quit` and go to the console window. Type each of these in.

```
player.inventory;
player.inventory.toString();
```

In the console, they're displayed differently. In the `alert()` popup, you only saw the second way. Try this exercise with one of our objects, like `rooms` or `player`.

```
player;                    //shows all player details
player.toString();         //shows [object Object]
```

We could override the `.toString()` method and make things display the way we want them to, but that's a bit more advanced at this point. Instead, let's talk about a neater way of showing the inventory.

Joining an array. Arrays have lots of useful methods, and `join` is one of them. Simply put, the join method takes each element in an array and joins them with whatever you tell it to and saves it as a text string.

Let's see an example.

```
var colors = ["blue", "red", "gold", "silver"];
var list = colors.join("***");
list;                    //blue***red***gold***silver
```

The default `array.toString();` is a simple `array.join(",");`.

Splitting a string. What's the opposite of `join`? It's `split`. For this, put in a string and the computer sends back an array of items. It finds what you put in, removes it, and sends the pieces back as array elements. It's `join` in reverse.

```
var myList = "catxdogxmonkeyxoxen";
var animals = myList.split("x");
animals;            // ["cat", "dog", "monkey", "o", "en"]
```

This one cuts out the letter "x" and sends back all the pieces. Oops, we accidentally split up the "oxen". I guess that means we need to be careful when using this.

Better control over the inventory output. We could use the `join` method to give us some control over how the inventory items appear onscreen. But what if we wanted to box them in brackets, `[like] [this]`? That's something `join` isn't built for.

We will need to make use of another type of loop, a `for` loop. And we're going to use it on the `player.inventory` array.

3.6 Anatomy of a 'for' Loop

We talked about `while` loops before (Section 2.16: While Loop). This is `while`'s twin, `for`.

We used the `while` loop to make sure the player entered a valid direction. We didn't know how many times we had to run the loop before we started. After all, the player could get it right on the first try, or they could keep hitting enter over and over to see if anything odd happened. For that, it made sense to use a `while` loop which continued to run until we had a valid direction.

> Loops are extremely important in computer programs. I'd really better study this.

A `for` loop is used when you *do* know how many times you need to run the loop. Let's say you specifically want something to happen five times. Or maybe you have a variable that represents a number and you want to run the loop *that* many times. For example, if we have an array with five items, we would want to run the loop five times.

Both loops have the same basic parts, but their syntax is different.

While Loop Syntax:

```
initializer
while (condition)                        //no semicolon
{
  //code block
  incrementor/condition-changer
}
```

For Loop Syntax:

```
for (initializer; condition; incrementor) //no semicolon
{
  //code block
}
```

Notice where semicolons are located and where they're missing. That's very important for your loops to run correctly.

The `for` declaration has three statements embedded in there all at once. Everything that controls the loop is right there. In the `while` loop, we need to have a situation set up ahead of time and we need to change that situation during the loop somewhere.

Let's start with an example of displaying the values 0 through 9 to get your feet wet. This will show the `for` loop and the `while` loop together.

For loop	While loop

`for (var i = 0; i < 10; i++)`
`{`
`  console.log(i);`
`}`
	`var i = 0;`
	`while (i < 10)`
	`{`
	`  console.log(i);`
	`  i++`
	`}`

- They both have a loop declaration: `for` or `while`
- They both have an initializer: `var i = 0`.
- They both have a condition to test for: `i < 10`.
- They both have an incrementor: `i++`.
- They both have a code block.

The `for` loop is a little more concise in its code because everything is on the declaration line. This is great for when you know how many times you need to go through the loop.

Initializer. We often use `i` for the variable in a `for` loop, meaning *index* or *increment*. You can use any variable you like. We still declare it with `var` like a regular variable. Typically, we also start loops at zero, `0`. Again, you can start this anywhere you need to.

Condition. Just like an `if` statement or a `while` loop, we need to test to see if we should run the code block. As long as this statement evaluates to `true`, we keep running the loop.

Incrementor. This is written in shortcut notation: `i++`. The `++` just means to add `1` to `i` each time through the loop. We could count up by anything here using a valid expression, like `i += 2` or `i = i * 4`. Most of the time, a `for` loop runs on a counter counting up by one, so `i++` became a very popular shortcut. Incidentally, there's also `i--` to subtract `1` each time.

Infinite loop. Yes, just like with a `while` loop, it's possible to make your `for` loop enter into an infinite loop. This is usually not what you want.

Check these examples.

```
//Infinite Loop 1:
for (var i = 0;  i < 10; i--) //counts  0, -1, -2...

//Infinite Loop 2:
for (var i = 10; i >= 0; i++) //counts 10, 11, 12...

//Infinite Loop 3:
for (var i = 0;  i < 10; i++) //looks fine, but...
{
  i = 0;  //...this resets i to 0 each time through!
}
```

Counting backward. Sometimes you need a loop to count backward. This is useful for a countdown timer or if you're examining an array that could shrink along the way. Be careful how you set up the conditions, but it's easy to do.

Counting down from 10 to 1:

```
for (var i = 10; i > 0; i--)
{
  console.log(i);
}
```

For as while? It is possible to make the `for` loop act like a `while` loop. It requires leaving out the initializer and the incrementor. When we were waiting for a good direction to be entered, we set the `while` header to be this.

```
while (!direction)
```

We could replicate this with a `for` loop by using this header.

```
for ( ; !direction ; )
```

It's weird, right? It needs those semicolons with nothing on the left or right. But *don't do this* in your code. It's bad practice. If you need a `while` loop, use a `while` loop. That's what it's for! (no pun intended)

3.7 Looping Through an Array

Our goal is to loop through our `player.inventory` array and format each element to look nice by wrapping it in `[square brackets]`. To do this, we need to loop through an array. We use a `for` loop. We also need to know how long the array is, which we find using the `length` property of the array.

> It would be really helpful if we could look at each item in our inventory.

Consider this.

```
player.inventory = ["batteries", "light bulb",
                    "new wire", "wrench"];

var length = player.inventory.length;

for (var i = 0; i < length; i++)
{
  var item = player.inventory[i];
  console.log(item);
}
```

Our example inventory has four items in it, so this will run `i` values of `0`, `1`, `2`, and `3`. Check out the `var item` line. It uses array notation to pull each item from the array. The first time through the loop, it pulls `player.inventory[0]`. The next time, it pulls `player.inventory[1]`, and so on. Each time, it looks at the next item in the array and reports it back. Then we display it to the `console.log()` window.

You don't have to create the `length` variable first, but it makes the code easier to follow.

Some programmers try to save memory by not creating extra variables. This really isn't something we need to worry about in our program.

But to show you, here's how it would look without either of the two extra variables.

Can you still understand it?

One common error when setting up loops this way is forgetting to include `.length` on the array. Without that, it won't work!

```
player.inventory = ["batteries", "light bulb",
                    "new wire", "wrench"];

for (var i = 0; i < player.inventory.length; i++)
{
   console.log(player.inventory[i]);
}
```

Updating the showInventory function. Now that we've talked about all of that, let's tidy up our inventory display function. We are going to create a text string that will set up the inventory items and, once the string is all set, we will display it. Ready?

```
function showInventory()
{
  var text = "Inventory: ";

  var length = player.inventory.length;

  for (var i = 0; i < length; i++)
  {
    text += "[";
    text += player.inventory[i];
    text += "] ";
  }

  alert(text);
}
```

Those three `text +=` lines are doing all the formatting. First, we add the open bracket [, then the name of the inventory item, then the closing bracket and a space], so it looks nicer.

Replace the old `showInventory()` function with this one and give it a whirl. If you'd rather use some other kind of formatting, go ahead and make it your own.

Can you get the display to show the inventory like any of these?

- `****light bulb****`
- `{ batteries }`
- `I've got the wrench in my pocket.`
- `--> screwdriver <--`
- `Don't tell anyone, but I'm carrying the new mirror.`

Wow, I have unlimited options! How am I going to decide what I want? I guess I can try them all and come up with my own!

3.8 Winning the Game

We've come so far, but we still can't win our own game! It's time to check to see if we've won.

We planned ahead and now we're ready to use that. Are you ready to win?

Winning condition. Our condition for winning is to fix all the broken things in the house. We already created a counter for this: `player.itemsLeftToFix`. Once that reaches zero, we've fixed everything, so the game is over.

Let's start by creating a function, `checkGameOver`, that tells us if we've won the game. If so, we will send back `true`. If not, we will send back `false`. All you need to do is see if `player.itemsLeftToFix` is equal to zero. If so, send back `true`, otherwise send back `false`. Remember to watch your capitalization.

At this point, you should be able to set up this function on your own. Go on and try, then check out what I've come up with.

I'm going to give this to you with another variation, so you can see another way to set up your code.

Long version of checkGameOver

```
function checkGameOver()
{
  var gameOver;
  if (player.itemsLeftToFix === 0)
  {
    gameOver = true;
  }
  else
  {
    gameOver = false;
  }
  return gameOver;
}
```

This creates an `undefined` variable `gameOver`. Then it checks the value of `player.itemsLeftToFix` and it adjusts the value of `gameOver` based on whether the player has things to fix or not.

We do have one possible bug condition here. What if, for some reason, the `itemsLeftToFix` counter goes negative? It shouldn't ever. But we can control for that with a simple tweak to the `if` statement. We change the strict equality `===` to less-than-or-equal-to `<=`.

```
if (player.itemsLeftToFix <= 0) //less than or equal to
```

We may not want to do this, because we may want to see the bug if it happens so we can fix it. The way we wrote our code, the `itemsLeftToFix` counter gets reduced by one. At that point, we will check for "game over" right away. There should never be a case where we have a negative `itemsLeftToFix`.

> There's always a lot of decisions to make when writing a program. But we can handle it.

Decisions like this have to made case by case. In our example, we don't have to worry about it. But let's say we were making a game where you lose hit points. If your hit points are zero or less than zero, it would also be game over (though not in a good way). For a case like that, we would want `<=` instead of `===`.

Short version of checkGameOver. Because of what our function is doing, we could really simplify this code a lot. This will do exactly the same thing as the full version, believe it or not.

```
function checkGameOver()
{
  return player.itemsLeftToFix === 0;
}
```

> There's lot of ways to solve problems in code. Use what makes the most sense to you.

What?! Yep. That does the same thing as before without any of the mess. Let's break it down.

We still test for the same winning condition `player.itemsLeftToFix === 0`, which will evaluate to either `true` or `false`. And we immediately send that result back with `return`.

A lot less code, right? For right now, it's all we need.

3.9 Implementing the Game Over State

You know what's coming next, right? We created a function, so now we have to make use of it. It won't run unless we tell it to. Think about our game flow. Where would we want to check for a game over situation? You've got to make decisions like this when you code.

> Give it some thought before reading ahead. Where do we put the checkGameOver function?

Current flow:
1. The player enters a room.
2. The room is described to the player.
3. If there's something the player can pick up, pick it up.
4. See if there's something to fix.
   a. If we have the right item, fix the broken thing.
      i. Adjust inventory and earn points.
5. Display the score.
6. Display the inventory.
7. Go to another room.

Where's the best place to check if the game is over? For us, how about right after fixing something and before going to another room?

This stuff all gets called from `moveToRoom()`. It's our main game function, isn't it? It's controlling everything. Unlike our other functions, we can't just insert the `checkGameOver()` function and have it work. *Do you know why?*

> Hmm. Our other functions just worked on their own. Why is checkGameOver different? What does it have that the others ddn't?

```
function moveToRoom()
{
  textRoomDescription();
  isThereAnItem();
  fixBrokenThing();
  showScore();
  showInventory();
  checkGameOver();          //this won't do anything

  var direction = getDirection();
  if (direction)
  {
    player.currentRoom = rooms[direction];
    moveToRoom();
  }
}
```

Think about what the `checkGameOver()` function does. It makes a comparison and sends back a `true` or `false`. That's it. There are no instructions on what to do if the game is actually over. We still have to control for that. We want to put it here in the `moveToRoom()` function because if the game is over, we have to stop the rest of this function from working.

Making the checkGameOver function work. We have to adjust our code a little. Consider the flow again.

If the game is over, we want to offer the player a chance to play again. Otherwise (if the game is not over), we want the player to choose another room to go to.

Can you figure out what we have to do?

We want to use return value of `checkGameOver` to figure out if the game ended or if we need to get a new direction. This calls for an `if`/`else` statement. In one branch, we end the game. In the other, we get a new direction by moving some of the existing code into an `else` statement. What are we going to use as the condition?

Hmm. Well, the `checkGameOver()` function returns a Boolean. It acts like a variable because it has a `return` value. We could actually stick *that* into the `if` statement! Crazy, right? Maybe, but useful!

```
if (checkGameOver())     //watch the parentheses
{
                          //handle Game Over
}
else                      //ask for a direction
{
    var direction = getDirection();
    if (direction)
    {
        player.currentRoom = rooms[direction];
        moveToRoom();
    }
}                         //close the if statement
```

Now the direction-asking part of our code only runs if there is *not* a game over situation.

So what are we going to do if there *is* a game over situation? We should first tell the player they've won. And then let's see if they want to play again.

Overkill? No way! Let's make lots of small functions! Then no one's doing all the work alone.

Would it be overkill to create two more functions for these things? Nope. Having small functions here and there makes it easier to adjust things later if we have to. Let's create them and put them where we need them.

First, the easier one.

```
function alertGameWon()
{
  var text = "Congratulations, " + player.name + "! ";
  text += "You fixed everything in the house! ";
  text += "You should be proud of yourself! ";
  text += "You finished the game with a score of ";
  text += player.score + " points! ";
  text += "Play again soon!";
  alert(text);
}
```

That's pretty straightforward. You can say however much or little as you want. Feel free to change up the dialogue.

Now the other function.

```
function checkPlayAgain()
{
  var text = "Would you like to play again? ";
  text += "Click OK to replay. ";
  text += "Click CANCEL to end. ";

  var again = confirm(text);
  if (again)
  {
    startGame();
  }
}
```

Remember that a `confirm` popup returns either `true` or `false`. We can use that response to either start the game again or let the game exit.

Do you know where the function calls go?

Our final version of `moveToRoom()`.

```
function moveToRoom()
{
  textRoomDescription();
  isThereAnItem();
  fixBrokenThing();
  showScore();
  showInventory();

  if (checkGameOver())
  {
    //handle Game Over
    alertGameWon();
    checkPlayAgain();
  }
  else
  {
    var direction = getDirection();
    if (direction)
    {
      player.currentRoom = rooms[direction];
      moveToRoom();
    }
  }
}
```

That's it! The basic game is finished. Have fun!

Looping technicality. The way we are running this game, we are looping a lot. Each time the player moves to a new room, there is a recursive loop that spirals deeper and deeper. At the end of the game, if the player decides to play again, that keeps the loop going deeper and deeper still.

If the player decides not to play again, all those loops unravel all at once until the game actually stops. We won't likely ever see the result of this anywhere, but if you really follow the flow of all the functions, that's what happens... a technically endless looping spiral of room-fixing fun.

3.10 Game Complete — What's Next?

You're done! You have a house. You can walk to all the rooms. You can pick up items. You can fix things that are broken. You earn points. And you can even win the game.

> You've come a long way. And guess what? We can improve the game if we want to. What would you want to add?

The learning and fun don't have to end here. There's a lot we can do to make improvements on this game.

Here are some ideas to consider:

Add randomization	• Start the player in a random room • Move each item found to a random room • Change up the point values for fixing things • Sometimes fail to fix things, based on the number of items you're carrying and the number of rooms you've visited • Randomize the layout of the house
Add more rooms	• Rooms are easy to add • What about a second floor?
More exits	• Not just north, east, south, west
Track the player's path	• At the end, tell the player how they navigated the house

Make a new endgame	• Require a passcode to finish the game • Find pieces of a passcode that let you leave the house • Can you leave the house without fixing everything?
Possibly lose points	• If you fail to fix something • If you enter the wrong passcode
Get rid of popups	• Popups are annoying • Wouldn't a clean interface be nicer? • Have buttons to click for rooms • Use colors • Add pictures

What else can you think of?

Chapter 4

A Required Upgrade

In Chapter 2 and Chapter 3, you created a text adventure game, walking around a house, picking up items, and using them to fix things in the house.

It's a fun game the first few times you play it. Then it gets repetitive. Typing directions can be annoying, especially if you're doing so with a keyboard that pops up and vanishes all the time.

We have a lot of improvements we can make to the main game. You don't have to include any of these. Most of them can be added in any order, so pick and chose the ones that interest you. You don't have to go in the same flow as this part of the book. There will be some parts that rely on other parts, but when that happens, I'll let you know.

We're going to update our code to make other features easier to work with.

This part you must do first and right away. The first thing we're going to do is tweak the `rooms` object and move the directions into something more useable for later, an `exits` property. A number of features will rely on it, so get this part done, then you can skip around to the features you want to add.

Let's go!

4.1 Update the Rooms Object with Exits

Our rooms have a lot of detail in them. We want to organize things a little better. We need to fix up our exits. Right now, north, east, south, and west are all separate properties in each room.

That's great, except we may want other directions. Plus, if you recall from Section 2.14: Checking for a Valid Room, we had to be careful other property names weren't incorrectly used as directions, like name.

Here is my current livingRoom object.

```
var livingRoom =
{
  name: "living room",
  points: 25,
  brokenThing: "fireplace screen",
  description: "A cozy room with a fireplace.",
  fixWith: "new wire",
  itemFound: "batteries",
  north: "dining room",
  south: null,
  east: "hallway",
  west: null
};
```

We're going to change the north, east, south, west by pushing them into an object inside the livingRoom object. Yep, it will be an object inside an object, but we already have experience with that, don't we?

The `rooms` object holds all the individual room objects. We already have an object with objects in it. (Have I said "objects" enough yet?) We're going to have `rooms` with each `room` that has `exits`. We are also going to do away with the `null` properties.

We've got some work to do. It won't be too bad, though.

Creating an object within an object. We did this before with our `rooms` object, but it didn't look like this. I was trying to keep things simpler and to allow us to focus on room creation instead of syntax.

When we created the `rooms` object, we started with an empty object and added each room through array notation. Remember this?

```
var rooms = {};
rooms[livingRoom.name] = livingRoom;
```

This let us create a `rooms` object that looked like this on the inside.

```
var rooms =
{
  "living room":
  {
    name: "living room",
    description: "A cozy room with a fireplace.",
        //the rest of the living room properties
  },
  //other rooms
};
```

We didn't see it this way because of how we created the rooms. We *could* have done this, but notice the braces `{}` living inside other braces. It can be confusing, especially when we're first learning.

Here's one more case where JavaScript did some of the work for us.

Notice the string property, `"living room"`, at the top. It has a colon, just like `name` and `description`. That's a special JavaScript feature that lets us use strings as properties so we could have multiple words and numbers. We ***can't*** use dot notation (`rooms."living room";`) for it. We ***can only*** use array notation (`rooms["living room"];`). We talked about this back in Section 2.7: Creating the Rooms Object.

4.2 Creating an Exits Property

We want to be more flexible with how we move around the house. Using north, south, east, and west is fine, but not perfect. We may need a `northeast`, or a `staircase`, or a `side corridor`. Who knows? Starting with basic compass points allowed us to visualize our house and make sense of how things connected. Let's make things a bit more adaptable.

We are going to shift all those directions into a new object called `exits`. Each room will have its own set of exits. We will also reduce our code a little by removing exits that don't go anywhere (the `null` exits).

Here is part of my `livingRoom` object.

```
var livingRoom =
{
  name: "living room",
  //other properties are here
  north: "dining room",
  south: null,
  east: "hallway",
  west: null
};
```

Right above the set of directions, we're going to stick in `exits: {` with the open brace and at the end of the directions, put the closing brace `}`. We should also indent the directions for readability.

That's this.

```
var livingRoom =
{
  name: "living room",
  //other properties are here
  exits:                          //<-- new
  {                               //<-- new
    north: "dining room",
    south: null,
    east: "hallway",
    west: null
  }                               //<-- new
};
```

Not too bad?

We can now access the exits as follows.

```
livingRoom.exits.east;                      //"hallway"
rooms["living room"].exits.east;            //"hallway"
rooms["living room"]["exits"]["east"]   //"hallway"
```

Wow, that last one is kind of crazy, but can you see how it works?

Mixed chaining. Yeah, it's a mix of array notation and dot notation. That's allowed, as long as you have things in the right order. The `rooms` object has a `"living room"` property and that now has an `exits` property and *that* has an `east` property. Whew.

How do I know which one to use? I guess it depends on the situation.

This works because `rooms`, `"living room"`, and `exits` are all objects that have their own properties. Accessing properties like this all in a row is called "chaining". Because I used dot notation and array notation, I call it "mixed chaining".

125

Let's make one more change. Let's get rid of any direction that's pointing to a `null` room. We're doing this to clean things up.

```
var livingRoom =
{
  name: "living room",
  //other properties are here
  exits:
  {
    south: null,           //delete lines with null
    north: "dining room", ///"south" and "west" are gone
    east: "hallway"        //I removed the comma here
  }
};
```

You can do it! Follow the example.

Go through all your rooms and make these changes to the exits. You need to go change them now before you do the next part.

When you have fixed all your rooms to give them each an `exits` property, you know what's next. You have to test it. Run your game. Type `quit` at the first prompt. Go to the console. Check your exits.

```
rooms["dining room"].exits;
```

```
: rooms["dining room"].exits
=> { south: 'living room', east: 'kitchen' }
:
```

Figure 14. My output for the dining room exits.

Do this and check all your rooms. I know it seems annoying sometimes to check everything, but getting into that habit will make it easier on you in the long run.

Once you do this to all your rooms, you will not be able to play your game again until you take care of the next task: making it work with this new property.

4.3 Making the Exits Property Work

You made important changes to your rooms. Your code no longer works. It doesn't recognize any of your exits, but we're going to fix that here and then move on with enhancements to the game.

If you did not complete the task in the last section, Section 4.2: Creating an Exits Property, then you must go there and do it first, before making these changes here. It's required.

Without it, the game won't work.

When we created the program, we made a lot of functions. Each function served a single purpose. We have one that makes the rooms, one that makes the player, one that starts the game, one that manages the moves, one that gets directions, and so on.

We need to edit the `getDirection()` function so it can make use of the new `exits` property in each room. You will see how this is more versatile than what we have now.

We have four sets of lines that check to see if it's possible for you to go north, east, south, or west. We also have a set of code that checks for use of the `name` variable. *All of these lines need to be deleted.*

Here is our current, edited, and *incomplete* `getDirection()` function.

```
function getDirection()
{
  var text = "Which way do you want to go? ";
  var direction;
  while (!direction)
  {
    text += "There are exits: ";
    //the code that was here has been deleted
    direction = prompt(text);
    direction = direction.toLowerCase();

    var exitTo = player.currentRoom[direction];
    if (rooms[exitTo])
    {
      return exitTo;
    }
    else if (direction === "quit")
    {
      break;
    }
    text = "You can't go " + direction + ". ";
    text += "Please try again. ";
    direction = null;
  }
}
```

Do you remember which line finds out if a typed direction has an exit?

```
var exitTo = player.currentRoom[direction];
```

This won't work anymore. Rooms no longer have a direct north or south property. They're now inside an `exits` property, so we have to change this line a little to fix that.

```
var exitTo = player.currentRoom.exits[direction];
```

This update was a cinch!

Yeah, *that's it.*

You need to put a dot `.` and the word `exits` in between `currentRoom` and `[direction];`.

Sometimes updates aren't a big deal.

There is one more thing we should add back in—telling the player which exits are available. But the game works again!

4.4 Using a for...in Loop

We made some major changes to the `getDirection()` function in the last section, but we have one more thing to fix. We want to tell the player which directions are available.

We used loops before when we were checking `player.inventory` in Section 3.7: Looping Through an Array. However, we can't use a regular `for` loop to check object properties, and we're using properties for our `exits`.

Another loop. Interesting.

We have to use a `for...in` loop.

Syntax:

```
for (var propertyVariable in object)
{
    //do something
}
```

It starts with the `for` keyword. Then we declare a variable, like in a regular loop. Next is the `in` keyword followed by the object we're looking at.

The variable will take the name of one property from the object. It can be used inside the code block to check or do something. The loop ends when all the properties have been checked.

Let's use this practice example.

```
var myFavorites =
{
  sport: "bowling",
  videoGame: "Final Fantasy VI",
  color: "royal blue",
  number: 317,
  iceCream: "mint chocolate chip"
};
```

Here is a loop that will display all the details in the console window.

```
for (var topic in myFavorites)
{
  var value = myFavorites[topic];
  console.log("Favorite " + topic + " is " + value);
}
```

Can you envision what the output will look like?

```
Favorite sport is bowling
Favorite videoGame is Final Fantasy VI
Favorite color is royal blue
Favorite number is 317
Favorite iceCream is mint chocolate chip
```
Figure 15. for...in loop result for my favorites

In the `console.log()` method, it says `"Favorite " + topic....` If you look at the output, it says `"Favorite sport"` or `"Favorite iceCream"`. Look back at the object; those are the names of the properties!

To get the value of what each thing is equal to, we need to use array notation. It's really useful, isn't it? To make the code easier to read, I set up a `value` variable to get the value before it tries to display it.

The first time through the loop, `topic` is `"sport"`. If I use array notation: `myFavorites["sport"];`, it would show `"bowling"`. You can even test that out in the console, you know.

Each time through the loop, it picks another property, gets its value, then displays it. Can you see where we're going with this?

When we ask the player to pick a direction, we want to let them know which way they can go. We have two choices now. Because we're using properties in `exits`, we could tell them the property name (`north`, `south`, etc.) or the *actual room* it connects to (`"dining room"`, `"den"`, etc.).

I'll show you both ways, but *I'm going to keep it as the direction*, myself. Later, I want to add a feature to the game that shows which room they can go to only if they've already been there, otherwise it will give the direction.

Version 1: Showing the direction. I only want the player to see the direction for now. I'm going to use a `for...in` loop to find all the possible `exits` and add it to the text string we started building in the first version of this function.

Here it is.

```
text += "There are exits: ";   //<-- already there

for (var exit in player.currentRoom.exits) //<-- new
{                                          //<-- new
   text += "[" + exit + "]";               //<-- new
}                                          //<-- new

direction = prompt(text);     //<-- already there
```

Because we are only displaying the property name, that's all we have to do! The game already checks for things like north and south so there's nothing else to change. I added the brackets for visual appeal: `[north]`. They're not needed, but you should at least have a space.

That's it. Done!

Version 2: Showing the room name. If you would rather show the name of the room the player can move to, then you need to make a similar `for...in` loop, but we have to change one other thing.

Here is the new `for...in` loop.

```
text += "There are exits: ";   //<-- already there

for (var exit in player.currentRoom.exits)
{
  var roomName = player.currentRoom.exits[exit];
  text += "[" + roomName + "]";
}

direction = prompt(text);   //<-- already there
```

It's using array notation on the `exits` object, but remember that the `exits` object is in the `currentRoom` that the `player` is in. That's why it looks clunky.

This won't work yet, though. We need to let the computer check for the direction based on what value was typed in (like `"hallway"`) instead of the direction (like `"north"`) which means we have to change one other thing.

Originally, the `exitTo` variable checked the room's exits based on the direction that was typed in and it returned the value. If you typed in `north` it said `"dining room"`. Well, now the player is typing in the name of the room, so if you simplify it, you would get this.

```
var exitTo = direction;
```

That looks really easy! Whew. Fun. Cool.

Um, but wait... What if the player types in a room somewhere else in the house? I'm in the `living room`, but I type in `office`. With this code, *I would teleport to the office!* Cool! But it breaks our game.

We need to control for this, so we can't simply use this one line of code. Bummer.

We need to first check to see if the room typed in is a valid exit for the room we are in. We need another `for...in` loop and an `if` statement.

```
var exitTo;          //leave this undefined
for (var exit in player.currentRoom.exits)
{
  if (player.currentRoom.exits[exit] === direction)
  {
    exitTo = direction;
    break;           //stops looping when room is found
  }
}
```

And that fixes the problem. No more teleporting.

We use the `break;` command to end the loop as soon as it finds a room. There's no reason for it to keep looping. If you leave this out, it's not a problem unless you have a loop that has a lot to run through.

The last thing I will add is this... What if you want the player to be able to say `"dining room"` *or* `"north"`? In other words, what if you want either option?

Just restore the original `exitTo` line instead of leaving it undefined.

```
var exitTo = player.currentRoom.exits[direction];
```

First, it sets a value to `exitTo` based on north, east, etc. Then it will check the properties for a room name. We could control this even better with an additional `if` statement.

```
var exitTo = player.currentRoom.exits[direction];

if (!exitTo)                           //<--new
{                                      //<--new
  for (var exit in player.currentRoom.exits)
  {
    if (player.currentRoom.exits[exit] === direction)
    {
      exitTo = direction;
      break;
    }
  }
}                                      //<--new
```

That's starting to look a bit complex, isn't it? When you want to check for different cases and allow for extra options, that's what happens.

It's your call if you want to use version 1, version 2, or this modified version 2. Your game, your call.

For now, I'm going to stick with version 1. I want the player to see directions only, unless they've been in the room before. This is a feature I'll be talking about in a little bit.

Remember, you can make your own decisions for your game. You don't have to use mine. I'm just here to teach you the basics so you can make the game your own.

This is the end of the required update. It will allow all the upcoming new features to work.

Chapter 5

Improving the Game — New Features

There is a lot we can add to the game. If you want to dive into HTML and make the game into a clickable adventure before adding more features, you can jump to Chapter 6 and come back here later.

We will improve our game in a few ways.
- Add more descriptive text after fixing a room
- Add more room possibilities
- Move the player to a random room in the beginning
- Shift the locations of all the items found in the house
- Change the point values for each task
- Have different possible broken items for each room
- Make the player tired as they travel through the house so sometimes they can't fix the broken thing, losing some points
- Make the game more interactive, asking the player to take and use items instead of it being automatic
- Make the gameplay more challenging with an alternate goal: finding pieces of a security code that let you leave the house
- Randomly mix up the layout of the house

In this chapter, there will be some new JavaScript concepts, but most of it will be stuff we've done before. You may need to look back at previous explanations if you don't remember how some things work.

5.1 Getting More Descriptive

There is a simple addition we can make to the game that will make it feel more dynamic. In each room, we have something that's broken. With the right item, we fix it, but aside from the game not mentioning it anymore, there's nothing that improves our experience.

What if the room's description changes when we fix something? In my dining room there is a chandelier with a broken bulb. Once it's fixed, the description could make note of that. "The room is bright and cheery. Let's eat!"

This is an easy addition. Go into your getRooms() function and add a new property, altDescription, to each room that provides this new description. Make it relevant to what's been fixed.

Here's the new altDescription property.

```
function getRooms()
{
  var livingRoom =
  {
    name: "living room",
    brokenThing: "fireplace screen",
    description: "A cozy room with a fireplace.",
    altDescription: "A cozy room. The new fireplace
       screen keeps the ashes from ruining the floor."
//rest of function
```

Go into the `fixBrokenThing()` function where we update the player's score and remove the `brokenThing` from the room. Then add this.

```
function fixBrokenThing()
{
  //start of function

  //remove item from room
  player.currentRoom.brokenThing = null; //already there

  if (player.currentRoom.altDescription) //<--new
  {
    player.currentRoom.description =
                        player.currentRoom.altDescription;
    display.description(player.currentRoom);
  }
```

We're putting this into an `if` statement in case there isn't an alternate description provided for the room. If we didn't check for this, we could end up with some rooms being described as `undefined`. We certainly don't want that. And we might as well display it immediately.

Go on and get those alternate descriptions in there!

Keep adding to your house every now and again.

Add more rooms. You're already making updates to each room. Take it one step further and add more rooms to your house.

It's a good idea to jump back to that first `getRooms()` function and add to it, making sure you remember how. Follow the example of your other rooms. Make sure you add any new rooms to the `rooms` object near the end of the function. That's the part with the array notation.

Get up to at least ten rooms but why not shoot for more? Make a mansion! Make a second floor. Create a `staircase` room to get from one floor to another. You don't even have to put a `brokenThing` and `fixWith` in it. You can just let it be a passage.

You also need to pop into the `getPlayer()` function and increase the `itemsLeftToFix` property so it matches your `brokenItem` count.

5.2 Randomizing the Player's Start Room

Right now, every time the game starts, the player is in the same place. This may be how you want your game to begin and that's cool. For instance, when you come home, you probably enter your house the same way every time, such as through the front door. But let's mix ours up and have the player start in a random room.

Using Math.random(). To randomize, we need help from a random number generator. We can adjust this number to do whatever we need it to do.

Randomizing stuff keeps things interesting. I'd better focus here.

Computers can't really come up with random numbers, but they use a seed to generate a long list of *pseudorandom* numbers. Sometimes you may notice patterns, like the player starts in the same room every third playthrough or something. But these are usually random enough for what you need.

The JavaScript Math object has a lot of great methods attached to it. `Math.random()` generates a pseudorandom number from 0 up to 1, *noninclusive* (not including 1). When you first hear it, this might not sound very useful. Go ahead, turn to a console window and type in `Math.random();` a bunch of times and see the results.

```
Math.random();   // 0.7103008247977285
Math.random();   // 0.5305054978326511
Math.random();   // 0.1735780971139378
```

Ah, right. Decimals!

When we multiply this by a number, we change the range of values. If we do `Math.random() * 15;` we will get values from 0 to 15 (again, not including 15). For example: `12.668657404169108`

Using Math.floor(). Oftentimes, we want whole numbers when we're picking random numbers. `Math.floor()` will truncate (erase) any decimal attached to a number. It does not round the decimal off. It just throws it away.

```
Math.floor(12.76); //12
```

Let's have the computer pick a whole number up to 15.

```
Math.floor(Math.random() * 15); //1
Math.floor(Math.random() * 15); //11
Math.floor(Math.random() * 15); //0
Math.floor(Math.random() * 15); //14
```

This has a lot of uses. If we were making a game where the computer wants you to guess a number from 0 to 14, we would have the computer pick a number with this and then begin the guessing game.

This will be really helpful. Let's see how it works.

Picking randomly from an array. We want to place our player into one of our rooms at random. We will need to use an array for that. Remember, an array is a list of things, like rooms, or numbers, or strings.

Each array has a length, which tells us how many elements there are in the array. If we multiply `Math.random()` by the `length` of the array, we will get a randomly selected index from the array (assuming we use `Math.floor()` to get rid of the decimal).

139

```
var roomsArray = ["den", "office", "hallway", "kitchen"];
var length = roomsArray.length;
var index = Math.floor(Math.random() * length);
console.log(index);                    //Example: 2
console.log(roomsArray[index]);        //Example: "hallway"
```

Here, I made a `roomsArray` variable with four rooms in it. That means the length is 4. If I multiply `Math.random()` by 4, I get a decimal number (called a *float*) from 0 up to 4.

When I use `Math.floor()`, I get a whole number 0, 1, 2, or 3. Those would be the index numbers of the array. (Remember that arrays are indexed starting at zero.)

The randomizePlayerStart function. The only complication we have is that our rooms are packed into an object, not an array. The first thing we will need to do is create an array of rooms, then we can pick one randomly and move the player into it.

```
function randomizePlayerStart(availableRooms)
{
  //create an array of available rooms
  var roomsArray = [];                   //this starts empty
  for (var roomName in availableRooms)
  {
    var roomToAdd = availableRooms[roomName];
    roomsArray.push(roomToAdd);
  }

  //randomly pick one room and assign the player to it
  var length = roomsArray.length;
  var index = Math.floor(Math.random() * length);
  player.currentRoom = roomsArray[index];
}
```

For this function, we are sending in a set of rooms. This may be the entire set of rooms or it may be a selection of rooms if we change that part of the game later. This function allows us to work with either option because of the `availableRooms` parameter. As long as we send in an object with rooms in it, we're good to go.

Turning our rooms object into an array. The `for...in` loop runs through all the properties in the `availableRooms` object. (If that name is confusing, think of it as the usual `rooms` object for now.) Those properties are room names. We convert each one to an actual room with `availableRooms[roomName]`. Those are added to the `roomsArray` with the `push` method. When it's finished, we will have array holding our rooms.

Picking the random room. After creating the array, we generate a random number based on the number of rooms and then give that room to the player as their `currentRoom`.

Updating startGame. All that's left is to add this to the `startGame()` function, after we create the `rooms` and the `player`.

```
function startGame()
{
    rooms = getRooms();
    player = getPlayer();

    randomizePlayerStart(rooms);        //<--this is new
//rest of function
```

Now the player will start in a random room with each run-through.

5.3 Randomizing the Item Locations

In this section, we are going to shuffle the items around the house. Each room still has the same thing to fix and the same item needed to fix it with, but the location of that item will change. For me, that means the *batteries* won't always be in the *living room* anymore.

This will be similar to the last section where we randomized the player's location. If you need a discussion on how to use the `Math.random()` function, scan back to the previous section.

The item randomizer will shuffle the items around the house. To accomplish this task, we need to first check through all the available rooms and see which items are needed. These are the `fixWith` items. We will create an array for them. We won't be looking at `itemFound` at all. We only need the `fixWith` items. Does it make sense why?

Why won't we need `itemFound` any more? How're we going to pick stuff up?

We want to make sure each room can be fixed. We want a list of the actual items, like a supply list for school. It doesn't matter where we put those items before, because we're moving them anyway.

The randomizeItems function. For this section, I'm going to put the comments right into the code. You don't need to type in the comments. You have seen all of these things before throughout the game. I'm pushing your comprehension skills here.

See if you can follow it now. Here's the first half.

```javascript
//we need to send in a rooms object when we
    call this
function randomizeItems(availableRooms)
{
  //reset this now and we'll count as we go
  player.itemsLeftToFix = 0;

  //we need to make a list of fixWith items,
      start empty
  var items = [];

  //loop through all the rooms that are
      available
  for (var roomName in availableRooms)
  {
    //helper variable for code clarity
    var room = availableRooms[roomName];

    //if you ever set a room without something broken
    //then skip the code and jump to the top of the loop
    if (!room.brokenThing)
    {
      room.fixWith = null; //make sure there's no fixWith
      continue;
    }

    //now we know there's an item, so let's count it
    player.itemsLeftToFix++;

    //add the fixWith item from each room
    //to the new items array
    items.push(room.fixWith);
  }
```

Think it through. I bet you can understand this code!

Here's the second half.

```
//now loop again through the available rooms
for (var roomName in availableRooms)
{
  //if no items are left, clear other default items
  if (items.length === 0)
  {
    availableRooms[roomName].itemFound = null;
    continue;
  }
  //pick a random fixWith item from the items array
  //the items array will shrink each time through loop
  var index = Math.floor(Math.random() * items.length);

  //set the random item to the current room
  //the loop is in
  availableRooms[roomName].itemFound = items[index];

  //remove the fixWith item from the items array
  //so we don't put it into two places at once
  items.splice(index, 1);
}
}                  //end of the randomizeItems function
```

And this will activate it in the game.

```
function startGame()
{
    rooms = getRooms();
    player = getPlayer();

    randomizePlayerStart(rooms);
    randomizeItems(rooms);              //<--this is new
//rest of function
```

The placement of this function is important. In the `startGame()` function, after this point, the text string is built where we tell the player how many things they need to fix in the house. Our `randomizeItem()` function updates the number of items dynamically.

If we add more rooms to the game, for instance, we don't have to go into the `player` object (in the `getPlayer()` function) to update the `itemsLeftToFix` number ourselves. This function now takes care of it for us automatically. Also, if you decide to have some rooms without a broken object, this function will take of that too.

144

5.4 Randomizing the Point Values

Let's vary the results of the game while we're at it. If you like the point values you came up with, you don't have to do this part. That's totally fine!

Not everyone would want point values to change. Think of this as a coding exercise. You may come up with another reason to use a function similar to this for some other purpose.

I am going to use the original point values and pick a random number up to twice the value. If something is worth 25 points to fix, I'm making the computer pick a new point value from 25 to 50. Of course, you can change that if you want.

We could do this in two loops, with one loop to change all the values, and a second loop to tally the maximum score. However, we can do all this at once if we're smart about it. Let's be smart.

To complete this, we are going to loop through all the rooms and change the point values. While we are at it, let's tally up the points so we can tell the player what the maximum score will be. It'll be a nice way for the player to see how much more they have to do. By randomizing the values, it still leaves some mystery.

Some of this is similar to the `randomizeItems` function. We could have combined the two, but it's usually better to keep functions separate so they serve a single purpose.

```javascript
//we need to send in a rooms object when we call this
function randomizePoints(availableRooms)
{
  //we need to tally the total point value
  var maxScore = 0;

  //loop through all the rooms that are available
  for (var roomName in availableRooms)
  {
    //helper variable for code clarity
    var room = availableRooms[roomName];

    //helper variable that gets the point value for item
    var base = room.points;

    //get a random number from 0 to base point value
    //add that to the base point value
    var value = Math.floor(Math.random() * base) + base;

    //set the room's point value to the new value
    room.points = value;

    //add these new points to the total point tally
    maxScore += value;
  }

  //let the player carry the total point value
  //just like the player carries the score
  player.maxScore = maxScore;

  return availableRooms;
}
```

Can you follow all that?

We are setting a new property to the player here. If it doesn't exist, this will create it for us. But we should probably do a neater job of it.

146

Updating the player object. For code clarity, we should add a `maxScore` property to the `player` object. This way, anyone reading over the code will see immediately that the player carries this information without having to look at the `randomizePoints()` function.

```
function getPlayer()
{
  return {
    name: "Lica",
    score: 0,
    currentRoom: rooms["living room"],
    inventory: [],
    itemsLeftToFix: 8,              //<--comma
    maxScore: 0                     //<--this is new
  };
}
```

If you added the `randomizeItem` function, you may wonder why we're leaving `itemsLeftToFix` as a number here. We're doing it in case you turn off the `randomizeItems` function at a later time. We want the game to work like it originally did if we disable the item feature.

Updating the score display to show the maximum score. Since we now have a maximum score tallied up, we should show it to the player. Originally, we sent the score immediately to an `alert`. We're going to use a text chain instead, so we can add the maximum score if there is one.

```
function showScore()
{
  player.score = Math.max(0, player.score);
  var text = "Score: " + player.score;

  //if there is a maxScore tally, then show it
  if (player.maxScore > 0)
  {
    text += " / Max: " + player.maxScore;
  }

  alert(text);
}
```

Now the player can have a sense of how well they're playing and how much further they have to go.

Updating startGame. One more thing to do, right? We have to call the function. Do you know the best place to put it?

```
function startGame()
{
    rooms = getRooms();
    player = getPlayer();

    randomizePlayerStart(rooms);      //if you created this
    randomizeItems(rooms);            //if you created this
    randomizePoints(rooms);           //<--this is new
//rest of function
```

If you created the `randomizeItem` function, then you want the new `randomizePoints` to come after it. In our case, it would also work if you placed it before, but from a logical game flow standpoint, setting the point values after placing the items makes more sense.

5.5 Tracking the Player Through the House

The player is going to wander around the house trying to find things and fix things. At the end, why not let the player know how they navigated through? It's a simple thing to add.

There are three things we need to update: the `player` object, the `moveToRoom()` function, and the `alertGameOver()` function.

Go to the `getPlayer()` function and add a new property to our player, `pathTaken: []`.

```
function getPlayer()
{
  return {
    name: "Lica",
    score: 0,
    currentRoom: rooms["living room"],
    inventory: [],
    itemsLeftToFix: 8,
    maxScore: 0,
    pathTaken: []                          //<--new
  };
}
```

Now that we have the empty array, each time the player moves we will add that room to the list. At the top of `moveToRoom()` add this.

```
function moveToRoom()
{
    player.pathTaken.push(player.currentRoom);    //<--new
//rest of function
```

The final task is to display the path at the end of the game.

```
function alertGameWon()
{
  //end game text string code
  //text += ...

  var path = "Here's how you traversed the house: ";
  var steps = player.pathTaken.length;
  for (var i = 0; i < steps; i++)
  {
    var room = player.pathTaken[i];
    path += room.name;
    if (i < steps - 1)
    {
      path += " --> ";
    }
  }

  text += " ***** " + path + " ***** ";
  alert(text);
}
```

Showing the path is a fun addition. The player may be curious how many times they passed through the living room. Have you ever had that thought when you're trying to find something you need?

This `pathTaken` feature will be used in some other updates, such in as Section 5.6: Making the Player Tired and Section 6.6: Creating Navigation Buttons, so be sure to add this one in if you plan to include these other features.

5.6 Making the Player Tired

There's no risk or penalty in our game (unless you add the passcode feature in Section 5.9: Intermediate: Creating a Passcode Goal). Usually, you want there to be some kind of risk involved in a game.

What if the player can't always fix the broken object? They try, but sometimes fail. We could take some points away for this.

Making it completely random would probably frustrate the player. Let's do something more logical. Let the randomness be based on how tired the player is. We can calculate tiredness based on how many inventory items they are holding and how many rooms they've trudged through (if you added that feature in Section 5.5: Tracking the Player Through the House).

Let's see… A random penalty but based on how long the player has played. Let's see how that works.

Let's create a function that determines how tired the player is and whether they're able to fix something. The function will make use of the `player.inventory` and (if it exists) the `player.pathTaken` array. It will send back a Boolean.

The hard part is figuring out what a good threshold would be. If it's too low, the player will fail to fix things too often. If it's too high, they'll never be penalized.

```
function playerIsTired()
{
  var items = player.inventory.length;
  var fixes = player.itemsLeftToFix;
  var steps = 0;

  if (player.pathTaken)
  {
    steps = player.pathTaken.length;
  }
  var tiredness = items + steps - fixes;
  var effort = Math.min(tiredness , 25);
  var threshold = Math.floor(Math.random() * effort);

  return threshold > 15;
}
```

We start by setting `steps` to `0` in case there is no `player.pathTaken` array. It's an edge case check, in case you didn't add the player tracking feature from Section 5.5: Tracking the Player Through the House.

Capping the effort. We're capping `effort` at 25. If the player runs around the house a lot and we don't cap this number, they may never be able to fix anything. We are using a method of the Math object to make sure the effort value doesn't get too large. We use `Math.min`. We can put any number of values into the method. It will pick the lowest one and return it. It seems backwards, but if we want a maximum limit, we use `Math.min`. If we want a minimum limit, we use `Math.max`.

```
var effort = Math.min(threshold, 25);
```

Returning the threshold comparison. When we `return` something like `threshold > 15`, we are asking the computer to make the comparison and `return` either `true` or `false`. It's the same thing that happens in an `if` statement. We could make a separate variable first but there's no reason to.

You should play around with the `threshold` check. Is 15 too high? Too low? Just right?

Updating fixBrokenThing. To use this new feature, we have to adjust the `fixBrokenThing()` function. Here's the skeleton of the function now.

```
function fixBrokenThing()
{
  //start of function
  if (brokenThing)
  {
    //test: if fixWith is NOT in inventory
    if (index === -1)
    {
      //it's not
    }
    else //the item IS in the inventory
    {
      //build text string
      //fix the broken thing
      //etc.
    }
  display.broken(text);
  }
}
```

We are going to nest one more `if` statement in there, inside the `else` block. All the code that's in the current `else` block is being pushed into the new nested `else` block. Like this.

```
    else //the item IS in the inventory
    {
      if (playerIsTired())
      {
        text += "You try to fix the " + brokenThing;
        text += " but you feel fatigued and couldn't.";
        text += " You lose 5 points. Try again. ";
        player.score -= 5;
      }
      else
      {
        //build text string
        //fix the broken thing
        //etc.
      }
    }
    alert(text);                    //already there
```

That's all you need to do.

5.7 Randomizing Broken Things

In each of our rooms, we have one thing that needs to be fixed, and it's the same thing every time we play. Let's add some variety.

In each room, we will add a new property: `brokenArray`. In this array, we will hold a list of small objects that describe the things that need to be fixed in the house. The object will hold a new `brokenThing`, the `fixWith` item, and an alternate description for the room once the `brokenThing` is fixed, to use the feature we added in Section 5.1: Getting More Descriptive.

We will also create a function that picks from these choices in each room and sets them for gameplay.

In order for this new feature to work, you will also have to create the `randomizeItems()` function in Section 5.3: Randomizing the Item Locations. The computer will be picking each `brokenThing` randomly, so we can't tell what things are going to be needed ahead of time. The `randomizeItems()` function takes care of that for us.

Initializing objects inside an array.
We will be adapting each current room object by adding the `brokenArray` to it. The array will be a list of objects with the following properties: `brokenThing`, `fixWith`, `points`, and `altDescription`. We've created objects before and we've used some arrays, but how do we create them all at once?

154

If we were creating a basic array, we would use the following syntax.

```
var array =
[
  element0,                   //first element in array
  element1                    //second element in array
];
```

When the elements are objects, it looks more like this.

```
var array =
[
  {                           //first object in array
    property1: value,
    property2: value
  },

  {                           //second object in array
    property1: value,
    property2: value
  }
];
```

> **What's different here?**

It looks confusing. Look at the parts. The array starts and ends with square brackets `[]`. Each object starts and ends with braces `{}`. The objects are elements in the array and they are separated with a comma.

We will be inserting our array as a *property*, so it has to look like one. It's a subtle difference from above, like other properties we've created. Instead of an equals sign `array =`, we use a colon `array:` .

```
var roomObject =
{
  array:
  [               //arrays start with [
    {                           //first object in array
      property1: value,
      property2: value
    },
    {                           //second object in array
      property1: value,
      property2: value
    }
  ]               // arrays end with ]
}               //end of object (or more properties)
```

You often want your array items to be of the same type, with the same structure. We will use the same set of property names in each object element of the array.

Adding to the room objects. Here are two new `brokenThings` I'm adding to my living room.

> This could really add to the game. Let's make a bunch of things!

```
var livingRoom =
{
  //other properties
  brokenArray:
  [
    {
      brokenThing: "sofa",
      fixWith: "leather repair kit",
      points: 30,
      altDescription: "The fireplace is great to watch
          now that you can sit comfortably on the sofa
          again."
    },
    {
      brokenThing: "lamp",
      fixWith: "light bulb",
      points: 15,
      altDescription: "The room feels so much brighter
          with the lamp fixed, even without the
          fireplace aglow."
    }
  ]                        //end of array property
}                          //end of living room property
```

You also have the option of putting the room's original `brokenThing` into this list. I'm going to leave them where they are in case we need to interrupt our upcoming `randomizeBrokenThings` function. I want the game to still work using the original `brokenThing` even if we disable this feature later for some reason. Our code will make sure the original item is still an option.

I did not include an `itemFound` here and that could be a problem. We need the `randomizeItem()` function from Section 5.3: Randomizing the Item Locations for this new function to work. It will make sure each item the computer chooses will be put in the house. Take some time and go add a bunch of things to each room to add variety to your game.

Duplicate items? You may have noticed that I used "light bulb" to fix the lamp in the living room. I also need a "light bulb" in the dining room. Will that be a problem? It shouldn't be, and you'll be able to use the light bulb in either place, but you'll need to find both to fix both lights.

The way we handled the inventory and the `randomizeItem` function, we make lists based on what we need. We never excluded any items, so duplicates work without a problem.

Creating the randomizeBrokenThings() function. You may already have an inkling of how this is going to work.

We need to:
1. pass in the available rooms (in case they're different)
2. for each room, pick a random element from the new array
3. set those values to overwrite the room's default properties
4. send back the updated rooms
5. insert a function call in `startGame()`

When we "pass in" something to a function, it means we're telling the function specifically what we want to use. It's like when we use `alert()`. We pass in the text it needs to display. For our new function, we want to control the rooms the rooms being sent in. Why? Well, there's an advanced feature later that could change up the rooms, so mostly we're planning ahead. That feature comes in Section 5.10: Advanced: Randomizing the Rooms.

With that out of the way, let's focus on our currect task.

Here's our new function.

```
function randomizeBrokenThings(availableRooms)
{
  for (var roomName in availableRooms)
  {
    var room = availableRooms[roomName];

    //helper object: make sure default set can be used
    var original =
    {
      brokenThing: room.brokenThing,
      fixWith: room.fixWith,
      points: room.points,
      altDescription: room.altDescription,
    };

    var brokenThings = [original]; //put default on list

    if (room.brokenArray)
    {
      brokenThings =
          brokenThings.concat(room.brokenArray);
    }

    var brokenLength = brokenThings.length;

    //pick a random thing
    var index = Math.floor(Math.random() * brokenLength);
    var chosenThing = brokenThings[index];

    room.brokenThing = chosenThing.brokenThing;
    room.fixWith = chosenThing.fixWith;
    room.points = chosenThing.points;
    room.altDescription = chosenThing.altDescription;
  }
  return availableRooms;
}
```

Take a look at this from the code above for a moment.

```
    var brokenThings = [original];

    if (room.brokenArray)
    {
      brokenThings =
          brokenThings.concat(room.brokenArray);
    }
```

158

We started by making an `original` broken object based on what we had originally created for the room long ago. We created a new `brokenThings` array and initialized it by putting the `original` broken thing inside of it.

The concat() array method. Next, we check to see if this room has a set of other broken things to pick from. If so, then we *concatenate* the two arrays. We've mentioned this with strings before. "Concatenate" means to "add together."

> Strings and arrays can be concatenated. In short, we can put things together into one bigger thing.

The `concat()` method attaches to an array and adds to the end of it any arrays you send it. You could do something like to this to combine a bunch of arrays together.

```
firstArray.concat(secondArray, thirdArray, fourthArray);
```

One nice feature of this method is that it *does not alter* your original arrays. They all stay untouched. This method sends back a new array with everything linked together. To use this, then, we need to assign it to a variable. In our case, we can overwrite the `brokenThings` we were already using.

```
brokenThings = brokenThings.concat(room.brokenArray);
```

Once we have our list of possible `brokenThings`, the computer can go ahead and choose one randomly. By the way, if you don't make alternate `brokenThings` for a room, that's ok. This will use the `original` because it will be the only one to choose from.

We use `Math.floor(Math.random() * brokenLength)` to grab a random index from the array. With that, we made a `chosenThing` variable to make the code easier to work with. That `chosenThing` has one of the objects we created with the alternate `brokenThing`, the new point value, and so on. All that's left is to set those values to the room we're working with.

That was a lot, huh?

159

Updating startGame(). There's one more thing to do. We need the function call to let this feature work. Go into the `startGame()` and add the call before `randomizeItems()`, but after we get the rooms.

You may not have some of the functions shown here. They are other features included in this guide. I marked them with "added feature". You can choose to create them at any time, if you haven't already.

```
function startGame()
{
    rooms = getRooms();
    player = getPlayer();

    rooms = randomizeRoomLayout(rooms);   //added feature
    rooms = randomizeBrokenThings(rooms); //add this
    randomizePlayerStart(rooms);          //added feature
    randomizeItems(rooms);                //needed feature
    passcode = getPasscode(rooms);        //added feature
    randomizeExits(rooms);                //added feature

//rest of function
```

This set of lines might look weird.
```
    rooms = getRooms();
    rooms = randomizeRoomLayout(rooms);
    rooms = randomizeBrokenThings(rooms);
```

We keep updating the definition of `rooms` because these functions all change the `rooms` object and we want to use the updated information.

It looks weird, but it works like this.
```
    rooms1 = getRooms();
    rooms2 = randomizeRoomLayout(rooms1);
    rooms3 = randomizeBrokenThings(rooms2);
```

If you follow the numbers, does it make more sense? The original `rooms1` is used to randomize the layout which is then saved to `rooms2`. Next, `rooms2` is used to randomize the broken things which is saved to `rooms3`. From there, we would need to use `rooms3` in our game because it's the most current version. But instead of making separate `room#` variables, we just rewrite the original `rooms` object.

Test it. We always end at this step. Give it a go!

5.8 Intermediate: Increasing Interactivity

Our game is really coming along. There's still something we can do to get a player into the game. This is tougher stuff, but you can handle it.

Right now, everything inside the room happens automatically. If there's an item, you pick it up without a second thought. If something is broken, you immediately try to fix it.

What if we required the player to tell us to do these things? When they input a direction, they could also have the option to `"take"` something or `"use"` something. If they try to take something that isn't there or use something that isn't needed, they could lose points for it.

We have several decisions to make. Does the player just have to type `"take"` or must they type `"take batteries"`? Can they still go north by typing `"north"` or are we going to make them say `"go north"`? Is it `"use batteries"` or `"use batteries on TV remote"`? This could get really complicated.

How complex should it be?

Let's be simple. The player can type `"take"` to pick up the item in the room without saying which item. We will let the player use directions like they have already. And when they want to use an item, they will have to tell us which item to use, but not what to use it on.

We've got some work to do, so let's go.

Updating getDirection(). This function needs to accept these two new commands. Let's change how this dialogue starts.

```
function getDirection()
{
    var text = "Which way do you want to go? "; //delete
    var text = "Take an item from the room using [take]. ";
    text += "Use an item in the room with [use item], ";
    text += "such as 'use batteries'. ";
    text += "You can also move to a new room. ";
```

Lower down in the function, immediately after we prompt the user for a direction, add these two checks.

```
direction = prompt(text);
direction = direction.toLowerCase();

if (direction.indexOf("take") !== -1)
{
    return "take";
}

if (direction.indexOf("use ") !== -1)
{
    return direction;
}
```

Showing that there is an item. Let's be kind and tell the player they should search the room for an item. We'll add the call for this in `moveToRoom` in a moment.

```
function showItemInRoom()
{
    if (player.currentRoom.itemFound)
    {
        alert("You see something useful in here.");
    }
}
```

That'll give the player a hint that they should use the `take` command. If you don't want to give this hint, you can leave out the function call `showItemInRoom();`. Then they'll have to remember which rooms they already searched. It's up to you.

Updating isThereAnItem(). This function currently checks that the room has the item and if so, it adds it to your inventory. That's great, but let's add a penalty if the player tries to take something from the room that isn't there.

```
function isThereAnItem()
{
  var item = player.currentRoom.itemFound;
  if (item)
  {
    alert("You found the " + item + "!");
    player.inventory.push(item);
    player.currentRoom.itemFound = null;
  }
  else                                              //new
  {
    alert("There's nothing to take. You lose 5 points.");
    player.score -= 5;
  }
}
```

If you already added the passcode feature fom Section 5.9: Intermediate: Creating a Passcode Goal, then you will have `if (direction === "exit")` and the game over status will be checked there. If you have that, then *don't* include the game over check in these changes. It's marked with a comment in the code.

Updating moveToRoom(). This function needs a bit of updating, too. Things are no longer happening automatically. We need to ask the player to do things, and then check for a game over situation. That's backward from what we have.

We need to tell the player if there is an item to pick up and if there's something to fix. Then we need to ask for input. We will deal with "take" first, then "use", then a direction. Because the player wins if they fix everything, we will move the game over check into the "use" block.

The new `moveToRoom` function. It may be easier to type this in from scratch instead of trying to update the original.

```
function moveToRoom()
{
    player.pathTaken.push(player.currentRoom);

    textRoomDescription();
    showItemInRoom();      //update from isThereAnItem
    showBrokenThing();     //update from fixBrokenThing
    showScore();
    showInventory();

    //most of this is different
    var direction = getDirection();
    if (!direction)
    {
      //player typed quit, don't do anything, exit game
    }
    else if (direction === "take")              //take item
    {
      isThereAnItem();
      moveToRoom();
    }
    else if (direction.indexOf("use ") !== -1)  //use item
    {
      var useItem = direction.substring(4);
      fixBrokenThing(useItem);

      //here's the game over check
      //if you made the passcode ending, don't add this
      if (checkGameOver())
      {
        alertGameWon();
        checkPlayAgain();
        return; //prevents moveToRoom below from running
      }
      moveToRoom();
    }
    else                                        //move player
    {
      player.currentRoom = rooms[direction];
      moveToRoom();
    }
}
```

This is a lot different, huh? We changed the automatic checks to "show" functions (`showItemInRoom` and `showBrokenThing`). We moved `isThereAnItem` into the check for "take". We moved `fixBrokenThing` into the check for "use ". We still have to fix that.

164

We are going to assume the player types in the `use object` correctly. We could do a lot of checking to make sure they typed it in right, but that can be a lot of extra code to parse the words.

The `substring` method returns part of a string. In this case, if the user types in `"use batteries"`, we want to get rid of the first four characters, `"use "`, and keep the rest, `batteries`.

Updating fixBrokenThing().

The changes here are even more drastic. We are going to break this into two functions. The first will display the name of the broken item if there is one. The second will deal with the logic of checking inventory and using it to fix things. This part is confusing. If it's too much, focus on the sections marked *Part 1*, *Part 2*, etc., and type in anything that doesn't have a ~~strikeout~~ line.

If splitting this function in half is confusing, just forget it and type in everything you see in Parts 1 through 5.

Here's the basic layout of the original function.

```
function fixBrokenThing()
{
  //helper variables
  var brokenThing = player.currentRoom.brokenThing;
  var fixWith = player.currentRoom.fixWith;

  if (brokenThing)
  {
    var text = "There is a broken ";
    text += brokenThing + " in this room. ";
//first half
//*************** break the function here ***************
//second half
    var index = player.inventory.indexOf(fixWith);

    if (index === -1)
    {
      text += "You need the " + fixWith;
      text += " to fix it.";
    }
    else //the item IS in the inventory
    {
      //text string, remove brokenThing, add points
      //update itemsLeftToFix, remove inventory item
    }
    alert(text);
  }
}
```

The top half of the old function gets updated like this.

Part 1:

```
function showBrokenThing()    //change from fixBrokenThing
{
  var brokenThing = player.currentRoom.brokenThing;
  var fixWith = player.currentRoom.fixWith;    //delete

  if (brokenThing)
  {
    var text = "There is a broken ";
    text += brokenThing + " in this room. ";
    alert(text);                                //add
  }                                             //add
}                                               //add
```

Don't throw out the rest of the original function; we still need it.

Add `function fixBrokenThing(fixWith)` to the top of the remaining code (the second half). Let's bring back the `brokenThing` variable and start a new `text` string. We will first check to see if something in the room is broken and, if not, give a penalty and exit the function.

Part 2:

```
function fixBrokenThing(fixWith)
{
  var index = player.inventory.indexOf(fixWith);

  var brokenThing = player.currentRoom.brokenThing;
  var text = "";

  if (!brokenThing)
  {
    text += "There's nothing to fix in here! ";
    text += "You lose 10 points. ";
    player.score -= 10;
  }

  if (index === -1)                   //already there
```

We already have the `var index` declaration, right? These new lines go right underneath it, before the existing `if (index === -1)`.

The next thing we'll do is see if the item sent in to the function is actually in the player's inventory. Originally, this check told the player what they needed to use to fix the broken thing. Make this change.

Part 3:

```
else if (index === -1)              //add 'else' to this
{
  text += "You're not carrying a " + fixWith + ". ";
  text += "You lose 5 points.";
  player.score -= 5;
}
```

We have one more check to make. Is the item the player used the same as the one needed to fix the broken thing?

Part 4:

```
else if (fixWith !== player.currentRoom.fixWith)
{
  text += "The " + fixWith + " won't fix ";
  text += "the " + brokenThing + ". ";
  text += "You lose 15 points.";
  player.score -= 15;
}
```

We'll keep the rest of the original function from this point on, but you have to *delete the last closing brace* or there will be an error. I'm giving you two versions depending on whether you add the feature from Section 5.6: Making the Player Tired.

*Part 5 — **Without** the playerIsTired function.*

```
else //the item IS in the inventory and correct
{
  text += "You fixed the " + brokenThing;
  text += " with the " + fixWith + "!";
  text += " You earn ";
  text += player.currentRoom.points;
  text += " points.";

  player.currentRoom.brokenThing = null;
  player.score += player.currentRoom.points;
  player.itemsLeftToFix--;
  player.inventory.splice(index, 1);
}
alert(text);
}
+                // delete this extra closing brace
```

167

*Part 5 — **With** the playerIsTired function.*

```
      else //the item IS in the inventory and correct
      {
        if (playerIsTired())  //optional feature
        {
          text += "You try to fix the " + brokenThing;
          text += " but you feel fatigued and couldn't.";
          text += " You lose 5 points. Try again. ";
          player.score -= 5;
        }
        else
        {
          text += "You fixed the " + brokenThing;
          text += " with the " + fixWith + "!";
          text += " You earn ";
          text += player.currentRoom.points;
          text += " points.";

          player.currentRoom.brokenThing = null;
          player.score += player.currentRoom.points;
          player.itemsLeftToFix--;
          player.inventory.splice(index, 1);
        }
      }                              //this was already there
      alert(text);                   //this was already there
    }                                //this was already there
+   }          // delete this extra closing brace.
```

All done. That was a lot. Yeah, sometimes making changes can be a headache. That's why I tagged this an an intermediate challenge.

It took a lot of work to add one feature but you did it!

The real problem was changing the `fixBrokenThing()` function, wasn't it? We didn't want to throw out all the code, but we had to break it up and alter its functionality.

We also had a lot to do for `moveToRoom()`, too.

But guess what? The game is even more fun for the player now. It's time to test it out and see what you think. Have fun!

5.9 Intermediate: Creating a Passcode Goal

Let's change the game's final goal. We will lock the player in the house and make them find pieces of a passcode by fixing different things in the house. Once they figure out the passcode, they can leave the house and end the game. They can still fix everything in the house to earn a higher score.

A brand new endgame will be a cool addition.

I am going to have three pieces of the passcode that the player needs to find. Each passcode will be made up of three digits. The player will have to enter the nine-digit passcode to leave the house.

To give the player some guidance, a random word will be attached to each part of the passcode, giving the player a hint about the order of the numbers. These will be in the inventory for the player to see.

Starting the process. When the game starts, a new passcode will be generated. Because the player is already carrying other game state information, like the number of items to be fixed and the score, we could give the passcode to the player. It's convenient, but not an ideal way to control the code. Therefore, we will create a new global `passcode` object.

This goes at the top of our code.

```
"use strict";        //this should always be at the top

//initialize global variables
var rooms;
var player;
var display = getDisplay(); //from optional HTML addition
var passcode = {};                            //add this
```

We will also need to call this from our `startGame()` function so it randomizes the passcode each playthrough.

```
function startGame()
{
    //reset the global variables
    rooms = getRooms();
    player = getPlayer();

    //Mix things up for each gameplay
    rooms = randomizeRoomLayout(rooms);        //optional
    rooms = randomizeBrokenThings(rooms);      //optional
    randomizePlayerStart(rooms);               //optional
    randomizeItems(rooms);                     //optional
    randomizePoints(rooms);                    //optional
    passcode = getPasscode(rooms);             //add this
```

We put this in the randomization section, not with the resetting of the global variables, because the other randomization functions (if you created them) may change other things in the house. We want to make sure the passcodes don't end up in a room that isn't being used.

Creating the getPasscode() function. We need to make sure we're only using the rooms that are available in this playthrough of the game, so the room set is passed into this function.

We start by defining some variables we need for the function to work. By keeping these at the top, it is easy to make adjustments later if we want to. We are using variables for the number of passcode pieces and for the number of digits in those pieces. This makes our code easier to understand and easier to debug. If we put the numbers into our loops directly, it would be unclear what the numbers are doing without adding comments.

This setup also allows us to change things up later. What if you want to add randomization to the number of passcode pieces and the number of digits needed? You could easily set that up right at the beginning and the rest of the function will work fine without any other updates needed.

Let's also offer a reward for when the player correctly guesses the passcode and a penalty if they get it wrong.

Let's declare our function.

```
function getPasscode(availableRooms)
{
  //reset the global password object
  passcode =
  {
    reward: 100,   //points for winning
    penalty: 25,   //lose points for mistakes
    exitCode: "",  //full unlock code
    codes: [],     //pieces of the code
    rooms: []      //list of rooms with passcode pieces
  };

  var numberOfCodes = 3;
  var digitsPerCode = 3;
```

We're adding a `rooms` property to keep track of which rooms get passcode pieces. For now, this is mostly for debugging. After running the program, you can go into developer tools and type `passcode.rooms` to see where the pieces were placed.

Setting up hints. The player is going to find pieces of code around the house, but what order do they go in? If you find 234 and 456, are you supposed to enter them as 234456 or 456234? We could leave it up to trial and error, but a player might get frustrated with this, so let's help them out a little.

This is going to take some setup.

I decided that I would attach the number to the name of a fruit and let the player figure out that the fruits have to be arranged in alphabetical order to assemble the passcode correctly. If you like this idea but want to use something other than fruit, go right ahead!

I included over twenty fruit names to make sure I have variability from play to play, and if I want more passcode pieces, there will be hint names available for them. Feel free to adapt this list.

This gets added to the start of the function from the last page.

```
//create a set of hints
var clues = ["apples", "berries", "cherries", "dragon
    fruits", "emu berries", "forest strawberries",
    "golden apples", "honeydews", "ilamas",
    "junglesop", "kumquats", "lemons", "mandarins",
    "nectarines", "olives", "papaya", "quince",
    "rangpurs", "strawberries", "tomato", "vanilla",
    "watermelon", "youngberry", "zucchini"];

var hints = [];
for (var i = 0; i < numberOfCodes; i++)
{
  var index =
    Math.floor(Math.random() * clues.length);
  hints.push(clues[index]);
  clues.splice(index, 1);
}
hints.sort();                    //alphabetize the list
```

The loop is using the number of codes we want in order to make sure we have a hint for each one. If we had hard-coded this as a 3, it would be fine unless we changed the number of codes at some later time.

Pulling randomly from an array has been useful a few times already. It's great to know how!

Is this loop familiar? If you added the other randomization functions, then it should be. Each time through the loop, we randomly pull an index based on the size of the `clues`. I opted not to make a `length` helper variable this time. Does it make sense?

With the index selected, we pull the hint with `clues[index]`. We push it into the `hints` array we initialized before the loop. The last thing we do is `splice` that hint out of the main list so it isn't used again.

Once the hints are selected, we use an automatic array method, `sort()` to alphabetize the list. This method uses character codes to sort the list, so make sure your hints are capitalized the same way, like mine are all lowercase. If the computer compares `melon` to `Monkey`, the `Monkey` would come first because capital letters have lower character codes than lowercase letters.

Picking the codes. For the next part, we want to pick a set of numbers for each code. The set of numbers (`digitsPerCode`) could potentially be different if we later decide to change this up. We can make it so this handles those changes automatically.

For example, if we wanted to keep things easy, we could pick a three-digit code like this.

```
var code = Math.floor(Math.random() * 900) + 100;
```

This would give us a three-digit code from 100 to 999. It would work, but if we later decide to use 2- or 4-digit codes, we'd also have to change this. This also prevents zero from being a first digit to account for leading zeros (054 → 54). The computer removes zeroes in the front, just like we do. You wouldn't say you have zero-five dollars ($05) in your pocket, right?

Nested loop. We can use a nested loop to create the digits we need dynamically. For a nested loop, make sure to use a different variable name than the main loop. Usually, `i` is used for the first loop, then `j`, `k`, etc. are used for loops within. Try not to nest them too deeply. If you have more than three nested loops, you may need to rethink your code, though sometimes there's nothing you can do about it.

Loops inside of loops? We can do that?

We will be using a string for the passcode, not a number. We do this for two reasons. If the passcode starts with a zero, we don't want it to be dropped. 054 would be carried as as 54 without the 0 if it was a number.

We also don't want the numbers to be arithmetically added together. If we have 234 and 456, we want the passcode to be 234456. This will happen automatically if we add the numbers like strings. If we used numbers, then adding these together would result in 690.

Continue adding to our function with this.

```
//get the codes we need
for (var i = 0; i < numberOfCodes; i++)
{
    var code = "";
    for (var j = 0; j < digitsPerCode; j++)
    {
        code += Math.floor(Math.random() * 10).toString();
    }
    var hint = code + " " + hints[i];
    passcode.codes.push(hint);
    passcode.exitCode += code;
}
```

The inner `j` loop creates a code to whatever length we need. I included a standard JavaScript method that isn't technically necessary. Notice that at the end of the `Math.floor()` function, there is `.toString()`. This is the proper way to convert a number into a string when you want to concatenate the numbers, like we are doing.

But because we started by making `code` a string (`var code = "";`), JavaScript will automatically make this conversion for us.

Ok, let's look at the hint line.

```
var hint = code + " " + hints[i];
```

This takes our three-digit code, adds a space, and then adds one of the fruit names we had pulled out in the first loop of this function.

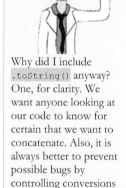

Why did I include `.toString()` anyway? One, for clarity. We want anyone looking at our code to know for certain that we want to concatenate. Also, it is always better to prevent possible bugs by controlling conversions like this ourselves instead of relying on a hidden set of rules.

We picked the hint names first because we needed to sort them so we could call these here in alphabetical order. Each of these hints gets added to the list of codes we are going to put around the house.

Lastly, we need to create the final passcode. Rather than doing this in yet another loop, we are using this loop to do the work. Using `passcode.exitCode += code;` simply tacks on the newly created code to the end of the final passcode, which will give us what we want.

Scattering the passcode pieces. Now that we have an array of rooms and all of our codes, it's time to put those codes into different rooms. First, we need to convert our `rooms` object into an array of rooms to make it easier to pull random rooms from. While doing this, we leave out any rooms that don't have a `brokenThing` in it (in case that happens). We do this because passcode hints are only given out when something gets fixed, so if nothing's broken then the hint would never be given out!

We will make one more loop based on the number of codes we need to stash away. For this, we are using the length of the `password.codes` array, not the original `numberOfCodes` variable. This is again for flexibility. If you decide later you want to add more code hints or distractions, you can add them to the `password.codes` array and this loop will automatically use them.

```
//create an array of available rooms
var roomsArray = [];
for (var roomName in availableRooms)
{
  var roomToAdd = availableRooms[roomName];
  if (roomToAdd.brokenThing)
  {
    roomsArray.push(roomToAdd);
  }
}

//put codes into rooms
for (var i = 0; i < passcode.codes.length; i++)
{
  var index =
    Math.floor(Math.random() * roomsArray.length);
  roomsArray[index].passcodeHint = passcode.codes[i];
  passcode.rooms.push(roomsArray[index]);
  roomsArray.splice(index, 1);
}
return passcode;
}                      //this finally ends our function
```

This is similar to the `hints` loop at the start of the function. The difference here is that we are creating a `passcodeHint` property for each room that gets randomly selected and we are attaching the code hint there.

Because our rooms are globally created, these changes happen to the rooms directly and can be used throughout the game. Therefore, we don't need to send the rooms back from this function. We do, however, need to send back the passcode itself and end the function.

We want the player to have a good experience. Let's give them a chance!

Giving hints to the player. That was a lot of work to set up the passcode, but we still have more to do. When the player fixes a broken object, if that room has a passcode hint, then we want to add it to the player's `inventory` so they can see it.

Where do we deal with fixing broken things? In our `fixBrokenThing()` function. Take a look at the structure of that function. We have an `if` statement that checks if there is a broken thing to fix. There is no `else` block for this check.

If something is broken, we check to see if the player is carrying it. If the item's `indexOf` comes back as `-1`, then the player does not have the item they need. If they do have the item, we fix the broken thing. If they fix it and the room has a hidden passcode, this is where we give it out to the player.

```
if (brokenThing)
{
  if (index === -1)
  {
    //player doesn't have the item
  }
  else
  {
    //player does have the item
    //fix the broken thing
    //check if there's a passcode hint to give out <--new
  }
}
```

Notice the placement? For the game to work the way we intend it to, this next `if` statement has to go *inside* the `else` block above right after we fix the broken thing. We're still inside `fixBrokenThing()`.

```
player.inventory.splice(index, 1);        //<--already there

if (player.currentRoom.passcodeHint)
{
  text += " You found a piece of the passcode! ";
  text += player.currentRoom.passcodeHint;
  player.inventory.push(player.currentRoom.passcodeHint);
}
```

We aren't doing anything with the passcode yet, just giving it to the player. That's all we do in this function, but we're not finished yet.

Note that if you added the increased interactivity from Section 5.8: Intermediate: Increasing Interactivity, then the original `if`/`else` block is more complex, but the new if statement goes in the same place.

Where is the exit? We need a place where the player can try to exit. That's where they can use the passcode to complete the game. So where is this exit?

Decisions, decisions.

This is up to you.
- We could have the exit chosen randomly.
  - That might be a little weird if the exit for the house ends up in the bathroom!
- We could have the exit be in the room where the player starts.
  - This would ensure there *is* an exit available.
- We could hard-code certain rooms to have an exit.
  - This is probably more realistic for an actual house.
  - If you create the randomized room layout, you need to make sure the room with the exit is in the house.

We will use the property `exitHouse`. It will be a `true` Boolean if you're allowed to leave the house from that room. It will remain `undefined` otherwise. You can have as many exits as you want (such as from the living room and kitchen).

Option 1: setting the exit(s) manually. If you want to specify the exact rooms that have exits, go to the `getRooms()` function, find the room(s) you want to give an exit to and add the property `exitHouse: true`.

```
function getRooms()
{
  var livingRoom =
  {
    name: "living room",
    points: 25,
    exitHouse: true,
//rest of function
```

Option 2: setting the exit based on player start. This is easy to do. Go to the `startGame()` function where we added the call to `getPasscode()`, then and the `exitHouse` property to the player's `currentRoom`.

```
passcode = getPasscode(rooms);
player.currentRoom.exitHouse = true;       //<--new
```

Option 3: setting exit(s) randomly. This one will require a new function and a function call. For the function call, put it right under the passcode creation inside the `startGame()` function.

```
passcode = getPasscode(rooms);
randomizeExits(rooms);                     //<--new
```

Flexibility gives us more options.

We could keep this simple, but let's stretch our coding legs and make this *flexible*. We will give the programmer an easy way to control which rooms *must* get exits, which ones *cannot* get exits, and *how many* exits are desired. See if the function on the next page makes sense.

I'll talk you through it after you see it. Try to make sense of it as you go through it, though. I think you'll be able to follow it pretty well at this point.

```javascript
function randomizeExits(availableRooms)
{
  //needed variables for the function
  //rooms we do and do not want to have exits
  var roomsToInclude = ["living room"];
  var roomsToExclude = ["bathroom", "hallway", "den"];
  var exits = 2;

  //convert the rooms object into an array
  var roomsArray = [];
  for (var roomName in availableRooms)
  {
    roomsArray.push(availableRooms[roomName]);
  }

  //make sure we have enough rooms for exits desired
  var roomsPossible =
      roomsArray.length - roomsToExclude.length;
  var numberOfExits = Math.min(exits, roomsPossible);

  //make sure the rooms we want exits for have them
  for (var i = 0; i < roomsToInclude.length; i++)
  {
    for (var j = 0; j < roomsArray.length; j++)
    {
      if (roomsArray[j].name === roomsToInclude[i])
      {
        roomsArray[j].exitHouse = true;
        numberOfExits--;
        break;
      }
    }
      //<--optional: break out if numberOfExits <= 0
  }

  //if we have exits left to add, add them
  while (numberOfExits > 0)
  {
    var index =
      Math.floor(Math.random() * roomsArray.length);
    var checkExclude = roomsArray[index].name;

    //if the room is on the exclude list, skip it
    if (roomsToExclude.indexOf(checkExclude) !== -1)
    {
      continue;
    }

    roomsArray[index].exitHouse = true;
    roomsArray.splice(index, 1);
    numberOfExits--;
  }
}
```

179

Code breakdown. We start by setting up all the variables for things the game designer (that's you) may want to control. For instance, I don't want the player to exit the house from the bathroom.

Setting definite exits. There is no control for `roomsToInclude`. We try to set all of them to an exit. If the room isn't in the list of available rooms, nothing happens. If you put three rooms in here but only wanted two exits, this loop would put *all three* exits, not just two.

If you want to control for that, you could, but I chose not to. I put a comment in the code for you; that's where the check would go. Do you know to code it?

```
if (numberOfExits <= 0)
{
  break;
}
```

Setting the number of exits.
Right now, the number of exits is set at
2. If you want to make this random, too, you can. Try to make it reasonable and a lower number, but make sure you get at least one exit.

You could replace `var exits = 2;` with something like this.

```
var exits =
  Math.floor(Math.random() * 3)
  + 1;
```

This gives you a small, random number of exits: 1, 2, or 3.

Sidenote. You know how `Math.floor()` rounds a number *down* to the next integerl? There's an opposite method called `Math.ceil()` that rounds *up* to the next integer (ceiling). To get the 1, 2, 3 with `Math.floor()` we had to add 1 at the end, otherwise we would get 0, 1, or 2. Instead, we could get 1, 2, 3 with `Math.ceil()`;

```
var exits =
Math.ceil(Math.random() * 3);
```

Checking the actual number of exits. The `numberOfExits` variable is important to control because we have a `while` loop coming that will keep trying to add exits even if we run out of rooms. Imagine accidentally typing in 100 exits but only having 8 rooms. The `roomsArray` would be emptied out and you would get a type error trying to set `exitHouse` to an `undefined` array element.

Because we have some rooms we don't want exits for, we subtract that value from the total number of rooms (giving us `roomsPossible`). We then use `Math.min()` to give us the smaller of the two values: number of desired exits and number of possible rooms. This makes sure we don't have problems later.

If we come across a room name that we want to exclude, we `continue` the `while` loop, starting it from the top without changing anything else.

That's our third option for setting the room exits. Incidentally, you could use this function for all three exit-setting options. Use the `roomsToInclude` array for all the rooms you want exits for (option 1). If you want the player's starting room to have an exit (option 2), you could add `player.currentRoom.name` to the `roomsToInclude` array.

```
var roomsToInclude = [player.currentRoom.name];
```

This could potentially mean that the living room, for instance, might be on the `roomsToInclude` list twice. It would ultimately give you one less exit if that happened, but you'd still have a proper exit. Although we could check for this edge case, I think it's a minor thing to worry about, so I'm ignoring it. Feel free to test your skills by checking for it. Think: If the player's current room isn't on the include list, then add it.

Breather time. That was a pretty hefty function, wasn't it? Take a breather because we aren't done yet. We still have to let the player try to exit the house when they type in a direction. We have to see if they have the right passcode. And we need to update the information at the start of the game so the player knows about the passcode.

> We're working through a lot. Pause now and then and let it sink in.

Updating getDirection(). Now that there is at least one exit in the house, we need to let the player use it. We have to update our `getDirection()` function to check for an exit to the house.

```
//beginning of function
  text += "There are exits: ";

  for (var exit in player.currentRoom.exits)
  {
    text += "[ " + exit + " ] ";
  }

  if (player.currentRoom.exitHouse)              //new
  {
    text += "[ exit house ]";
  }

  direction = prompt(text);
  direction = direction.toLowerCase();

  if (player.currentRoom.exitHouse &&            //new
      direction.indexOf("exit") !== -1)
  {
    return "exit";
  }
//rest of function
```

Using `direction.indexOf("exit")` allows the user to type anything with `exit` in it to try to leave the house, even **exit**orious! or compl**exit**y.

We could control this more if we wanted to. One way would be to check for `"exit "` with the space in there or check specifically if `direction === "exit house"`. You can go ahead and change that if you'd like. I wanted you to see how `indexOf()` can even read through strings.

We also check to make sure there *is* an exit available in this room. Otherwise they could try to exit from anywhere. We use the AND (`&&`) operator to check for two conditions at once. Both must be true for the code block to run. If *either* one is `false`, the entire condition is `false`.

```
if (player.currentRoom.exitHouse && //is there an exit
  direction.indexOf("exit") !== -1) //and was exit typed
```

Updating moveToRoom(). Now the player can type in "exit house" to leave the house. That sends back `"exit"` as a direction. We need to address what to do with this, but we also have another thing to fix.

Currently, if all broken things in the house are fixed, the game ends. But we are changing our endgame to make the player enter a passcode to end the game. Therefore, we need to make some more changes, this time to the `moveToRoom()` function.

> Different features mean we have to do some different things here.

The next change depends on whether or not you added the interactivity addition from Section 5.8: Intermediate: Increasing Interactivity.

Version 1 shows the changes to make if you *did not* add the interactive feature. Version 2 shows the change *with* the interactive feature.

When you make this change, pick a point value as a penalty if the player guesses the passcode incorrectly. I went with 25 points, but you may want a steeper or lesser penalty for your game.

Version 1 — **Without** *the added interactive feature*

If you *did not* add the interactive feature yet, then you have this near the end of the `moveToRoom()` function.

```
if (checkGameOver())
{
  alertGameWon();
  checkPlayAgain();
}
else
{
  var direction = getDirection();
  if (direction)
  {
    player.currentRoom = rooms[direction];
    moveToRoom();
  }
}
```

Replace all of this to reflect our new goal. First, we will have to ask the player for the direction every time now. If that direction comes back as `"exit"` then we need to ask for and check the passcode. If it's correct, the game ends. Otherwise, we move the player and keep going.

Replace the *entire* `if` statement above with this.

```
var direction = getDirection();

if (direction === "exit")
{
  var guessPasscode = prompt("What's the passcode?");
  if (guessPasscode === passcode.exitCode)
  {
    alertGameWon();
    checkPlayAgain();
  }
  else
  {
    alert("Sorry, that is not the correct passcode. You
      lose " + passcode.penalty + " points.");
    player.score -= passcode.penalty;
    moveToRoom();
  }
}
else if (direction)
{
  player.currentRoom = rooms[direction];
  moveToRoom();
}
```

*Version 2 — **With** the added interactive feature*

If you added the interactivity, then you already have most of the changes done. You will need to add one `else if` statement to check for the `"exit"` command. In there, you'll have to check for a game over status. The other change to make is to remove the original call for a game over check.

```javascript
var direction = getDirection();
if (!direction)
{
  //player typed quit, don't do anything, exit game
}
else if (direction === "take")
{
  isThereAnItem();
  moveToRoom();
}

else if (direction === "exit")      //add this block
{
  var guessPasscode = prompt("What's the passcode?");
  if (guessPasscode === passcode.exitCode)
  {
    alertGameWon();
    checkPlayAgain();
  }
  else
  {
    alert("Sorry, that is not the correct passcode.
          You lose " + passcode.penalty +
          " points.");
    player.score -= passcode.penalty;
    moveToRoom();
  }
}                                   //end of new block

else if (direction.indexOf("use ") !== -1) //use item
{
  var useItem = direction.substring(4);
  fixBrokenThing(useItem);
  //here's the game over check    //delete this block
  if (checkGameOver())
  {
    alertGameWon();
    checkPlayAgain();
    return;
  }                               //end of delete
  moveToRoom();
}
```

Updating the game text. Now that we have this passcode feature, we need to update our game text at the start and at the end.

Inside `startGame()` change the text string to something like this.

```
var text = "Welcome to the Room Adventure!";
text += " You are " + player.name;
text += " and you are in a house";
text += " Go from room to room";
text += " to find the items you need";
text += " to fix what's broken.";
text += " Earn points for fixing things.";
text += " There are " + player.itemsLeftToFix;
text += " things that need to be fixed.";
text += " Along the way, you will find pieces";
text += " of a passcode. Find the exit, and";
text += " enter the correct passcode to win!";
text += " You start in the ";
text += player.currentRoom.name + ".";
text += " Good luck!";
```

Finally, in `alertGameWon()`, update that text string too. While we're at it, let's reward the player with some points!

```
var text = "Congratulations, " + player.name + "! ";
text += "You entered the correct passcode ";
text += "and escaped the house! ";

text += "You earn " + passcode.reward + " points! ";
player.score += passcode.reward;

text += "You finished the game with a score of ";
text += player.score + " points!";
text += " Play again soon!";
```

It took a lot of changes to get to this set up, but it'll be a fun addition to the game.

5.10 Advanced: Randomizing the Rooms

After a while, the player is going to know exactly where all the rooms are located. If you expand your game with lots of rooms, you may want this. However, sometimes it's fun to play in a world that is randomly generated. We are going to create a function that will randomly lay out your rooms. You still need to create the rooms ahead of time, but any directions you give will be overwritten by this function. It will create its own set of north, south, east, and west connections.

This is an advanced design concept.

We are making a complex function here. We have a lot to account for and it will be confusing to look at. We're pushing into difficult territory here. You've come a long way. Take it one part at a time and you'll see that you can handle this.

You've handled a lot of challenges already. I know you can do this!

Here is our plan:

- Create a room array based on the rooms object
  - Optional: randomly ignore a room
- Get a number of rows of rooms based on the room count
  - At least 3 rooms per row
  - At least 2 rows (if there are more than 3 rooms)
- Link all rooms in a row, connecting them east and west
- Connect each row north-to-south at least once

Samples: (dark lines represent walls)

9 Rooms		
L.R.	D.R.	Kit
Base	Bath	Den
Off.	Hall	Cat

8 Rooms	Base	Hall	Kit	L.R.
	Off.	Den	D.R.	Bath

9 Rooms	Den	Kit	L.R.	Off.	Bath
	D.R.	Cat	Hall	Base	

> I need to look at this for a minute. Ok, the rooms going left to right all pass into each other, and sometimes they also connect up and down.

We could get even more complicated, but this is difficult enough for the purposes of this book. From this design, the player will be able to run east-west across the length of the house in whichever row they are on. This is to ensure all the rooms are connected and reachable without getting into complicated logic.

We're going to use two-dimensional arrays and parallel arrays. Let's talk a little about those before looking at our new function.

Two-dimensional array. Arrays are a single list. But what if you had a list of lists? Let's say you need to get a bunch of supplies from different stores. You would have a list of things you need from the supermarket, another list for the toy store, a third list for the clothing store, and so on. Each list is an array. If you have a notepad and each page is a different list, that notepad acts like a two-dimensional array.

Store	Things needed from the store			
supermarket	milk	bread	candy	eggs
toy store	video game	teddy bear	board game	clay
clothing	shirt	shoes	shorts	pants

If we put this into code, the stores would look like this.

```
var supermarket = ["milk", "bread", "candy", "eggs"];
var toyStore = ["video game", "teddy bear", "board game",
    "clay"];
var clothing = ["shirt", "shoes", "shorts", "pants"];
```

Each store is a separate list. Let's put those lists into a bigger list.

```
var stores = [supermarket, toyStore, clothing];
```

Make sense so far? Well, what if you want to see what you need from the toy store?

```
stores[1]; //shows the list for the toyStore
```

What if you wanted to see the third item for the toy store? Here's where it starts looking complicated.

```
//if it's just the toy store array:
toyStore[2]; //"board game"

//but we saw that stores[1] is also the toyStore, so…
stores[1][2]; //"board game"
```

Do you see the double set of brackets? We are looking at the main list of stores and pulling the store at index 1 (toyStore), and within that, we are looking at *that store's* index 2 ("board game").

There's a lot we can do with arrays depending on our needs. Something to keep in mind.

It's a bit like chaining object properties:

```
rooms.office.exits.west;              //"hallway"
rooms["office"]["exits"]["west"];     //"hallway"
```

One main difference is that arrays have to be accessed by index numbers, not words or property names.

This would be a good time to hit the console and play around with this example and try to make sense of it.

Parallel arrays. Let's say you wanted to keep two lists that link up somehow. How about a food shopping list and the person who wants each item? Each food item would need a matching person. You could use parallel arrays to track this.

Consider:

Food	popcorn	apples	M&Ms	tuna
People	Lois	Joseph	Kevin	Steve

```
var food = ["popcorn", "apples", "M&Ms", "tuna"];
var people = ["Lois", "Joseph", "Kevin", "Steve"];
```

If I check index 2 of both arrays, I would get this.

```
food[2];     //M&Ms
people[2];   //Kevin
```

Let's say Kevin changed his mind and he doesn't want the M&Ms. If we spliced it out of the food array, we'd have this.

```
food.splice(2, 1); //["popcorn", "apples", "tuna"];
people = ["Lois", "Joseph", "Kevin", "Steve"];
```

Remember what splice() does? It delete elements from an array and shifts the other elements down to fill the empty space.

Now if I check index 2 of both arrays, I would get this.

That's not what we wanted!

```
food[2];     //tuna      <--not what we want
people[2];   //Kevin
```

And poor Steve…

```
food[3];     //undefined  <--not what we want
people[3];   //Steve
```

If we had assigned `food[2] = null;` instead of splicing, we'd have a different story.

```
var food = ["popcorn", "apples", "M&Ms", "tuna"];
var people = ["Lois", "Joseph", "Kevin", "Steve"];

//Kevin no longer wants M&Ms
food[2] = null;

food[2];      //null        <--This is correct
person[2];    //Kevin       <--This is correct

food[3];      //tuna        <--This is correct
person[3];    //Steve       <--This is correct
```

Working with parallel arrays means taking care to add or remove from both arrays at the same time, or to set things equal to `null` (or `undefined`) if something is meant to disappear. This allows the index number to relate to both arrays correctly.

Do some practice in the console.

The randomizeRoomLayout function.

With all that groundwork out of the way, let's see the main `randomizeRoomLayout()` function for our game. Take your time reading this and do your best to make sense of it. This is tricky stuff. It may not all make sense the first time. I'll break it down into chunks. These chunks are all part of the same function so keep adding to it as you go.

> We know a lot more about arrays so let's use that info now.

Part 1: Create the roomsArray. This code is written to sometimes use the original layout. It's set to a 5% chance of *not* randomizing the rooms. You can increase the percentage (as a decimal so 13% would be entered as 0.13). Or if you want to, you can set the percent to `0` and always randomize the layout.

When the game doesn't use the original layout, it will create the `roomsArray`, but sometimes leave a room out for variety. You can also play with the percentage here. Don't make it too high, though, or you may drop a lot of rooms.

```
function randomizeRoomLayout(availableRooms)
{
  //optional: randomly return the original layout
  if (Math.random() < 0.05) //5% chance
  {
    return availableRooms;
  }

  //create the roomsArray
  var roomsArray = [];
  for (var roomName in availableRooms)
  {
    //optional: randomly drop a room
    if (Math.random() < 0.05) //5% chance
    {
      continue;
    }

    roomsArray.push(availableRooms[roomName]);
  }
```

Part 2: Figure out the size of the house grid.
As the programmer, you decide how many rooms are in each row. I
went with 3 to 6 rooms per row. You can change these or randomize
them further.

```
//determine the number of rooms per row
var minimum = 3;
var maximum = 6;
var range = Math.abs(maximum - minimum) + 1;
var roomsPerRow =
    Math.floor(Math.random() * range) + minimum;

//determine the number of rows of rooms
var totalRooms = roomsArray.length;
var numberRows = Math.floor(totalRooms / roomsPerRow);
numberRows = Math.max(numberRows, 2);
```

How does this work? We create the variables `minimum`
and `maximum`, which you set, as the designer. To get
the range, we subtract those two values and then add
`1`. We add `1` because the `Math.random()` method never
includes the maximum value, so this allows it to include that.

> There's a lot of detail
> here for a small
> amount of code.

I also used `Math.abs()` for the subtraction. This is just a
precaution in case you accidentally make the maximum
value smaller than the minimum. `Math.abs()` returns the
absolute value, a fancy way of saying it removes a negative
sign if there is one.

We then randomly pick the number of rooms per each row of the
floorplan within the range of values we gave. For me, that's a number
from 3 to 6.

The length of the `roomsArray` we created in *Part 1* tells us the total
number of rooms we have available to use. If we divide the total
number of rooms by the number of rooms we want on a row, then we
figure out the number of rows. So if we had 13 rooms and we
ranmdomly get 4 rooms per row, that would leave us with 13 / 4 or
3.25 rows. We round down with `Math.floor()` to get 3 rows because
we can't have a fraction of a row. You either have a row or you don't.

The last thing we do with the `Math.max()` line is make sure we have at
least 2 rows.

Part 3: Initialize the two-dimensional array
There isn't an automatic way to set up a two-dimensional array in
JavaScript, like you can in some other languages. We have to do this
manually. We loop through the number of rows and set each one of
them to an empty array.

```
//initialize two-dimensional 'rows' array
var rows = [];
for (var i = 0; i < numberRows; i++)
{
  rows[i] = [];   //creates an empty array on each row
}
```

Part 4: Shuffle the rooms into different rows.
Our next job is to take all the rooms we have and shuffle them into
the number of rows we created. It's sort of like dealing cards out
players. The cards are shuffled and then you deal one to each person
around the table. Each time you deal a card, it's no longer in the deck
because it was removed.

We are going to do the same thing with the rooms. We have a "deck"
of rooms (roomsArray). We will dole out all of them (totalRooms). We
give one to each "person" (row). We go from person to person in order
(% or *modulo*), thus removing the room from the deck (splice). While
doing this, we also have to clear out the exits in each room so we can
make new ones.

```
//shuffle rooms into the rows
for (var i = 0; i < totalRooms; i++)
{
  var r = Math.floor(Math.random()* roomsArray.length);
  var row = i % numberRows;   //alternate between rows

  rows[row].push(roomsArray[r]); //add room to row
  roomsArray[r].exits = {};      //erase existing exits
  roomsArray.splice(r, 1);       //remove room from list
}
```

I'm using the modulo operator (i % numberRows) to alternate between
rows so the rooms get scattered. Modulo does regular division but
returns the whole number remainder. If you do 13 divided by 4, the 4
goes in 3 times, and you have a 1 left over. Modulo gives back that 1.

If modulo (%) feels confusing, it's ok. Think of modulo as dealing cards at a table to yourself and two other players (3 players total, for this example). You get a card (player 0), then the next person gets a card (player 1), then the next person gets a card (player 2). Then it's back you (player 0), then player 1, and so on until you run out of cards. That's all modulo is doing.

If there are three rows of rooms (so `numberRows` is `3`), the possible remainders are 0, 1, and 2. You get `0` if the number divided in equally, because there is no remainder. These remainders would relate to the row numbers (actually, their indexes).

Once modulo has picked the row *number* (`row`), we use `rows[row]` to pick the *actual* row we want (`row[0]`, `row[1]`, etc.). Then we push the randomly selected room (`roomsArray[r]`) onto the row.

We also need to clear out the original set of exits because we're changing them to make new ones. We do this by setting the `exits` property equal to an empty object.

```
roomsArray[r].exits = {};
```

Finally, now that the room is placed, we take it out of the list of options for the next iteration in the loop. You've seen that done before, right?

```
roomsArray.splice(r, 1);
```

At this point, all the rooms have been placed into different rows. Next, we need to start linking them together.

Part 5: Connect rooms west and east along each row.

We need to connect our rooms from west to east, and make sure we will be able to connect north and south somewhere. We need to make sure two rooms are lined up for that. If there are three rooms on the top row but only two rooms on the bottom row, then we don't want to connect the third room north-to-south. To watch for this, we want to keep track of the minimum number of rooms on each row, keeping only the smallest value among all the rows. This will be used later.

We begin a nested loop. The first loop (i) picks each row. The second loop (j) runs through each room in that row. Then we set the exits. Take a look. I'll explain it all afterward.

```javascript
//minimum number of rooms per row is needed to figure
//out how many north/south connections to make later
var minRoomsPerRow = totalRooms;

//connect rooms east-through-west across each row
for (var i = 0; i < rows.length; i++) // pick a row
{
  var row = rows[i]; //select current row in the loop

  //only keep the smallest number of rooms per row
  minRoomsPerRow =
    Math.min(minRoomsPerRow, row.length);

  for (var j = 0; j < row.length; j++) // pick a room
  {
    if (j === 0)      //west wall of house: no west exit
    {
      //row[j] is current room
      //row[j + 1] is room to the right
      row[j].exits.east = row[j + 1].name;
    }
    else if (j === row.length - 1) //east wall of house
    {
      //row[j - 1] is room to the left
      row[j].exits.west = row[j - 1].name;
    }
    else                  //room is an inner room
    {
      //add neighboring room to the left and right
      row[j].exits.west = row[j - 1].name; //left room
      row[j].exits.east = row[j + 1].name; //right room
    }                            //close else block
  }                              //close j loop
}                                //close i loop
```

It's a lot to take in.

> I'm gonna have to give this some thought. So if `j` is a room, then `j + 1` is the room on the right and `j - 1` is the room on the left.

Our goal is to add connections east and west along each row. So we pick the first row (`rows[0]`). We then go through every room in that row to add the connections between those rooms.

We have three conditions to watch out for on each row:

1. If the room is on the **west** side of the house, there can't be a room connected to its west side.
   a. This happens when `j` (the room looper) is zero `0`.
   b. So, only add an east exit to the room by setting east equal to the name of the *next* room (`j + 1`) in the row.
   c. `row[j].exits.east = row[j + 1].name;`

2. If the room is on the **east** side of the house, there can't be a room connected to its east side.
   a. This happens when `j` is one less than the row's length.
      i. Why one less? Because arrays are indexed from zero so all the numbers are off by one.
   b. So, only add a west exit to the room by setting west equal to the name of the *previous* room (`j - 1`).
   c. `row[j].exits.west = row[j - 1].name;`

3. If we're **not at either** end of the house, we add both west and east exits.
   a. `row[j].exits.west = row[j - 1].name;`
   b. `row[j].exits.east = row[j + 1].name;`
   c. We added west before east so west shows up first when we display the available directions.

Part 6: Making the north/south connections.

Remember that `minRoomsPerRow` variable we made in the last part? We let it figure out the smallest number of rooms per each row. It's time to use it. We want to have at least one connection, so we are using `Math.ceil()` to round *up* to the next whole number.

I chose to make an average of one north/south connection for every other room in a row. It's still a bit random. You can change the 2 to get a different result.

The loop here runs until `rows.length - 1`, not the usual `rows.length`. This is because the last row doesn't have any more rows under it and we don't want to link those rooms to a row that doesn't exist.

We randomly pick an index based on the minimum rooms per row. This makes sure we have two rooms lined up.

The last thing to do is to set the *south* exit of the top room (`rows[i]`) equal to the room under it (`rows[i + 1]`), and set the bottom room's *north* exit to the room above it. Can you picture it?

```
//choose number of north/south connections
//use Math.ceil() to ensure at least 1 connection
var connections = Math.ceil(minRoomsPerRow / 2);

//connect north and south at random along each row pair
for (var i = 0; i < rows.length - 1; i++)
{
  for (var j = 0; j < connections; j++)
  {
    var index =
    Math.floor(Math.random() * minRoomsPerRow);

    //rows[i] is top room, rows[i + 1] is bottom room
    rows[i][index].exits.south =
                            rows[i + 1][index].name;

    rows[i + 1][index].exits.north =
                            rows[i][index].name;
  }
}
```

Part 7: Creating the new rooms object.

We're almost done. We need to make a new rooms object and send it back where this function was called from so it can be used in the game.

It's all coming together now!

Remember when we made our rooms? We created each one as a separate object and then we used array notation to add them in to the rooms object there. We're doing the exact same thing here, except the computer is doing it in a loop, where we had added each room by hand.

We use one more nested loop to capture all the rooms and add them.

```
//create new 'rooms' object to return
var newRoomLayout = {};
for (var i = 0; i < rows.length; i++)   //loop the rows
{
  var row = rows[i];
  for (var j = 0; j < row.length; j++) //loop the rooms
  {
    var room = row[j];
    newRoomLayout[room.name] = room;    //look familiar?
  }
}
return newRoomLayout;
}  //finally, the end of the randomizeRoomLayout function
```

Wow, that was a lot, huh?

Updating startGame(). We still need to activate this feature by including it in the startGame() function. This is the best place it can go. It needs to be created after the initial set of rooms, but before we randomly move the player or set the items around the house. We need the house's layout set up first. We need the rooms = at the beginning because the rooms object is changing in this function.

```
function startGame()
{
    rooms = getRooms();
    player = getPlayer();

    rooms = randomizeRoomLayout(rooms);
    randomizePlayerStart(rooms);
//rest of code
```

Chapter 6

Improving the Gameplay: HTML

We have unlimited options for what we can do going forward. This chapter focuses on linking our JavaScript file to a webpage through HTML. This will not be a comprehensive look at HTML or CSS. We will only cover the essentials that we need for our game.

What will we cover in the chapter?

- Learning basic HTML
- Creating an HTML table
- Removing all pop-ups
- Moving by clicking buttons
- Adding images for each room
- Some CSS styling

If you are using a Web Project at `http://repl.it`, then you already have an HTML file started for you (index.html). If you used a JavaScript repl, go into it, select all the JavaScript code (Ctrl-A) and copy it (Ctrl-C). Start a new repl under HTML, CSS, JavaScript, and paste (Ctrl-V) into the index.js file. Now you're ready.

If you are coding elsewhere, you may have to create your own file system. If you need help, refer to Section 1.5: Basic File Setup.

6.1 Learning Basic HTML

HTML stands for **H**yper**t**ext **M**arkup **L**anguage. Every webpage you see on the internet is formatted with HTML. We use HTML to set the *structure* of a webpage. It sets up where things are located. It is a completely different language than JavaScript, which determines the *behavior* of a webpage.

Another offshoot of HTML is CSS, or **C**ascading **S**tyle **S**heets. This is a third language, which governs how things are *styled*, or how they look. Why are some fonts bigger, smaller, or different colors? Why are images shown at certain sizes? Why does a webpage look different on a smartphone than it does on a laptop or computer screen? That's all because of CSS.

These three languages are designed to work together.

HTML tags. There are many HTML tags and they all have specific uses. Some set up the information in the browser's title bar, some make paragraphs or tables, and so on. Some of the tags overlap in their purpose. Some are considered outdated, but they are still supported by modern browsers.

The key to using a tag is to know what it's for, of course. But you also need to open and close your tags. Like brackets and quotes in JavaScript, you need to close everything you open. There are some special tags, though, that close themselves.

```
<!-- Some tags that need to be closed. -->
<html></html>        <p></p>          <table></table>

<!-- Some tags that close themselves. -->
<img />              <br />           <hr />
```

For the self-closing tags, you don't need the slash if you're using HTML5 (the current standard). It is recommended to include the slash.

HTML comments. It's a different language, so everything is different, even the way we create comments. In JavaScript, you could use `//` or `/* ... */`. Here, you open a comment with `<!--` and you close it with `-->`. HTML comments are multi-line comments, so you can split up the open and close tags.

```
<!--
   This comment spans several lines.
   The computer won't do anything in here.
   Use comments in your code to document what you're
      doing.
-->
```

Starting an HTML document. Every HTML document is just a basic text file with a line that tells the browser that it's HTML. The current version, HTML5, uses a very simple indicator.

That's how we get it started!

```
<!DOCTYPE html>
```

This *always* goes at the *very top* of the document so the browser knows right away how it should interpret the page.

Inside a webpage, there is an `<html>` tag, and inside of that, there is a `<head>` and a `<body>`. The `<head>` holds information about the page, like the character set (letters) you're using, the title of the page, and if you're using a stylesheet (CSS). The `<body>` holds everything else, and that's what you see on a page.

Basic HTML page structure. You must start with the `<!DOCTYPE html>` declaration, then you open an `<html>` tag. You set up the `<head>` tag, include what you need, then close it with `</head>`. You open a `<body>` tag, put in whatever you need, then close that with `</body>`. Last, you close the `</html>`.

```
<!DOCTYPE html>
<html>
  <head>
    <meta charset="utf-8">
    <meta name="viewport" content="width=device-width">
    <title>repl.it</title>
    <link href="index.css" rel="stylesheet"
      type="text/css" />
  </head>
  <body>
    <script src="index.js"></script>
  </body>
</html>
```

This is the default "boilerplate" HTML code that **http://repl.it** uses. A *boilerplate* is a code template that is automatically loaded when you start a new file. You can edit it, but repl.it does a great job of setting up the basics. You can use this boilerplate code in your own html files.

Do you see the `<html>`, `<head>`, `</head>`, `<body>`, `</body>`, and `</html>` tags? They always have to be in that order.

Inside the <head> tag. The `<meta>` tags tell the browser some things. The first one (`<meta charset="utf-8">`) tells the browser to use the standard font set. The second one (`<meta name="viewport" content="width=device-width">`) tells the browser to zoom in to fill whatever screen you're using, from a smartphone to a monitor.

The `<title></title>` tag is what displays in the browser bar at the very top of the screen or in the browser tab for the page you're on.

The `<link />` tag attaches a CSS stylesheet. The default stylesheet in repl.it is completely blank. But as soon you add to it, this self-closing `<link>` allows it to be used instantly. If you create a CSS stylesheet, but don't link it in, it won't do anything.

Looking at a page's HTML. Try this:

Go to a webpage. Right-click on it and select "View Source" or "View Page Source". You should see the HTML inside. Some sites (like google.com) are very hard to read because they have been *minified*.

Here's our `moveToRoom()` function in minified version.

```
function moveToRoom(){if(textRoomDescriptio
n(),isThereAnItem(),fixBrokenThing(),showSc
ore(),showInventory(),checkGameOver())alert
GameWon(),checkPlayAgain();else{var e=getDi
rection();e&&(player.currentRoom=rooms[e],m
oveToRoom())}}
```

The word *minified* means that all comments and whitespace are removed from the code. Most variables get replaced with single or double letters. It's hard to read!

Inside the <body> tag.

In the boilerplate code on the previous page, all you see is a `<script>` tag and nothing else. Usually, this is loaded with lots of HTML elements.

Go to my coding site `http://coding.stephenjwolf.com` and look at the page source. You will see the same basic structure I mentioned above.

That `<script>` element is really important. Can you tell what it's for? That's right, it links in your JavaScript file.

This tag is generally best placed at the very bottom of your HTML file, immediately *above* the closing `</body>` tag. If your JavaScript is going to interact with your webpage, then the other HTML elements need to load first. Putting this at the bottom allows for the page to be translated before your JavaScript tries to do anything to it. It's safer.

<div> tags.

A `<div>` tag is a standard for organizing your webpage. It's a division of your page. You can style each `<div>` separately and use them for lots of things. They are versatile and can hold pretty much any webpage structure you want.

\<p\> tags. These tags denote paragraphs. By default, the text inside a `<p>...</p>` tag will have some space around it to separate paragraphs visually.

\<img /\> tag. The `<img />` tag is self-closing, so you don't use `<img>...</img>`. This is how you put pictures onto a webpage. You need to give the `<img>` tag a source (`src=""`) for the image you are using. This is a link to an image file.

```
<img src=" http://coding.stephenjwolf.com/Merlin.jpg" />
<img src=" http://coding.stephenjwolf.com/Monty.jpg" />
```

Like most elements in HTML, you can add an `id` and a `class` tag. There's a lot more you can do too, like control the display size (width and height). I'll discuss then when we put images into our game.

If you're testing things on your computer, you can link to a picture file on your computer. If you're on the web, you need a place to upload your images and then link to them there. You should never link directly to an image on another person's website unless they say it's ok. You would use up *their* bandwidth every time someone looks at *your* page. It's not good etiquette.

HTML id attribute. When you have elements on your page, you want to be able to access them. It's like giving your cats different names. You want to find Monty, so you give him an id (his name). Basically, every tag in HTML can be given an `id`. However, each `id` on a page *must* be unique. There can't be two "Monty" tags.

```
<div id="Monty"></div>
<img id="Merlin" />
<p id="Shadow"></p>
```

We can use JavaScript to change what's inside an element by using its `id`. They are unique names, so we can always find the specific one we want. We'll talk about how to do this later on.

HTML class attribute. What if you want to group all your cats together so you can find them easily? Then you use the `class` keyword. This is used to access a set of different tags. You can use classes and ids together, but you don't have to.

```
<div class="cat" id="Monty"></div>
<img class="cat" id="Merlin" />
<p class="cat" id="Shadow"></p>
<div class="dog"></div>
```

This has two different classes, `cat` and `dog`. Now you can find all your cats at once.

These are just some of the basics. There's a lot more to HTML than what we're covering in this book.

6.2 Adventure Game Page Setup Plan

If you want to design a good webpage, you should take some time to plan it out first. It will save you a lot of fidgeting.

We are going to make a user interface (UI) so the player can interact with a mouse or touchscreen to play our game. Because they often involve graphics, these can also have the name GUI (Graphical User Interface).

I'm going to create an arrangement for our adventure game using a basic table here in my word processor. It's like when we made the floorplan for the house. This is a plan that we will turn into code.

Room Adventure UI. This is the setup for my user interface. You can use something different. I chose an `id` for each section and gave some a `class` as well. We won't be using the `class` until we talk about CSS.

<table>
<tr>
<td colspan="2" align="center">

The Room Adventure
id="gameTitle"

Information
<div> id="info"
</td>
</tr>
<tr>
<td>

Current Room and description
class="text" id="description"
</td>
<td rowspan="4">

Picture of the room
<div> wrapper for <img>:
   id="imagewrapper"
<img>:
   id="image"
   src=""
<div>:
   id="caption"
</td>
</tr>
<tr>
<td>

Item broken/fixed information
class="text" id="broken"
</td>
</tr>
<tr>
<td>

Item found information
class="text" id="found"
</td>
</tr>
<tr>
<td>

Player's Score
class="text" id="score"
</td>
</tr>
<tr>
<td>

Navigation buttons
id="navigation"
</td>
<td>

Inventory
class="text" id="inventory"
</td>
</tr>
</table>

HTML <table>. In HTML, a `<table>` is an element that lets you set up rows and columns. In my layout, I have five rows and two columns. It is easy to set up a table to display everything.

Disclaimer. Professionals in the industry often say that the `<table>` element is meant only for displaying data, like if you were doing a lab in science class. It's not meant for laying out things like our game. I do understand their point. However, we're just starting out here and using `<div>` elements with CSS formatting to create a table is a bit more than we need. Be aware that there is another way to do this using `<div>` elements. For simplicity, we're going to stick with the `<table>` element.

> For what we're doing, using a <table> is all we need. But it's good to know there's another way.

Tags we need. To use a table in HTML, you need to use three specific tags. First is the `<table>` tag that tells the browser where the table starts and where it ends `</table>`. We need to also declare each row in the table using `<tr>...</tr>`. And finally, we need to create each table data cell with `<td>...</td>`. We can have as many rows and columns (cells) as we want inside the table.

The HTML structure for a table looks like this.

```
<table>                          <!--open/start the table-->
    <tr>                         <!--start the first row-->
        <td>...</td>             <!--create 1st column-->
        <td>...</td>             <!--create 2nd column-->
    </tr>                        <!--end the first row-->
    <tr>                         <!--start the second row-->
        <td>...</td>             <!--create 1st column-->
        <td>...</td>             <!--create 2nd column-->
    </tr>                        <!--end the second row-->
</table>                         <!--close/end the table-->
```

> This is such a mess! We can make it look better, can't we?

Remember whitespace? We can indent wherever we want to make things easier to read. Here, we are indenting the rows and columns to show how they are nested one inside the other. We could remove the whitespace and have this too:

```
<table><tr><td>...</td><td>...</td></tr><tr>
<td>...</td><td>...</td></tr></table>
```

Seems messy. It doesn't look like the shape of the table we want to make. How about this?

```
<table>
    <tr><td>...</td><td>...</td></tr>
    <tr><td>...</td><td>...</td></tr>
</table>
```

Now it looks like the table we want. Each row is on its own row and the columns (data cells) are next to each other inside each row. Guess what? The browser sees all three of these versions the exact same way. It doesn't care if we split up the tags on different lines. It only looks for the arrangement of the tags. This is why the `<td>` tag must be inside the `<tr>` tag. If it's outside, it won't work correctly.

Now that we covered that...

210

We will also be using a special `<table>` attribute called `rowspan`. If you look again at the plan on the earlier page, you'll see that the picture of the room takes up four rows. That's `rowspan=4`.

For the picture, we are going to use the self-closing `<img />` tag wrapped in a `<div>`. We will use a heading tag `<h1>...</h1>` for the title.

The buttons will be created with the `<button>...</button>` element. We could create these as `<div>` elements and make them clickable. More web designers are doing it that way these days, but we have a `<button>` element. Why not use it?

Finally, we will wrap the entire interface in a `<div>`. Technically, we do this first. You'll see.

I know I'm going a little fast on this HTML stuff, especially the tables. The focus of this book is on JavaScript, so I'm keeping this part brief.

There's way too much to cover if we wanted to go in detail. Let's stay focused on what we need.

There are many, many tags that can be used in HTML and they would fill a book all their own. Just do your best to follow along. The code will be provided for you, so if you don't want to master HTML, you can simply type in the code at the end of the chapter and move back to JavaScript.

6.3 Laying Out the Tags

We still need the "boilerplate" code that was discussed in Section 6.1: Learning Basic HTML. I want to focus on the new code, so first, I'm going to ignore the boilerplate. All of this code below will go inside the `<body>` element, immediately above the `<script>` tag. If you put it after the `<script>`, then the JavaScript will crash when we run it.

First the basic structure. We are wrapping the entire UI in a `<div>` called `interface`. Inside that, we put the title of the game in a large header `<h1>`, and a place we can share some information. Then we will start the table. Here's what it looks like so far.

```
<div id="interface">
  <h1 id="gameTitle">The Room Adventure</h1>
  <div id="info">Information</div>
  <table>
                <!--we need to put the rows here-->
  </table>
</div>
```

Notice how every tag that gets opened has to be closed? Also notice that the tags don't overlap. You don't have `<div><h1>` then `</div></h1>`. You have to close the `<h1>` before you can close the `<div>`. You always have to close inner sections before you close the ones that wrap around them.

212

Adding rows. We need five rows to match the original plan. Therefore, we will need five `<tr>...</tr>` sets. We have two columns, so we also need two `<td>...<td>` sets inside each row. (Well, except that the image spans four rows...)

Row #1: This has the room description and the image. The image is going to span 4 rows. In the layout on the previous page, I had planned ahead and chose `id` and `class` name for each table cell. Here is an example of how we put that into a tag.

```
<td class="text" id="description">
```

Not bad, right? You don't need both a `class` and an `id`. You only include what you need. They go inside the angle brackets after the name of the tag.

> Ok, so we can give things names so we can update them later.

We already gave `class` and `id` names to everything we need. This is what row 1 will look like.

```
<tr>
    <td class="text" id="description">Description</td>
    <td rowspan=4>
      <div id="imagewrapper">
        <img id="image" src=""/>
      </div>
      <div id="caption">Caption</div>
    </td>
</tr>
```

You may notice I added the word *Description* and *Caption* right before the closing data tags `</td>`. Those are only there so we can see where things are when we run the code. We'll remove them later and our room descriptions and captions take their place.

Rows 2, 3, and 4: These are going to be a little different. We won't have two columns. Do you know why? It's because the cell with the `<img>` tag inside has a `rowspan` of `4`. That means it will take the place of the second cells in these next three rows.

Here are the next three rows.

```
<tr>
    <td class="text" id="broken">Broken</td>
</tr>
<tr>
    <td class="text" id="found">Found</td>
</tr>
<tr>
    <td class="text" id="score">Score</td>
</tr>
```

Row 5: The last row needs to have the second column in there because the image cell's `rowspan` from the first row has run out.

```
<tr>
    <td class="text" id="navigation">Navigation</td>
    <td class="text" id="inventory">Inventory</td>
</tr>
```

If you have all these in the right place and you run your repl, you will see the table setup in the *result* tab (next to the console tab we've been using). If you're typing this into your own file structure, load the html file in a web browser to see it.

If you had trouble knowing where to put everything, the whole thing is coming up in a page or two.

Everything is laid out where we want it, but it's hard to tell it because the table has no borders that you can see.

A tiny dip into CSS. Open up your CSS file (index.css). I'm not going to go into any real detail yet, but we want to be able to see where things are. In your CSS file, put the following.

```
#interface {
  border: dotted;
  padding: 15px;
}

h1 {
  text-align: center;
}

table {
  border: solid;
  width: 100%;
}

td {
  border: dashed;
  width: 50%;
  padding: 10px;
}
```

We just want to be able to see how our table is set up.

You might see a warning in repl.it that says using width and border together may make elements larger than you expect. Don't about this for now.

Can you figure out what the code is doing just by reading it? You may recognize that h1, table, and td are HTML elements.

Selector	Command	Effect
#interface	border: dotted;	# targets id, not tag; dotted border
	padding: 15px;	Add space between border & table
h1	text-align: center;	Text is centered
table	border: solid;	Solid line border wraps the table
	width: 100%;	Table fills 100% of interface div
td	border: dashed;	Dashed line border wraps cells
	width: 50%	Cell fills 50% of table (2 columns)
	padding: 10px;	Add space between border and text

Give it a test run and see where it all ends up. Resize the window and watch the table and cells.

215

HTML Code for the Basic UI. This is all of our HTML.

```
<!DOCTYPE html>
<html>
 <head>
   <meta charset="utf-8">
   <meta name="viewport" content="width=device-width">
   <title>The Room Adventure</title>
   <link href="index.css" rel="stylesheet"
       type="text/css" />
 </head>
 <body>
  <div id="interface">
   <h1 id="gameTitle">The Room Adventure</h1>
   <div id="info">Information</div>
   <table>
    <tr>
     <td class="text" id="description">Description</td>
     <td rowspan=4><div id="imagewrapper">
          <img id="image" src="" />Image</div>
          <div id="caption">Caption</div></td>
    </tr>
    <tr>
     <td class="text" id="broken">Broken</td>
    </tr>
    <tr>
     <td class="text" id="found">Found</td>
    </tr>
    <tr>
     <td class="text" id="score">Score</td>
    </tr>
    <tr>
     <td class="text" id="navigation">Navigation</td>
     <td class="text" id="inventory">Inventory</td>
    </tr>
   </table>
  </div>
  <script src="index.js"></script>
 </body>
</html>
```

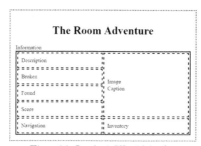

Figure 16. Our basic UI with borders.

6.4 Connecting to the HTML Layout

Now that we have the UI laid out, we will start making use of it. We are going to get rid of the alerts and add buttons that allow the user to navigate by clicking, instead of typing, their destination. We will make use of the new `exits` property in our rooms to do that, as well as a bit of a trick to make it happen.

The first thing we need to talk about is how JavaScript can communicate with the different HTML tags, even though they're in different languages. We will be accessing the DOM, the Document Object Model, to talk to each of the elements we created in the previous section.

The window object. We've talked about objects. You've even created a bunch of them. Your browser runs in a window; that's where everything gets displayed. Guess what? That's one big object!

The commands we've been using, like `alert()`, `console.log()`, and `prompt()` are all methods (or functions) of the `window` object. You could write `window.alert();` and it will do the same as writing `alert();`.

All of your JavaScript is tucked into that window object when you're running it in a browser. We don't need to keep saying `window` when we do things because it's understood that you're using it. You could even call the functions you've created by attaching them to the window object. `window.startGame();` would run your program and `window.getDirection();` would ask you which way you want to go.

If you open Developer Tools in a browser and type `window` in the console, you'll see a huge list of properties and methods that are defined for the `window` object. If you're logged in to your browser, you may even see which email address is logged in. I don't suggest doing this in the repl.it console, though. It's not meant to handle displaying the window object.

The document object. Your HTML page is a document that lives inside the browser window. You may know what's coming next... the document itself is also an object. It holds all the HTML tags and a host of functions meant for communicating with the document.

If you type `document` in a Developer Tools console (not in repl.it), you will see the basic HTML for the current webpage displayed there. It will give you a display that's very similar to using View Page Source from the menu.

Some document methods.
There are a lot of methods predefined for the `document` object. We need to use

> It sounds like these things are how webpages get updated in real-time.

those to make changes to the page using JavaScript. We can have JavaScript change what the page looks like entirely, or just in small parts, like adding text to our table.

Jumping back into JavaScript to access HTML. We have our HTML set up and we can use JavaScript to alter it. Let's see how. You'll want to head back to your JavaScript file (index.js) and you'll be switching back and forth between repl.it's console and result windows.

document.getElementById();. When we set up our table, we included an `id` for different tags. This allows us to target each `id` as we need them. Be careful of the capitalization here.

```
var nav = document.getElementById("navigation");
```

This sets a variable, `nav`, as a pointer to the HTML tag where we will have our navigation buttons. We can now use `nav` to make changes to the "navigation" panel on the webpage. Notice how we passed in `"navigation"` as an argument? (Like passing `"Hello!"` into an `alert`). That's the `id` for the navigation box in the HTML.

innerHTML. There are different ways we can change what is inside the cell. Some are more complex-looking than others and need a few steps to add them in. These are necessary for certain dynamic changes to a webpage. However, as with other aspects of this book, I'm going to keep this simple.

`innerHTML` is a property of an HTML tag, so we add it to a tag with the dot operator (see the example below). We pass in a string and it gets translated as HTML. We could put in any HTML tags we want, really, and the page would be updated with them. Let's start with a simple example. Type these into the console **one at a time** and look at the result window after each one.

```
var nav = document.getElementById("navigation");
nav.innerHTML = "We are updating the HTML live!";
nav.innerHTML += "<p>So cool!</p>";
nav.innerHTML += "<h1>Dynamic!</h1>";
```

Here, we create the `nav` variable so the code is easier to read. We use `nav.innerHTML =` to assign a new value to the `innerHTML`. This will replace anything else that was inside because we just used the assignment operator (=).

219

The next line uses `+=`. Remember when we did this for math and text strings? This adds to the current value and then assigns it back. In other words, we add to what's in there already and keep it. The `<p>` tag wraps the sentence in a paragraph, so it will have extra spacing around it. The final line adds more space, using the big header tag `<h1>` for emphasis.

You know what to do… Test it out. Go to repl.it and run your game if you haven't recently. Quit the game as soon as you're able to. Go to the console window and type in the first two lines. Then click on the result window so you can see it. Go back to the console, add the next line, and switch back to the result window so see the change. Try adding your own stuff while you're at it.

Here's what this looks like.

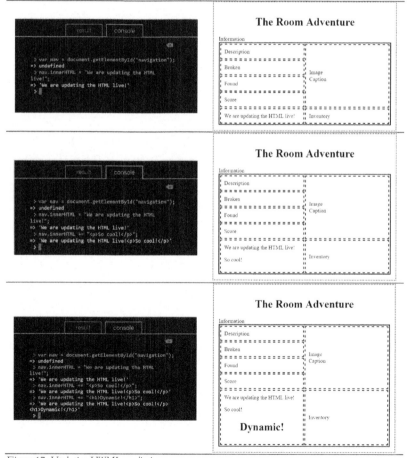

Figure 17. Updating HTML… live!

6.5 Preparing to Remove Popups

Now that we access the information on the webpage, it is time to start getting rid of the alerts we are using. Those are annoying to a user, so cleaning this up is a great idea.

Let's go through our game, find all the alerts, and make the needed changes.

startGame alert. Our first function of the game explains to the player what they need to do to play the game. We built a `text` string that explains the game and then we pass that to an alert. Instead, let's pass this to our info paragraph under the heading for our game.

Find this line in the `startGame()` function.

```
alert(text);
```

Delete it (or comment it out by putting two slashes in front of it `//`). Now add this.

```
var info = document.getElementById("info");
info.innerHTML = text;
```

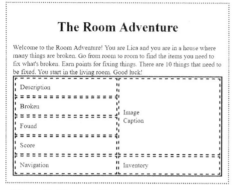

Figure 18. Using our HTML information box.

Make sure your result tab is selected (if you're using repl.it), then run your game. You won't see the new text until you quit, because alerts take over the entire user interface.

Pretty cool, right?

We can, of course, make this text look better with some HTML tags that help us to format things. Let's do a little bit of that so this is more presentable.

Making the introductory text look better. I'm not going to get into much here, but let's update our introduction text.

```
var text = "<h3>Welcome to the Room Adventure!</h3>";
text += "You are " + player.name;
text += " and you are in a house";
text += " where many things are broken.";
text += "<p>Go from room to room";
text += " to find the items you need";
text += " to fix what's broken.</p>";
text += "<p>Earn points for fixing things.";
text += " There are " + player.itemsLeftToFix;
text += " things that need to be fixed.</p>";

//only add these next three lines if you created the
//optional passcode ending; keep the rest regardless
text += "<p>Along the way, you will find pieces";
text += " of a passcode. Find the exit, and";
text += " enter the correct passcode to win!</p>";

text += "<span style='color: slateblue;'>";
text += "You start in the ";
text += player.currentRoom.name + ".</span>";
text += "<h3>Good luck!</h3>";
```

The `<h3>` tags are like the `<h1>` but smaller. I added some `<p>` tags to make paragraphs.

The <span> tag. I used a `<span>` tag to add some color with the `style` attribute.

The format of the value (`color: slateblue`) is CSS notation. There are numerous predefined colors, like the basics (`red`, `green`, `yellow`, `gray`) and common colors (`silver`, (`darkmagenta`, `deeppink`, `maroon`). Hexadecimal numbers (`#FF0000`, `#008080`) are also used to get the full range of values for red, green, and blue light (0 to 255).

Figure 19. Our intro text with some style.

Colors. All colors you see on your TV or computer screen are from red, green, and blue pixels. They light up from 0 (darkest) to 255 (brightest), which is 256 possibilities. Combining them creates all the colors you see. This is an 8-bit system, allowing for over 16.7 million colors! New 4K TVs have a 10-bit system, allowing for 1,024 colors per red, green, and blue (over 1.07 billion colors). For now, CSS is sticking with 8-bit.

You can play around more with CSS and styling the text, but we're going to get back to JavaScript for now.

6.6 Creating Navigation Buttons

> It would be easier for a player to click buttons rather than typing directions in.

Right now, the player has to type in whichever direction he or she wants to go. We're switching the game to use HTML here, so let's get rid of the typing by making some buttons.

There are several ways we could do this. Some are technically more "correct" than others. We are still going to keep this simple. We are going to create a text string for each button we need that contains the HTML it needs to work, then we will update the navigation bar of our page.

Building the text string will look a little confusing, so hang in there. Be careful of single and double quotes here, as well as spaces inside the quotes.

I also added a toggle to the code in the middle of making the buttons. A *toggle* is a `true`/`false` flag that gets flipped off and on each time it's used. It's like clicking a pen.

To flip a toggle from `true` to `false` (or vice-versa), you set set it equal to the `not` version of itself, `!toggle` in this case.

We're using the toggle here to add the `even` class to every other button. This will let us style those buttons differently with a different color later when we talk about CSS.

```
function createNavigationButtons(player)
{
  var buttons = "<h3>Navigation</h3>";
  var toggle = false;

  for (var exit in player.currentRoom.exits)
  {
    var button = "<button id='" + exit + "' ";

    if (toggle)  //add 'even' class to every other button
    {
      button += "class='even' ";
    }
    else
    {
      button += "class='odd' ";
    }

    toggle = !toggle;               //flip the toggle switch

    button += "onclick='movePlayer(this.id)'>";
    button += exit;
    button += "</button>";
    buttons += button;              //add to buttons string
  }
  var nav = document.getElementById("navigation");
  nav.innerHTML = buttons;
}
```

We begin with a `for...in` loop. It will cycle through all the possible exits for the room. This will pull any property that's inside that room's `exits` property object. We talked about this in Section 4.4: Using a for...in Loop. Each time through the loop, the variable `exit` is a direction, like `north` or `south`.

In HTML, we can use the `<button>` tag to create a button. We start by giving it an `id` so we can identify each button. We are using the name of the property as the `id`. So when `exit` has a value of `east`, the button gets an `id` of `east`.

Making the buttons clickable. When you click, you want the buttons to do something. It's up to you to tell the computer what to do, so we assign it a function it should call when it is clicked.

We use an attribute called `onclick` for this. This adds an *event handler* to the button. While there is another, more JavaScript way to do this, we'll be using this HTML shortcut.

We send the button to call `movePlayer` and we pass in an argument, `this.id`. Can you tell what that will be? If the button has an `id` of `"east"`, then it will send `"east"` to the function. We have to create this new function in a minute.

We want the button to show which direction is available, so we need some text in between `<button>` and `</button>`. We are using the direction here now, but we could make it show the room instead.

Next, the button itself is ended with the closing tag `</button>`.

Remember, there's more than one way to do things.

The final thing is to add each button to the `buttons` string. This becomes a long text chain that has HTML in it. It looks kind of weird that the `buttons` string starts with the *Navigation* title, right? Then we add buttons to it, one after another.

Why aren't they separate things? Well, we could have had the title in its own box, but I kept the UI design simpler. The browser puts `<h3>` tags on their own lines, so this will look fine the way it is.

When we pass the `buttons` string to the navigator display, it gets uploaded to HTML on the page, creating our buttons. Whew.

After all that, what does the actual HTML for each button look like?

```
<button id='north'
        onclick='movePlayer(this.id)'>north</button>
```

That's the `button` text string we create each time through the loop, one for each available direction.

We had changed our room objects so they had an `exits` object inside of them. This was one major reason why we did it. It makes creating the buttons so much easier. You can even have some fun and create an exit that says `teleporter`, and this new function would make a `teleporter` button automatically now.

To display the buttons, we created a temporary variable, `nav`, to get the navigation element on the webpage, then we update the `innerHTML` by sending it the `buttons` string. Soon, we will replace these two lines.

We need to do two *move* things. First, we will create the `movePlayer()` function, then we'll update our `moveToRoom()` function.

Optional: showing room names instead of directions.

Instead of showing "north" and "south", you could instead show "dining room" and "living room". This is entirely your call and it depends on how you want your game to run. I'm going to show you two versions: one that shows the room name all the time and one that only shows the room name if you've been to that room before.

Version 1 — Always showing the room name. You only need to change one line in our `createNavigationButtons()` function for this to work. Instead of sending in the name of the exit (the direction) we can use the value (the room's name).

```
for (var exit in player.currentRoom.exits)
{
   var button = "<button id='" + exit + "' ";
   button += "onclick='movePlayer(this.id)'>";
   button += player.currentRoom.exits[exit];        //update
   button += "</button>";
   buttons += button;
}
```

Version 2 — Showing the room name only if you've been there before. For this, we need two things, an `if` statement, and a list of places the player has been to, which is an optional feature we created in Section 5.5: Tracking the Player Through the House. If you want to use this version, then make sure you're implementing `player.pathTaken`. We're still inside the `createNavigationButtons()` function. Here's the code inside the `for...in` loop.

```
for (var exit in player.currentRoom.exits)
  {
    var button = "<button id='" + exit + "' ";
    if (toggle)
    {
      button += "class='even' ";
    }
    else
    {
      button += "class='odd' ";
    }
    toggle = !toggle;
    button += "onclick='movePlayer(this.id)'>";

    var exits = player.currentRoom.exits;         //<--new
    var roomName = exits[exit];
    var room = rooms[roomName];

    if (player.pathTaken &&
        player.pathTaken.indexOf(room) !== -1)
    {
      button += room.name + "<br>(" + exit + ")";
    }
    else
    {
      button += exit;                             //already there
    }                                             //<--end of new code
    button += "</button>";
    buttons += button;
  }
```

The three variables (`exits`, `roomName`, and `room`) are there to make the code easier to read.

We test to make sure the `pathTaken` array exists before trying to find the room inside of it. This is to prevent the game from crashing if the `pathTaken` property doesn't exist. If it does exist, *and* (`&&`) the room is on the list, then we show the room name and the direction. The HTML tag `<br>` inserts a line break (like hitting enter on your keyboard).

Creating the movePlayer() function. For fun, let me show you our entire `movePlayer()` function without any helper variables.

```
function movePlayer(direction)
{
  player.currentRoom =
      rooms[player.currentRoom.exits[direction]];
  moveToRoom();
}
```

At this point, are you able to read and understand that crazy line? It takes a minute, but maybe you can. This is an example of code that isn't very readable. It will work, but it's hard to look at and understand.

> That's code-heavy. We can understand it, but let's make it clearer.

You are welcome to leave it that way, but I'm going to break it down with this more readable version.

```
function movePlayer(direction)
{
  var exits = player.currentRoom.exits;
  var roomName = exits[direction];
  var roomToGoTo = rooms[roomName];
  player.currentRoom = roomToGoTo;
  moveToRoom();
}
```

Now when the player clicks a direction button, the proper room is picked, the player is moved there, and the `moveToRoom()` function is called to perform the next game loop.

Updating the moveToRoom() function. At the top of the `moveToRoom()` function, we need to create the navigation buttons by calling `createNavigationButtons();`. Then we need to get rid of the other process that handles getting the directions, because our buttons will take care of that now.

First, make this change. If you did not add the path-tracking feature from Section 5.5: Tracking the Player Through the House, then you won't have the first line with `player.pathTaken` in it.

229

```
function moveToRoom()
{
  player.pathTaken.push(player.currentRoom); //optional
  createNavigationButtons(player);              //add this
```

If you added the "take" and "use" commands from Section 5.8: Intermediate: Increasing Interactivity, they won't work anymore, until new functionality is added. That'll be discussed in Section 6.8: Removing the Alerts.

The other change we need to make to this function is different depending on whether you added the passcode feature in Section 5.9: Intermediate: Creating a Passcode Goal.

I'll walk you through these possibilities.

Version 1 — **Without** *the passcode feature*
If you did not add the passcode, then follow the edits here. We have an `if` statement that checks to see if the player won the game, else we make a move. We need to delete the entire `else` block.

```
if (checkGameOver())
  {
      //if all fixed, end the game
      alertGameWon();
      checkPlayAgain();
  }
  else                      //this all gets deleted

      //if NOT all fixed, get next destination
      var direction = getDirection();

      //allows player to "quit" game
      if (direction)
      {
          player.currentRoom = rooms[direction];
          moveToRoom();
      }

                            //<-- delete up to here
}                           //<-- but don't delete this }
```

That does it.

*Version 2 — **With** the passcode feature*
If you added the passcode feature, then this part feels crazy. Find the place where we get the direction… and ***delete everything*** until the ending brace, which you need to keep. There's a special section up ahead to reconnect the passcode feature so it works again with HTML. See Section 6.10: Updating the Passcode Ending: HTML.

> The passcode feature changed a lot, and this part's no exception.

```
var direction = getDirection(); //delete!
//everything else to the end    //delete!
}        //end of function (keep this)
```

> We're not done, but you can test things again!

Ok, you're ready. Big moment here. **Test it out!**

You're still getting popups and you can't do more than run around the house again, but updates like these take a bit of work. Hang in there.

Reorganizing the buttons. If you don't like the order the buttons appear in, the fastest way to change that is to rearrange the order inside the room's `exits` property. Typically, they will be displayed in that same order. Watch your commas if you move them around. Can you see the difference below?

Example 1	Example 2
```exits:\n{\n north: "kitchen",\n east: "office",\n teleport: "basement",\n west: "living room"\n}```	```exits:\n{\n teleport: "basement",\n east: "office",\n west: "living room",\n north: "kitchen"\n}```
Navigation: north | east | teleport | west	**Navigation:** teleport | east | west | north

Figure 20. How property order affects button order.

Yes, I made one say `teleport`!

6.7 Creating a Display Object

We went and changed one of the alerts to display on the webpage directly by creating navigation buttons. Now we will go through and change all the others, too. But let's help ourselves out a little.

For each `alert` we change, we will need to grab the tag from the `document` object and then update the `innerHTML` by directly accessing it. This is fine. It will work.

But why don't we create an object that will help us out? You know how `console.log();` works, right? There's a `console` object that has a `log()` method. We pass in what we want to the method and it displays it on the console. Let's make a `display` object that will help us write to our webpage.

This is a bit of an undertaking, but you're ready for it. Creating this will allow us to easily clear our UI each time we need to, and it makes the code easier to read throughout.

You've got this!

Creating a Function in an Object.

Here's another reason why we're doing this... to learn something we haven't done yet. We're going to create a function inside an object. We can do this with an object literal (defining it when we create the object) or by adding it to an object with array notation (like we did with our `rooms` object).

Here's our plan.

- We need a list of properties that will be easy to remember.
  - Why not use the ids we gave them?
- Each property will be a function.
- That function needs a parameter that tells us what to display.
- The function will then find the `id` it needs and update the `innerHTML` property for the tag.

You already know how to make a function. However, we haven't passed any information into the function directly (unless you've been adding the extra features). We let our functions use the global `player` and `rooms` objects to do what we needed. If we are going to display text, it's not as easy. We will have to tell the function what to display each time we call the function.

You know how we use `alert();`, `prompt();`, `confirm();`, and `console.log();` by putting something in the parentheses? That's called an *argument*. Each of these is a function and it uses the value of the argument as a *parameter* to do something with.

If we wanted to make a function that displays to the info box on our webpage, we could do this.

```
function displayInfo(whatToDisplay)
{
  var element = document.getElementById("info");
  element.innerHTML = whatToDisplay;
}

displayInfo("Ok, let's test it out!");
```

233

That last line was a hint. Go try it! Put something else in the parentheses, like `"Woo hoo!"` or `256 * 256 * 256` or `player.name` or `rooms["living room"].description`.

Whatever you put in gets displayed, unless you pass in an object like `player`. That only shows `[object Object]`.

This stand-alone function is great, but we have many different things to update. We can make a single object that we can use to display anything we need to. We want to move this function into that object.

We will be assigning an *anonymous function* to a property. That means we won't be giving the function a name like `displayInfo`. Instead, the property itself will run the function. Let's get started.

The initial display object. We start with an object literal, then we will add one property, `info`. We will make that property a function that displays text to the info box in our user interface.

```
var display =
{
  info: function (text)
  {
    var element = document.getElementById("info");
    element.innerHTML = text;
  } //<--a comma goes here when you add another property
};
```

You can use it like this.

```
display.info("Well, hello there.");
```

Do you see how it works? We have the `display` object (like we have a `player` object). It has the `info` property (like our player has a `name` property). We pass in the words we want to say as a string and the function does the work of putting it on our webpage.

We could actually shorten the function code a little by getting rid of the variable and attaching `.innerHTML` to the end of the `getElementById()` method, like this.

```
document.getElementById("info").innerHTML = text;
```

Both ways are fine. The first way (with the variable) is easier to read and works well if we were doing more to the tag (like changing its style), so I will continue to use that format.

We need a handful of `display` properties. I'm going to create them all at once, but you should challenge yourself first and try to do this part without me.

You've already got the base code for one property. Challenge yourself to create the others on your own!

How would you update the `display` object above to allow us to print to the following boxes: `gameTitle`, `found`, `broken`, `navigation`, and `inventory`?

We're going to do something different with `description`, `score`, and `image`.

See if you can do it. Remember, properties get separated with commas, so you'll need to add a comma after each function's closing brace.

Our display object. Here it is. Take your time with it. This goes at the top, right under where we create the `rooms` and `player` global objects and before `startGame()`.

```
var display =
{
  info: function (text)
  {
    var element = document.getElementById("info");
    element.innerHTML = text;
  },

  found: function (text)    //it's a lot like the last one
  {
    var element = document.getElementById("found");
    element.innerHTML = text;
  },

  broken: function (text)   //Do you see a pattern yet?
  {
    var element = document.getElementById("broken");
    element.innerHTML = text;
  },

  navigation: function (text)
  {
    var element = document.getElementById("navigation");
    element.innerHTML = text;
  },

  gameTitle: function (text)
  {
    var element = document.getElementById("gameTitle");
    element.innerHTML = text;
  },

  inventory: function (text)
  {
    var element = document.getElementById("inventory");
    element.innerHTML = text;
  }
};
```

The code is very repetitive. I used the same variable name (`element`) for all the functions. All I changed from property to property was the name of the property and the `id` it was pulling from.

When we want to display something, we can now call its display method and send it the information we want to show.

```
display.broken("Let's play!");
display.found("You found the " +
        player.currentRoom.itemFound + "!");
```

display.score(clear). Let's add another property to the display object that will update the score. We're going to tackle this differently and give it a parameter that lets us clear the box. This will be different than how the other boxes get cleared, but this is another case where I want to show you more than one way to handle a situation.

Add this to the display object as a new property. Don't forget to add a comma after the inventory property.

```
var display =
{
  //other properties; make sure previous one has a comma

  score: function (clear)   //this is a little different
  {
    var element = document.getElementById("score");

    if (clear)                      //lets us clear the box
    {
      element.innerHTML = "";
      return;
    }

    player.score = Math.max(0, player.score);

    element.innerHTML = "Score: " + player.score;

    //if there is a maxScore tally, then show the max
    if (player.maxScore > 0)
    {
      element.innerHTML += " / Max: " + player.maxScore;
    }
  }
}                                   //end of display object
```

The display.score() method takes a Boolean argument. If we send display.score(true); the function clears the cell and exits.

However, we can also access this by calling `display.score();` with nothing in the parentheses, like we've done for all of our other functions. That will set the `clear` parameter as `undefined`, which gets evaluated as `false` in the `if` statement.

We're making use of the global `player` object in this method, so it will figure out its value all by itself. And it's automatically going to add `"Score: "` before the number each time.

> For proper code control, we really should send in `display.score(false);` or rewrite this to send in the actual score, but this shortcut is used often in JavaScript and I thought you should see it.

The `if` statement will check to see if there is a `maxScore` property for the player greater than zero. If so, it will show the maximum score. This property was added to the `player` object in optional Section 5.3: Randomizing the Item Locations.

display.description();. We want to take some control over this display function to do something different. Like the `score` method, we should add some formatting. When we display the description of the room, we should show the room name and the room's description.

If we left this method like the others, we would have to format the information before we sent it in to this method. But the purpose of this function is to do the displaying, so we should let it do the formatting for us.

We are going to still send in some information, namely the room the player is currently in. Why not use the global `player` object and call its `currentRoom`? We could. However, we give ourselves more control over the display if we send in the specific room.

What if we change our game later and allow a player to look through a window or get information from a room they haven't been to yet? We would have to change this function and any place that calls it. That happens a lot when you're coding, but the more places you have to change, the more likely you'll miss something. By planning ahead for a potential change, we can have the feature in place now.

238

Go back up to the `display` object and add this property to it. Remember your commas when you insert this. The last property you added shouldn't have a comma, so add one and then put this in.

```
var display =
{
  //other properties; make sure previous one has a comma

  description: function (room)
  {
    var element = document.getElementById("description");

    if (!room)
    {
      element.innerHTML = "";
      return;
    }

    var innerHTML = "<h3>You are in the ";
    innerHTML += room.name + ".</h3>";
    innerHTML += "<p>" + room.description + "</p>";
    element.innerHTML = innerHTML;
  }
}                                    //end of display object
```

There is an `if` statement here that will allow us to clear this part of the user interface if we don't send in a room. If `room` is `undefined`, then `!room` will be `true`, so this code block would activate. It sets the `innerHTML` to an empty string, and then it leaves the function by using the `return` keyword. This keeps anything from being printed inside.

Once you add this property, run your game and click through until the navigation buttons appear. The game isn't running until you click something. Then go to the console window and type this in.

```
display.description(player.currentRoom);
```

Then check the result. What do you think? Feel free to add your own styling to it.

display.image(source);. We haven't talked about images at all yet, but now is a good time. There are several differences between this method and the others.

Our image will be displayed in one of the table cells we created. Remember this part of the HTML?

```
<td rowspan=4><div id="imagewrapper">
    <img id="image" src=""/></div>
    <div id="caption">Caption</div></td>
```

We are targeting the `<img>` tag directly, not the the `<div>` wrapper we have around it, nor the table data cell `<td>`. The `<img>` tag needs a source file that gets loaded and displayed. This means we need a web address or path where the image is located. Image files end with extensions like `.jpg`, `.gif`, and `.png`.

To use our `display.image();` method, we are going to have to add another property to each room. But before we do, let's stay focused on our `display` object and get it finished.

Courtesy warning. You should never link to an image on someone else's website unless they give you permission to do so. You're supposed to host your own files on your own website or server. There are places where you can build your own site and place files there, like Google Sites.

Disclaimer. Some images I have paid for. Others I created myself. The rest I have downloaded from free-to-use sites such as http://www.unsplash.com. Always check a license agreement before using anyone else's images, and you should always give credit for your sources. The images I use all have open licenses for such use.

Add this property to the `display` object we've been making.

```
var display =
{
  //other properties; make sure previous one has a comma

  image: function(source)
  {
    //if no image exists, set up a blank one
    if (!source)
    {
      source = { src: "", caption: "" };
    }

    document.getElementById("image").src = source.src;

    //set up the caption
    var cap = source.caption;

    //if image has a link, include it with the caption
    if (source.link)
    {
      cap += "<br><a target='_blank' ";       //in a new tab
      cap += "href='" + source.link + "'>";
      cap += source.linkInfo + "</a>";
    }

    document.getElementById("caption").innerHTML = cap;
  }
}                                   //end of display object
```

We are using an `if` statement to make sure a source is given to the function. If not, we set up a blank one so the program doesn't crash and so the last image doesn't stay on screen. This also allows us to call `display.image();` to clear the image cell completely.

Right now, images will display to whatever size they happen to be. This won't look great all the time. You can make a quick change to your CSS file to help control for this temporarily. We'll talk about a better solution in Section 6.11: Styling with CSS. Don't put this in your JavaScript file; it goes in your CSS file.

You can add this to your CSS file temporarily.

```
img {
  width: 450px;
  height: 300px;
}
```

Hyperlinks. I am also adding an option to let the user click on a hyperlink to go to the source of the image. I feel this is important for people to get credit for their work. A hyperlink in HTML is created with an `<a>` anchor tag with the following syntax.

```
<a href='web address to go to'>text to click on</a>
```

Updating room objects with images. For the image displayer to work, we need to add a new `image` property to each room. Remember when we made the `exits` property back in Section 4.2: Creating an Exits Property? That's what we need to do here.

If you want an image to display in your rooms, then add this for each room you have a picture for. Add a `caption` that gives credit to the source of the image if it's not your own or add descriptive text.

```
"den":
{
  name: "den",
  //other properties are here
  image:
  {
    src: "http://coding.stephenjwolf.com/roomadventure/
          /roomimages/den.jpg",
    caption:"Photo by Daniel Barnes",
    link:"https://unsplash.com/photos/z0VlomRXxE8",
    linkInfo:"Courtesy: unsplash.com"
  }
},
```

I have four properties for the image. One is the host source (`src`) where the file is located on my server. One is the `caption` text I want to show. Because I am using another person's image with permission, I am giving him the credit and linking to the original source of the image.

Life lesson: Always give credit to those who deserve it.

I always believe that credit should be given where credit is due.

Clearing the display. There is one last thing we need to add to our `display` object: a helpful clear-all function. When we go room to room, we will change many parts of the display, but if there isn't a new item to find or there isn't something broken, we need to empty out those cells in the UI.

Let's create one last property for the `display` object. We will call this at the start of each turn and then allow the rest of the game to fill in what it needs to.

```
var display =
{
  //other properties; make sure previous one has a comma

  clear: function ()
  {
    this.found("");
    this.broken("");
    this.navigation("");
    this.inventory("");
    this.image();
    this.description();
    this.score(true);
  }
}                                    //end of display object
```

We can now use `display.clear();` to empty every cell of our UI.

The `clear` method is inside the `display` object, and so are all the other methods we are calling. Because of that, we use the `this` keyword rather than using the name `display`.

> The keyword `this` sounds a little tricky. I'm guessing there's more to it than we're getting into in here.

It's like when you're at home and you describe where something is. You wouldn't say, "The TV is in the *317 MyHouse Street* den." In computer-speak, you would say, "The TV is in *this* den."

Wrapping the display object in a function. At last, the `display` object is finished! Let's do one very last clean-up piece. It's the same thing we did with `player` and `rooms`. Let's wrap this in a function and then move the code away from the top of the file. Do you recall how?

```
//this goes near the top, immediately under var player
var player = getPlayer();
var display = getDisplay();                    //new
```

Next, wrap the original `var display` object like this.

```
function getDisplay()                          //new
{                                              //new
  var display =
  //all the code for the object
  return display;                              //new
}                                              //new
```

Now you can move the function down below the first call to start the game (`startGame();`) to keep it out of the way of the things we need to begin the game.

Quick HTML cleanup. While we're updating display-related things, let's get rid of the placeholder words we put into our original HTML (index.html file).

It's good to clean things up, even if it feels like more work.

Most of these will already be overwritten as we update the displays, though `Image` won't. Still, we don't need them, so let's take them out. Find the following lines and delete the placeholder words that are crossed-out. These all start with a capital letter in my code.

```
<div id="info">Information</div>
<td class="text" id="description">Description</td>
<img id="image" src=""/>Image</div>
<div id="caption">Caption</div>
<td class="text" id="broken">Broken</td>
<td class="text" id="found">Found</td>
<td class="text" id="score">Score</td>
<td class="text" id="navigation">Navigation</td>
<td class="text" id="inventory">Inventory</td>
```

6.8 Removing the Alerts

We have a number of things to do, but this will be easy now. We took care of the hard part already. It's going to feel a bit like a sprint, running through most of our game's functions.

As you go through this part, you should be impressed with how far you've come!

This depends upon you making the display object in the last section. These changes will not work if you don't have the display object we created in Section 6.7: Creating a Display Object.

Updating startGame(). We made a change to this earlier, in Section 6.5: Preparing to Remove Popups.

If you made this change, then you should have these two lines.

```
var info = document.getElementById("info");
info.innerHTML = text;
```

If you didn't make the change earlier, then you have this line.

```
alert(text);
```

Whichever version you have, delete it and replace it with this.

```
display.info(text);
```

Updating createNavigationButtons(). We need to make a similar change to the button-maker function.

Delete these lines.

```
var nav = document.getElementById("navigation");
nav.innerHTML = buttons;
```

Add this line.

```
display.navigation(buttons);
```

Updating moveToRoom();. First, we want to clear the board to allow the game a clean slate it can use to update whatever it needs to. We also should show the room's image if there is one.

Let's stay motivated and get these updates done!

Add these.

```
function moveToRoom()
{
    display.clear();        //add this line at the top
    display.image(player.currentRoom.image); //add
    //rest of function
```

Also here, we call `textRoomDescription();` to show an `alert` that describes the room. We no longer need that function at all. Replace this line.

```
textRoomDescription();              //<--delete this line
display.description(player.currentRoom);    //<--add this
```

Similarly, we no longer need the `showScore()` function. Make this change.

```
showScore();                        //<--delete this line
display.score();                    //<--add this
```

Updating isThereAnItem(). We have an alert to change here, too. Replace `alert` with `display.found`. Add the inventory update.

```
alert("You found the " + item + "!");   //change this...
display.found("You found the " + item + "!");   //to this

player.inventory.push(item);           //already there
player.currentRoom.itemFound = null;   //already there

showInventory();                       //add this
```

Note: If you added the interactive item feature from Section 5.8: Intermediate: Increasing Interactivity, then there's more you need to do. At the end of the `isThereAnItem()` function, change the second `alert` to `display.found`. You also need to replace the whole `showItemInRoom()` function.

```
alert("There's nothing to take. You lose 5 points.");
display.found("There's nothing to take. You lose 5
        points.");
```

You need to *replace* the entire `showItemInRoom()` function with this to make a button that lets the player pick up the item.

```
function showItemInRoom()
{
  if (player.currentRoom.itemFound)
  {
    var button = "<button class='item'
      onclick='isThereAnItem()'>You see something useful
      in here.</button>";
    display.found(button);
  }
}
```

Updating fixBrokenThing(). We have an `alert` to change here. Replace `alert` with `display.broken`. Add score and inventory updates.

```
alert(text);                     //change this...
display.broken(text);            //to this
display.score();                 //add this
showInventory();                 //add this
```

Note: If you added the interactive item feature from Section 5.8: Intermediate: Increasing Interactivity, then you also need to change the `alert` inside of `showBrokenThing()`.

```
alert(text);                 //change this...
display.broken(text);        //to this
```

Updating showInventory(). We have an `alert` to change here. Replace `alert` with `display.inventory`.

```
alert(text);                     //change this...
display.inventory(text);         //to this
```

Optional: If you want to make the inventory title stand out a little more, make this change at the top of the function.

```
var text = "Inventory: ";                //change this...
var text = "<h3>Inventory</h3>";         //to this
```

Note: If you added the interactive item feature from Section 5.8: Intermediate: Increasing Interactivity, then there's more you need to do.

Right now, the player needs to be able to use inventory items. These items need to be clickable.

First, add the parameter `disable` to the function declaration: `function showInventory(disable)`. This is for the passcode feature, but putting it in won't hurt if you didn't add that feature.

Next, the `text` string that gets built inside the `for` loop needs to be replaced. Delete the text `+=` lines and add the code here, including the `if` statement.

Inside the `if` statement, there's a complicated set of punctuation you have to be very careful about. Take your time to make sure you have the single quotes, double quotes, slashes, and parentheses all in the right places. In particular, you have this to watch for `(\""` and this `"\")'"` so take care.

> Whoa! We really have to pay close attention here.

```javascript
function showInventory(disable)
{
  var text = "<h3>Inventory</h3>";
  var length = player.inventory.length;
  for (var i = 0; i < length; i++)
  {
    text += "<button class='inventory' ";

    if (!disable)
    {
      //pay very close attention to punctuation here
      //watch the single and double quotes!
      text += "onclick='fixBrokenThing(\"";
      text += player.inventory[i] + "\")'";
    }
    text += ">";
    text += player.inventory[i];
    text += "</button>";
  }
  display.inventory(text);
}
```

This creates a button for each inventory item that looks like this, with "batteries" as an example.

```html
<button class='inventory'
        onclick='fixBrokenThing("batteries")'>
        batteries</button>
```

We've mostly just used double quotes so far. Why are we switching back and forth here?

We need to alternate the single quotes and double quotes for this to work. We used double quotes to make it a string in the first place, so we couldn't put more double quotes inside, even though we needed them around `batteries`. We had to use the escape character `\"` to add those double quotes *inside* the string without closing the string early. It's confusing, but the thing to remember for now is to copy the punctuation exactly.

Updating alertGameWon(). We have an `alert` to change here too. Replace `alert` with `display.info`.

```
alert(text);                        //change this...
display.info(text);                 //to this
```

Once you've completed all these small changes, you've gotten rid of all the alerts, but we still have a problem. We don't get to see the start and end text. That's next on our list.

By the way, if you added the path-tracking feature from Section 5.5: Tracking the Player Through the House, you may want to update this section a bit to make a nicer path display, like this.

```
function alertGameWon()
{
  //create a text string ... already there

  display.info(text);  //you just added this, move it up
  var path = "<h3>Here's how you traversed the
      house</h3>";

  var steps = player.pathTaken.length;
  for (var i = 0; i < steps; i++)
  {
    var room = player.pathTaken[i];
    path += room.name;
    if (i < steps - 1)
    {
      path += " &rarr; "; // &rarr; = HTML right arrow →
    }
  }
  display.broken(path);
  display.found("");
}
```

6.9 Fixing the Start and End Game

If you play the game now, you can have a lot of fun. But the text that explains how to play the game doesn't show up. Also, at the end of the game, we get a `confirm();` popup that's a bit out of place compared to the rest of the user interface.

Let's make a couple of quick changes to make this a better experience.

Fixing the start game. Let's start at the start... Right now, the `startGame()` function initializes the `rooms` and `player`. (If you added the optional randomization section, that happens here next.) Then the function creates a text string, sends it to the info box in our user interface and activates the `moveToRoom()` function, which clears the screen and shows the first room. This prevents us from even seeing the welcome text.

> We want to be able to get the party started... with the click of a button!

Let's interrupt this action and let the player see the instructions. At the bottom of the `startGame()` function, we need to remove the call to `moveToRoom();`, so go ahead and delete that. While you're there, have your game clear the screen before it displays the welcome text.

```
function startGame()
{
    //initialize player, create the welcome string

    display.clear();                //<--add this
    display.info(text);             //this is already here
    moveToRoom();                   //<--delete this
                    //button code will go here in a moment
}
```

We are going to create a button that lets the player start the game when they are ready. The button itself will call the moveToRoom() function.

We are going to create this button using text, like we did for the navigation buttons. But we only need the one button, so this will be easy. Here we go. Put this right under display.info(text); where moveToRoom(); was.

```
var button = "<button id='start' onclick='moveToRoom()'>
        Start Game</button>";
display.navigation(button);
```

Ok, that's it. Really. We have a start button now.

Fixing the End Game. Right now, we use a `confirm();` popup to ask if the user wants to play again. We can't see the game over information before this popup because of the way these boxes appear. It is time to get rid of our final popup box.

We will create a button that lets the user play the game again from the beginning. If you added in the optional features discussed in Chapter 5, the player will have a different experience each time they play.

If you want to add a second button for a player who does not want to play again, you can do that, too. But what will you have them do instead? You could direct them to another website or to a page of your own that has other creations, and so on. It's all up to you.

Let's *replace* the entire `checkPlayAgain()` function with a new version. This will be similar to what we did in `startGame()` above.

```
function checkPlayAgain()
{
  //create the replay button
  var buttons = "<button id='replay'
      onclick='startGame()'>Replay Game</button>";

  //optional: add a second 'leave game' button
  var url = "http://coding.stephenjwolf.com";
  buttons += "<a href='" + url + "' target='_blank'>
      <button id='leave'>Learn to Code</button></a>";

  display.navigation(buttons);
}
```

The optional section button is a bit weird here. We are wrapping a button with a link that opens a new tab. This isn't the ideal way to handle this situation, but it's a workaround for a site like repl.it that prevents you from changing sites directly.

The `target='_blank'` tells the browser to open a new tab for the link.

Adding images to the start and finish. The game is looking great, but we have a bland opening screen and ending screen. Let's take a moment and add a picture of the outside of the house. If you want, you could add a separate image for each situation, but I'm going to stick with the same image.

For this to work, we're going to create an object of `houseImages` that only hold information for images. Then we will pass that in to `display.image()` and that'll do it. Because I want to use this in more than one place, I'm going to make this a global variable.

Add this to the very top of the code, *before* `startGame();`

```
var display = getDisplay();
var passcode = {};                       //optional feature

var houseImages =
  {
    outside: {
      src: "http://coding.stephenjwolf.com/roomadventure/
            roomimages/house.jpg",
      caption: "Photo by Rowan Heuvel",
      link: "https://unsplash.com/photos/bjej8BY1JYQ",
      linkInfo: "Courtesy: unsplash.com"
    },

    exitSign: {
      src: "http://coding.stephenjwolf.com/roomadventure/
            roomimages/exit.jpg",
      caption: "Photo by Elliott Stallion",
      link: "https://unsplash.com/photos/wweHSdXdAgA",
      linkInfo: "Courtesy: unsplash.com"
    }
  };

startGame();   //this has to be after the new object
```

254

Displaying the new images. Remember how we made the `display.image()` method work? We have to pass in the information for the image itself. We didn't just use the `player.currentRoom.image`. Nope, we made a more flexible function and this is one reason why.

Our `houseImages` object doesn't have the full information for a room. But it has more than one image. We could add more if we wanted to. Do you want a different image for the start and end game screens? You can do that! Just add another image property and then call it where you want it.

Inside `startGame()`, at the end of the function, let's show the house.

```
display.navigation(button);
display.images(houseImage.outside);
```

I also want to show the house when the player wins, so inside `alertGameWon()`, I want to show this again. This goes anywhere in the function. I'm putting it at the end.

```
display.info(text);
display.broken(path);   //optional
display.images(houseImage.outside);
```

You may have noticed that I created a property called `exitSign` but I didn't use it here. It's for the optional passcode feature. I included it in this section because this is where we made the `houseImages` object, and I wanted you to see more than one image in the new object.

Ready to play! At this point, you can go ahead and play the game. However, if you added the passcode feature, there's a little more work to do in the next section.

We can also jazz up the user interface with some styling, which we'll get to in Section 6.11: Styling with CSS.

6.10 Updating the Passcode Ending: HTML

In Section 5.9: Intermediate: Creating a Passcode Goal, we created an optional new ending for the game. If you added it to your game, then you have some updating to do to make it work properly with your new HTML interface.

We've got a few things we need to do to get the passcode working again, but we can totally handle it!

In the text version, the player can just type the passcode numbers in. Here, though, we need a way for the player to enter the numbers. We will create a number pad.

For this to work, we will create a button set like we did for navigation. These buttons will call a helper function that creates the passcode string. When the player submits the passcode, we will call another function to check it and to deal with ending or continuing the game.

Updating createNavigationButtons(). If the player is able to exit the house from a room, we need to offer an option to do so. We will add an `if` statement to include such a button. This goes at the end of `createNavigationButtons()` after all the other buttons are made but before they are displayed.

In the code below, the code starting with `var button` is three lines long here in print. When you type it in, make it all one line of code.

```
function createNavigationButtons(player)
{
   //rest of function to create other buttons in for loop

   if (player.currentRoom.exitHouse)             //<--new
   {
      //this is all on one line from var to </p>";
      var button = "<p><button id='exit'         // all
         onclick='enterPasscode();'>Exit          // one
         House</button></p>";                     // line

      buttons += button;
   }

   display.navigation(buttons);
}
```

This creates a new button for the navigation window. It's wrapped in a `<p>` element to put it on its own line. It has the `id='exit'` so we can style it differently from the other buttons if desired. The function that's being called, `enterPasscode()`, has to be created next.

Creating the enterPasscode() function. This will clear the player's current passcode guess and create a numberpad for the player to click on. We clear the text from the screen and show the inventory. We'll make use of the `"broken"` display box to give instructions.

```
function enterPasscode()
{
  display.clear();
  var text = "Enter the correct passcode to exit the
      house.";
  display.broken(text);
  showInventory(true);        //true disables item usage

  player.guessPasscode = "";

  //make passcode buttons
  var buttons = "";
  var digits = [7, 8, 9, 4, 5, 6, 1, 2, 3, 0];
  var toggle = false;

  for (var i = 0; i < digits.length; i++)
  {
    buttons += "<button ";

    if (toggle)
    {
      buttons += "class='even' ";
    }
    else
    {
      buttons += "class='odd' ";
    }
    toggle = !toggle;
    buttons += "onclick='addToPasscode(" + digits[i] +
        ")'>" + digits[i] + "</button>";

    if (i % 3 === 2) // line break after 3 buttons
    {
      buttons += "<br>";
    }
  }
  buttons += "<br><button id='passcode'
      onclick='checkPasscode()'>Try Passcode</button>";

  display.navigation(buttons);
  display.image(houseImages.exitSign);        //optional
}
```

We're using that toggle idea again so the buttons can be styled differently later. And if you want an image to show here, you can!

If you created the interactive items from Section 5.8: Intermediate: Increasing Interactivity, then `showInventory(true);` needs the `true` value to keep the buttons from being clickable. If you didn't create that feature, the `true` won't do anything. You could delete it.

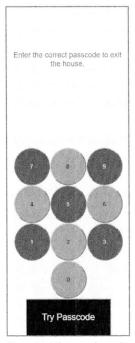

I created the `digits` array to control how the buttons are shown on the screen. If we didn't do this, the buttons would have been in order: 0, 1, 2, 3, 4, 5, 6, 7, 8, 9. That's not how we usually see number pads, and with a simple array, we can control it.

Does it help you to visualize the digits if we add whitespace?

```
var digits =
[7, 8, 9, 4, 5, 6, 1, 2, 3, 0];
```

```
var digits = [
    7, 8, 9,
    4, 5, 6,
    1, 2, 3,
       0        ];
```

Figure 21. The passcode numberpad.

Creating the addToPasscode() function.

Next up, we need to build the string that holds the passcode. When the player clicks any of the buttons on the numberpad, this function will be called, and the button's number will be sent as an argument. Our new function adds the number to the `player.guessPasscode` string. As the player clicks, we will also show what has been entered in the `found` display box.

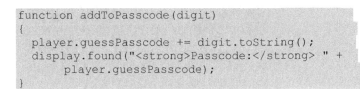

When the player clicks on the numbers, we have to keep track of that, right?

```
function addToPasscode(digit)
{
    player.guessPasscode += digit.toString();
    display.found("<strong>Passcode:</strong> " +
        player.guessPasscode);
}
```

259

Creating the checkPasscode() function. When the player clicks Try Passcode, this new function is called to see if the passcode is correct. This is the last step and it handles the logic for ending the game.

```
function checkPasscode()
{
  var text = "";

  if (player.guessPasscode === passcode.exitCode)
  {
    alertGameWon();
    checkPlayAgain();
  }
  else
  {
    var penalty = 25;
    text += "<h3>The door does not open. ";
    text += "You lose " + penalty + " points.</h3>";
    player.score -= penalty;
    display.clear();
    display.broken(text);

    var button = "<button class='text'
      onclick='moveToRoom()'>OK</button>";

    display.navigation(button);
    display.image(houseImages.exitSign);        //optional
  }
}
```

And that does it!

That last line of code with `houseImages.exitSign` was part of Section 6.9 where we talked about adding images to the start and end game. If you didn't include an image for the exit, you can go back there to see how to do it. Or you can leave this optional line out entirely.

> This update required a lot of hard work, but your game is now suitable for use on a webpage or a smartphone!

You may also want to go into `alertGameWon()` and add some HTML styling to the text string like we did in `startGame()`, but it's entirely up to you.

The game has been fully updated for HTML.

260

6.11 Styling with CSS

I am not going to get into a lot of detail with styling, but I think it's important for you to see some of what we can do visually. I'm no graphic designer and you may have more creative ideas for color schemes and so on. But that's the point! Change it up, have fun with it, and make it all yours.

Let's jazz things up! It's our third language: CSS.

For this section, you need to be inside your CSS file. You will still test things out by running your HTML code, but all this goes in CSS.

CSS uses *selectors* to target individual parts of a webpage. You can use tag selectors, class selectors, and id selectors. It is possible to target things even more specifically than that, too.

If you typed in the CSS code I gave you earlier, then you have the following in your CSS file already. We're going to change most of it.

```
#interface {                /* id="interface" selector */
    border: dotted;         /* make a dotted border */
    padding: 15px;          /* spacing: border <--> table*/
}

h1 {                        /* heading 1 selector */
    text-align: center;     /* center the test */
}

table {                     /* table selector */
    border: solid;          /* show a solid border */
    width: 100%;            /* make table 100% div width */
}

td {                        /* table cell selector */
    border: dashed;         /* make a dashed border */
    width: 50%;             /* make cell 50% table width */
    padding: 10px;          /* spacing: border <--> text */
}

img {                       /* image tag selector */
    width: 450px;           /* keep image width  at 450px*/
    height: 300px;          /* keep image height at 300px*/
}
```

To select an html tag, use the name of the tag, like `table`, `h1`, `p`, and so on, with nothing around it. If you want to select a class, use a dot (.) in front of the class name you want to select, like `.text` for ours (not shown above). If you want to target an id, use a number sign (or hashtag), like `#interface`.

Updating #interface. Update your `#interface` selector to this.

```
#interface {
  border-style: solid;
  border-width: 5px;
  border-color: orange;
  background-color: black;
  padding: 15px;
}
```

We can control the border in a lot of ways. Here, we are setting the style to solid instead of dotted. Borders default to 1px wide, so I'm overriding that and making it 5 pixels wide. I'm also making the border orange.

All of these instructions for `border` can be shortened to a single line.

```
border: solid 5px orange;
```

Replacing the three border statements above with that, you get the same result. They must be in that order: style → width → color.

The next attribute we are changing is `padding`. This defaults to 0. Padding is the amount of space *inside* the border before anything else inside is displayed.

> We have a lot of control over how things look.

We could set a margin. This sets up empty space *outside* the border, adding a buffer area around the element.

We can also control the borders, margins, and padding by selecting each side with `-top`, `-right`, `-bottom`, or `-left`.

```
margin-left: 10px;
border-top: solid 5px;
border-right: dashed 10px;
```

Last, we set the background color to `black`. I tend to use a lot of the predefined color names, like `royalblue` or `cornsilk`, because they're easy to remember and I'm not always that picky about the exact shade I use. We could also use RGB values and hexademical values to get more precise hues.

RGB (red, green, blue) values can range from 0 (none) to 255 (all). Combining them in different amounts gets you all the colors you see on your screen. Get yellow with 255, 255, 0. Create orange with 255, 165, 0. Make different levels of gray with all three values the same.

Let's give our info box `cornsilk` text and an orange background.

```
#info {
  color: rgb(255, 248, 220);      //cornsilk
  background-color: orange;
}
```

Using the class selector. We have a few boxes set up that we gave the class `"text"`. Let's select them all and do some formatting.

```
.text {
    padding: 0 10px;   //top & bottom: 0, left & right: 10px
    background-color: cornsilk;
    color: slateblue;
}
```

See the `.text` at the beginning? That selects all the elements that have `class="text"` set as an attribute.

Updating the table cells. Let's adjust the cell style, too.

```
table {
    border: solid;
    border-collapse: collapse;
    width: 100%;
}

td {
    border-right: solid black;
    width: 50%;
    text-align: center;
    vertical-align: middle;
    background-color: black;
    height: 75px;
}
```

I added `border-collapse: collapse;` to the `table` tag. This squeezes the cells together so the background color from the interface doesn't peek through. Without this, you get a thin line around the cells. I also adjusted the border of each cell to remove horizontal lines between cells. Adding the `height: 75px;` helps the UI look more uniform.

We will center the text inside each cell. Horizontally, we use `text-align: center;` Vertically, we use `vertical-align: middle;`. It'd be nice if they were the same word, but this is just how it is.

I made the `<td>` background color `black` so the image will stand out when we put one in. This will be a problem for the caption, though, because the text defaults to black, so we won't see the caption. We can fix that with more styling!

264

If we set the background of the table cells to black, will they all be black? What about the ones we changed to `cornsilk` using the `.text` class selector?

There are priorities in CSS. Ids have the highest priority, then classes, then tags, then the "all" selector, `*`. Since classes have a higher priority than tags alone, the cells with the `text` class with still have the `cornsilk` color.

Setting the caption style. This will only matter if you put in captions for your images. They may take away from the experience of the game, but I'm going to include them because I want the photographers to get credit for their work. All of my photographs for this project are used with permission from http://www.unsplash.com.

If you don't want to display any captions, you don't have to. There are a few lines of code in the program (in all three files) to delete, or you simply add this attribute to the `#caption` CSS selector, which would let you use captions later if you change your mind: `display: none;`

```
#caption {
    color: silver;
    font-size: 0.9em;
    font-style: italic;
}
```

To change font color, we use the `color` attribute. It's assumed to be a font color when you use this.

The font-size can be set in a few ways. You can set the exact pixel size you want, such as `16px`. This is great for directly specifying how big your text is on the screen. You could also set the point size, `12pt`, but it is meant for printed text and isn't ideal for displaying to the screen.

Using `percent` and `em` are similar to each other. 100% or 1em is equal to whatever font size is currently being used by the element. If your font is at 12 pixels, then 50% or 0.5em would change the element's font to 6 pixels for that section.

The benefit to using `%` and `em` (instead of `px` or `pt`) is that they scale with the font size of the page, so if you zoom in your browser, they will stay in proportion. Which one should you use? They're about the same. Older browsers may support them a little differently.

The link I have included in the caption is purple by default and hard to see. We can target the anchor `<a>` link that is inside the `#caption` paragraph by nesting the selector like this.

```
#caption a {
    color: silver;
    font-size: 0.8em;
    font-style: normal;
}
```

Remember that a link is part of the `<a>` tag, so this allows us to target any link that's inside the caption.

To italicize or not to italicize. Smaller font? Why not?

I made the caption italicized, but then I removed the italics for the link by adding `font-style: normal;` If I left this out in this second selector, then the link would also be italicized because it *inherits* from the parent `#caption` style.

Changing the img style. When you test the game, the images you link to may distort the table and make everything look stretched. It's a good idea to control this a bit so we have a cleaner look.

We could control the size of the image with something like this.

```
img {
    width: 450px;
    height: 300px;
}
```

The problem is this will distort any image that isn't in the same size ratio. It won't look nice. When you don't have an image, like on the start screen, you see a broken image icon. There are things we can do to the `<img>` tag directly, but they don't work as well as the second option.

266

We haven't talked about it much, but we wrapped our `<img>` tag inside a `<div>` called `imagewrapper` when we created the HTML.

Instead of controlling the image size directly, we will control this wrapper and let the image resize itself within the `<div>`.

Don't remember wrapping the image tag? Look at the HTML for this and note the `<div>`.

```
img {
    width: 100%;
}


#imagewrapper
{
    max-height: 300px;
    overflow-y: auto;

}
```

```
<td rowspan=4>
    <div id="imagewrapper">
      <img id="image"/>
      <div id="caption">
        </div>
    </div>
</td>
```

With this set of attributes, we have a much better design (though not perfect). The `<img>` tag will grow to fill the width of the `<div>`. By default, the `<div>` will grow to fit the width of the table cell `<td>` it's in. The image's height will scale to whatever the width stretches out to, so the image won't be distorted.

But if we had an image with a narrow width and a tall height, this would stretch our table and make the UI look funny. We control the size of the `<div>` using `max-height: 300px;`. The wrapper won't ever be any taller than 300 pixels. Try other numbers to get a size you like.

The second attribute, `overflow-y: auto;`, will give you a vertical scrollbar if the image is too tall. Then the player can scroll to see the whole image. On a touchscreen, they may not see an actual scrollbar, but they can still scroll the image.

What if you don't want the player to be able to scroll the image? A simple solution is to change the setting to `overflow-y: hidden;`. This means that any part of the image that is taller than 300px is cut off, hidden from view, impossible to see. We're controlling the y-axis here (the height) of the image by cropping off the excess.

It's your choice.

Styling the headings. We are using two different headings, `<h1>` and `<h3>`. There are 6 heading types preprogrammed in HTML, from `<h1>` through `<h6>`, and they are all the same except for their size. `<h1>` is the largest and `<h6>` is the smallest. They scale with the page and they have `font-weight: bold`.

Let's use a different font set for the large `<h1>` heading. Some fonts are safe to use because most browsers support them. You can give several fonts in a `font-family` to allow for backup fonts to be used if the font you want isn't available.

The `font-family` for the `<h3>` tag will be inherited from the `<body>` tag, which is coming up next.

```
h1 {
   text-align: center;
   font-family: "Lucida Console", Monaco, monospace;
   color: orange;
}

h3 {
   color: black;
}
```

Setting the default font. This will set the default style for the text inside the body of the page. Other selectors can override this.

```
body {
   font-family: Arial, Helvetica, sans-serif;
}
```

Lift navigation buttons from the bottom. In the `.text` selector, we set the top and bottom padding to 0. This is fine for most of the boxes, but the buttons in the navigation pane will sit on the bottom of the frame. So, let's bring them up a little by padding the cell on the bottom.

```
#navigation {
   padding-bottom: 10px;
}
```

Styling the buttons. Let's do something different with the buttons. We will employ a feature of CSS and use a `border-radius` to make the buttons round. We'll add some color while we're at it.

Using `border-radius` will give you rounded edges of whatever element you are styling. Like other attributes, you can use pixels and percents.

I'm going with a purple, orange, and black theme, but you can use whatever colors you want!

```
#navigation button {
    background-color: slateblue;
    color: white;
    height: 80px;
    width: 80px;
    border-radius: 100%;
    font-size: 0.8em;
    vertical-align: top;
    padding: 0;
}
```

The values here are from playing around a bit. You may want a larger (or smaller) width and height for your buttons. This will create round buttons that are light purple (`slateblue`) with white text inside.

Remember when we made the buttons for the navigation and the passcode numbers? We used that `toggle` variable to add the `even` class to every other button. This is why. We're going to leave the `odd` (first, third, etc.) buttons `slateblue` from the attribute above, but make the even (second, fourth, etc.) buttons `orange` with black text. If you want a separate definite for the `odd` buttons and give them addition stylings, you can.

```
#navigation .even {
    background-color: orange;
    color: black;
}
```

Item and inventory buttons. We have a set of special buttons we use in our game. We have buttons to start, replay, and leave the game. We have inventory buttons, a button for taking something from the room, and (if you added this feature) buttons that exit the house and let you try your passcode. Let's give them all some style.

Let's start with a default button style that makes the buttons purple (slateblue) with white text. Why not also give them some padding so they stand out even more?

```
button {
  background-color: slateblue;
  color: white;
  padding: 15px;
}
```

If you test this, you may notice that the buttons in the navigation panel are not affected. This is because we have a #navigation button selector already, and it will override this. That's ok, though. It's important to see how selectors show their priority.

Let's make the font of the *take-item* (.item) button a little bigger and let's make the inventory items have rounded corners. Both of these are tagged with classes in our code. They will still be slateblue, with padding and a white font, because they *inherit* from the button selector.

Finally, let's make the inventory box stand out with a different color.
```
.item {
  font-size: 1.1em;
}
.inventory {
  border-radius: 15px;
  background-color: slateblue;
  color: white;
}
#inventory {
  background-color: orange;
}
```

Notice that .inventory and #inventory are different things.
- We used the *class* selector .inventory to tag each of the items.
- We used the *id* selector #inventory to target the inventory box.

Exit House and Try Passcode buttons. If you made the passcode feature, then you have an Exit House and a Try Passcode button. I'm making them the same so you can see that we can have two different selectors use the same style setting by using the comma. Both `#exit` and `#passcode` are inside the `#navigation` so we need to target them inside their parent selector in order to reach them. That's because we have a `#navigation` selector being used elsewhere.

```
#navigation #exit, #navigation #passcode {
   background-color: #2f2475; /* dark slateblue */
   color: white;
   font-size: 1.2em;
   padding: 10px;
   width: 75%;
   border-radius: 0;
}
```

I made these rectangular again by setting `border-radius` back to `0`, so the `#navigation` setting that makes circular buttons doesn't apply to these. I made the width `75%` of the cell they're in so they're big. I'm using a hex value for the color to get a more exact shade. There are other ways we could control all these things, but I wanted you to see how you can override inherited settings.

Start, replay, and leave buttons. I want the `#start` and `#replay` buttons to be big. They're inside the `#navigation` id, so we have to target them inside there or else the new scheme won't take. We'll make the `#leave` button smaller. We don't really want them to leave, do we?

```
#navigation #start, #navigation #replay {
   background-color: slateblue;
   font-size: 1.2em;
   height: 150px;
   width: 150px;
}

#navigation #leave {
   background-color: orange;
   color: black;
   font-size: 0.8em;
   height: 70px;
   width: 70px;
   border-radius: 5px;
}
```

Changing styles using JavaScript. It is possible to use JavaScript to change features, too. Naturally, these would have to be in your JavaScript file. Here's a small example.

```
var title = document.getElementById("gameTitle");
title.style.backgroundColor = "cornsilk";
title.style.color = "slateblue";
title.style.fontSize = "3.0em";
```

We have to access the CSS style object and then the attribute we want to change. The CSS attributes have dashes when they have multiple words, but that won't work in JavaScript so we have to convert them to camelCase. Thus, the CSS attribute `background-color` becomes `backgroundColor` in JavaScript.

You could use this to change any style elements you want throughout the game. Maybe each room has its own color background. You can even make elements disappear (`visibility: hidden;`) and reappear (`visibility: visible;`).

Go ahead and have some fun. Maybe add a property to your rooms and make use of that in the rest of your code. For instance, give each room a `backgroundColor` and change the interface's background color to match. Where would be a good place to put that? How about where the player is moved to a new room?

Go wild! What colors do you want? Do you want buttons that are more rectangular with rounded edges? Larger buttons? Different fonts? You have lots of choices!

Give it a shot!

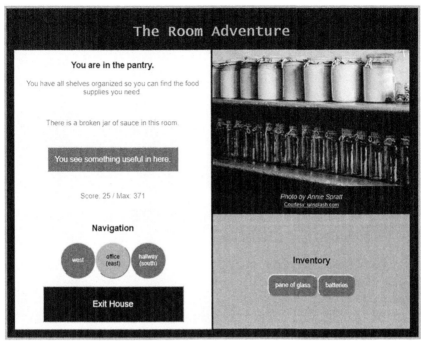

Figure 22. User interface with styling.

6.12 Code Cleanup

Before you step away from a project, it's a good idea to clean up your code structure if you can. Disable or delete any parts that are no longer needed. Add comments for yourself, so when you come back you'll know what you were doing. Reorganize the order of your functions and CSS attributes to something meaningful if you can (it's not always easy). There are several strategies for organizing things. Find a system that works for you.

If I do this now, I'll understand my code better when I look at it again later.

Organizing JavaScript. I tend to move larger functions toward the bottom so they're out of the way. I try to keep related functions together, like our functions that deal with finding items and fixing things. I move key functions toward the top, like our `moveToRoom()` function.

Deleting unnecessary functions. With all these changes, there are some functions we no longer need. If you made all the changes in this chapter, then you can get rid of these functions and all the code contained inside them. You may want to start by commenting them out and running your code to make sure it all works without these first.

To comment out a block of code, use `/*` at the beginning and `*/` at the end.

```
/*
function noLongerBeingUsed()
{
  //code
}
*/
```

You can delete all of these functions.

```
function textRoomDescription()
function getDirection()
function showScore()

//if you created the passcode feature, delete this too
function checkGameOver()

//optional test function from the text version
function testForTrue(condition)
```

Add helpful comments. I put a lot of comments in the code as we went along. These weren't just for you. They're also for me. If I don't look at this project for a while, I may forget what I intended certain things to do. I may also wonder why I coded something one way when I could have done it another way. The more you code, the more techniques you learn and you may find easier ways to do certain things.

Make things easier for yourself so you can work with this project in the future and adapt it for something else.

If you haven't put any comments into your code, it's a good idea to go back through it all and add notes to yourself for things that aren't obvious or things that were confusing or whatever else will be helpful to you later.

Organizing JavaScript into separate files. When you have a lot of code in a file, it can be helpful to split it up into smaller files. Also, you may have parts of your code that are useful for other programs you'll write. Having those functions in separate files makes it easy to load them into another project.

You don't need to break your game into smaller files. You can leave all your JavaScript in a single file. I just wanted to show you one more new coding concept before we wrap things up here.

If you do organize your code into separate files, you do have to be careful of what goes where. The order you load the files is vital. If you have a call to a function in your first file, but the function isn't defined until the second file, you'll get an error.

Using multiple files has its drawbacks, too, one of which is considering the load order. The other has to do with accessing the website they're loaded on. Each different file means the browser has to send another request to the server. With lots of files running lots of code, or with a bad connection, or if the host has a busy server, these can all lead to some issues. There's a balance to it.

To load multiple JavaScript files, just add a `<script>` tag to the bottom of your HTML file. They will load from top to bottom. Generally, if you have any code that runs automatically (like the ones that create our global objects and the `startGame()` function), then those should be loaded *last*.

```
<script src="firstFile.js"></script>
<script src="secondFile.js"></script>
<script src="thirdFile.js"></script>
</body>
```

Our `getRooms()` function is really big because of all the properties and text we have for each room. I ended up creating ten rooms for this tutorial and it adds close to over 400 lines of code for that function alone! I'm giving it its own file.

File organization for the room adventure. Here is how I organized my functions. The order presented here represents the order in which I load the files (numbers) and how I grouped the functions (letters) together within each file.

1. display.js
   a. showItemInRoom
   b. showBrokenThing
   c. showInventory
   d. createNavigationButtons
   e. getDisplay
2. rooms.js
   a. getRooms
3. randomizers.js
   a. randomizePlayerStart
   b. randomizeItems
   c. randomizePoints
   d. randomizeExits
   e. randomizeBrokenThings
   f. randomizeRoomLayout
4. passcode.js
   a. getPasscode
   b. enterPasscode
   c. addToPasscode
   d. checkPasscode
5. main.js
   a. *initialize global variables*
   b. startGame
   c. getPlayer
   d. movePlayer
   e. moveToRoom
   f. isThereAnItem
   g. fixBrokenThing
   h. playerIsTired
   i. alertGameWon
   j. checkPlayAgain

Organizing CSS code. For CSS, I try to stay close to the webpage layout, grouping related selectors together, like `img` and `#caption`. Some programmers keep all tags together, then classes, then ids. Figure out what works best for you.

This is my order of CSS selectors.

```
/* overall structure */
body
#interface
table
td

/* text effects */
h1
h3
.text

/* image-related */
img
#imagewrapper
#caption
#caption a

/* button-related */
button
.item
.inventory
#inventory
#navigation
#navigation button
#navigation .even
#navigation #start, #navigation #replay
#navigation #leave
#navigation #exit, #navigation #passcode
```

Organizing HTML. Actually, you really can't do much with the HTML because it is already set up in the order you need it to be. If you move things around, it will change the layout of your page. As long as your stylesheet link is in the `<head>` tag and your `<script>` tag is at the end of the `<body>` immediately before the closing `</body>` tag, then you should be fine.

Chapter 7

Final Thoughts

We covered a ton of things in this book. From creating variables and functions, to letting the computer make decisions, you've come a long way.

You've learned a lot more than just code itself.

Here are some of the major points I hope you take away from this book.

- Spelling and punctuation matter a great deal
- Planning things out makes it easier to code what you want
- Variables are versatile and easy to create
- Functions are just code you can reuse when you need to
- Computers make decisions with `if`/`else` statements
- Computers repeat actions with `while` and `for` loops
- You have different options for collecting and displaying info
- There is more than one way to solve a problem through code
- Test your code often as you create it
- Be patient with errors and resolve them right away
- Share your creations with others
- Be creative and remember to have fun!

7.1 Other Enhancements

As with most projects, there's never really an end. You can always update parts of it, add new ideas, and sometimes even change whole sections so they work better. The same is true of this project. There may be some things you've seen that you would like to change. Here are some of my ideas.

- The user interface changes size as you play. We could restructure the UI to allow us to fix that using CSS.

- Make the game fit smaller screens like a smartphone.

- When randomizing item placement, sometimes you find an item inside the room it's needed for instead of being found somewhere else, which isn't much of a challenge. Let's fix it.

- Maybe you really want a certain item to always be found in a specific room but let everything else be randomized.

- What about a visual map of the house? It could show which rooms you've been to and how they're connected.

- A more complex layout randomizer, allowing for other directions like *northwest* or *through the passage*.

- Multiple floors of the house. We can make this now, adding a stairway "room," but if we randomize the layout, then we may want to control the rooms for each floor.

- Different color schemes for each room, updating parts of the UI to reflect those schemes.

- Locked doors you can't get into until you have a key, or dark rooms for which you need a flashlight.

The list can go on forever. You will find these add-on features (and more) on my website at http://coding.stephenjwolf.com.

The point is, allow yourself to be creative. Don't limit yourself to what we did here. Our goal was to learn JavaScript and to use this game as a way to bring it all together.

Most games follow a format like our game, where you have certain areas that look a certain way. You find things you need and you can use them when you have to. Look at some of your favorite games and see how they're similar to what we built here.

I know games today are heavy on graphics, animation, and sound. For that we need to use HTML's `<canvas>`, which is a whole book unto itself. But without a solid programming foundation, making those games is a lot harder. And besides, a lot of what we built here is needed for those games too!

I mentioned a number of possible enhancements on the last page. There's one more I want to talk about in more detail because I think it will really open up your creativity and allow you to make some cool changes for your games.

The big idea? Changing the theme of your game. Instead of a house, what else could your game be?

7.2 Change Your Game's Theme

Not everyone wants to make a game where you run around a house. It was a useful idea because we all have places we call home. What if you wanted to change the theme of your game? What if you wanted to create a fantasy world instead? Or a space outpost? A labyrinth? A museum? The universe?

Why not have one more thing to think about before you go?

Well, go ahead and do it!

Let's talk for a minute about how you could change the theme. I'm not going to get into much actual code here. That's for you to do. You know how. I'll point out the things to look for.

Fantasy theme. Let's consider a fantasy setting instead of the house. You roam around a forest looking for certain herbs and mushrooms. You bring them back to villagers who need them. You earn experience points and collect weapons and armor. Learn different runes and create a magic spell that defeats the Dragonlord.

How do you convert our current game into this? It's not as hard as you might think!

Make a map. You need to plan out your map. What does the forest look like? Where can the player go? What herbs or materials can they find there? Each section of your forest is a "room." Make a dozen of them to really give your player a lot of ground to cover. You don't need to put a `brokenThing` in any part of the forest if you don't want to.

Create a village too. Maybe a castle. Lay out the places (rooms) the player can and cannot go to. You don't need to use actual rooms anymore. A passageway could be a room. Give it several exits, like "around the bend", "southwest", "over by the torch", or "behind the tree." A tavern, a prison cell, a well, and a small one-room cottage could each be a "room".

Code tip. To make properties with multiple words, use quotes. Inside the room's `exits` property, you could add properties like this.

```
exits:
{
    "secret room": "lab",
    north: "cottage",
    "magic tree": "lair"
}
```

You would get buttons that say *secret room*, *north*, and *magic tree*.

Update the items to be fixed and found. For each room's `brokenThing`, put a person here and there who needs you to fetch something, either from another character or from the forest. The more detail you have, the more interesting and fun your game will be.

You will want to update the text for dealing with broken things if you plan to have people needing things. Instead of saying, "there's a broken Dariak," you might want to change it to say, "Dariak needs you to find him a purple mushroom." In this case, "Dariak" is the `brokenThing` and the "purple mushroom" is the `fixWith`.

Put monsters into the game. You need certain weapons to defeat them. If you don't have the *magic sword of embers*, you can't slay the *ice behemoth*. Make the monster the `brokenThing` and the weapon you need is the `fixWith`. You can use the `altDescription` property to comment to the player about how much fun they had slaying the ice behemoth.

Would a weapon break or disappear after being used? If not, you could add an `if` statement to `fixBrokenThing()` so it doesn't remove it from the inventory.

Change the passcode to magic runes. Remember how we created the passcode? We made a host of hints and then picked random numbers, joining the random numbers together into a passcode. Change the hints from the fruit I used to other hints, like "essence," "token," "statue," and "bracelet." Or whatever you want.

To replace the random passcode numbers, create a new array of magic runes, then have the computer randomly pick from those (just like it already picks the hints). You could use elements, like *fire* and *ice*, or make up your own words, like *frashenor* and *krellexine*.

In the function that lets the player enter the passcode, change the `digits` array to the new runes array. Instead of an "Exit House" button, change it to "Slay the Dragonlord." You have to update some text in places to be consistent with these changes.

It's similar to how we handled the `itemsLeftToFix` in the non-passcode version.

You could really up the ante if you wanted to. You only get three chances to defeat the Dragonlord before he eats you.

Add a property to your player to count the number of tries. If the player fails to cast the spell (the passcode), then reduce the number of tries by one (instead of losing points). If the number of tries goes below zero, have a different end game function that tells the player they were eaten. I hope they were delicious.

Require certain conditions for tasks. Your player earns points. Let them level up for every 50 or 100 points. You could simply do a `Math.floor(player.score / expPerLevel) + 1;` to calculate the player's level. Show the level with the score.

Code tip. Check the level when the player tries to move. You need to do two checks: one to see if the room has a level requirement, and if so then does the player meet it? In our HTML `movePlayer()` function, we have a `roomToGoTo` variable. Use it.

```
if (roomToGoTo.minLevel)
{
    //then check if player's
    //level is >= the minLevel
    //if so, move them in
    //else, tell them they're
    //not quite ready
}
```

The challenge then is how to control things based on your level. You would need at least one `if`/`else` statement somewhere and perhaps a new property for a given room, `minLevel`. Maybe you can't enter the castle unless you're level 10. When the player tries to enter the castle below level 10, you keep them in their current room and tell them why.

Or maybe you're not allowed to pick something up without a required item. You can't lift the forged sword without the blacksmith's tongs. When you try to use the pickup button (or "take" command), check the inventory and decide.

Reduce randomization. If you make a new theme like this, you probably want to have more control over things and have less randomization. Turn off the randomization features that won't fit your game. If you've made an intricate forest layout, you don't want its layout getting randomized.

> Comment things out instead of deleting them. This lets you put them back in later.

You might still want to randomize the items. It's up to you. You could exclude certain places for items to go to, like we did in `randomizeExits()`. Or just the opposite and specify which locations (rooms) they *could* go to.

To disable any of the randomization features, just comment them out with a double slash `//` in front. Do this where the functions are called, which is usually inside another function. You don't need to delete the function you're disabling. Hey, you may find a way of modifying and using it later.

7.3 Enjoy Your Coding Adventures

Enjoy yourself. The final point is to have fun. Make changes here and there and enjoy the process. Share your game with friends and family. You'll be surprised how cool it feels to see someone else playing your game.

Keep coding. The best way to really learn to code is to keep doing it. Use what you learned here and build your own creations. Practice makes perfect and testing often keeps things working as you go.

Check my website for updates. As people play the game, they'll have ideas for improvements. I'll post updates on my site for these so you can add them to your game too!

Let me know what you think. Now that you've gotten this far, let me know what you think. What did you like? What could be better? And while you're at it, send me a link to your game! Repl.it gives you a share link you can send. I'd love to see what you've come up with. Tell me if you want me to add it to a list of playable games others can see!

Above all, happy coding!
—Stephen J. Wolf

Email: coding@stephenjwolf.com
Website: http://coding.stephenjwolf.com

Chapter 8

JavaScript Crash Course

This chapter is a short reference guide that covers the main details you need to code in JavaScript. This is not an intensive manual.

Use Strict. The `"use strict";` imperative causes JavaScript to evaluate your code more distinctly. It forces you to control for variable types more strongly, which is a better coding practice. You should always include this imperative at the top of your script to ensure your code is as clean as possible.

Punctuation. To code properly, you need to follow a set of rules. Some of these are coding conventions; they're not rules, per se, but they're used commonly by programmers, so everyone understands what they're for.

Case-Sensitivity. JavaScript is case-sensitive, like most passwords. A capital "J" is different than a lowercase "j".

Keywords. Keywords instruct the computer what to do, like declaring a variable or a function, or starting a loop. Keywords are all lowercase.

No spaces in names. Developer-created variables and functions must have a single-word name with no spaces.

CamelCase. We use camelCase to show different words in a chain. CamelCase is like a hashtag with each word starting with a capital to make it easier to read: `carStartingPosition`, `testScore2`.

Allowed characters. Variable and function names can be made up of letters, numbers, underscores, and the dollar sign. Where possible, use only letters. Names cannot start with numbers.

Naming conventions. All basic variables and functions should start with a lowercase letter. Special constructor functions, used for making classes, begin with a capital letter. Start a variable name with an underscore to let other programmers know it's a private variable and should not be changed. The dollar sign is often used by external libraries, like jQuery. Variables that are meant to remain constant and whose values should never change are named with ALL_CAPS.

Semicolons. Every statement should end with a semicolon unless the statement is followed by a required code block (as with functions, conditionals, and loops). Though the browser will understand the majority of your code without semicolons, it is better practice to include them.

Quotes. JavaScript understands 'single quotes' or "double quotes". Either is fine, but be consistent. I stick with double quotes except in special circumstances. Every open quote must have a closing quote.

Brackets. Parentheses `()` are for functions and math operations. Square brackets `[]` are used for arrays. Braces `{}` are used for code blocks and objects. Every open bracket must have a closing bracket.

Comments. Insert comments in your code to explain what your code is meant to do. You can also comment out lines of code to skip over them while you debug your work. There are two ways to add a comment. Use a double slash `//` to comment out a single line of code. Wrap a comment block with `/*`   `*/` to hide several lines of code.

Variables. These are used to store values in a program. They allow for values to change and be substituted into other places, like using formulas in math class. Variables are declared using the `var` keyword. You can declare an undefined variable, or you can assign its value when you declare it.

```
var x;                      //undefined
var y = 33;                 //a number
var myName = "Steve";       //a string
```

There are three types of primitive variables: numbers, strings, and Booleans.

Numbers. A number is what you'd expect: `3.14`, `42`, `-12`. Use `e` for scientific notation. `4e-6` is 4 x 10^{-6} or 0.000004.

Strings. A string is any collection of characters, like words, set inside quotes: `"hello!"`, `"This is a test."`, `"32"`. Yes, you can treat a number like a string, which can cause different behaviors.

Booleans. A Boolean is a flag that is either set to `true` or `false`.

Undefined and null. An `undefined` value means no value was ever assigned to it. Functions return this if they don't have a return value. A `null` value has to be set by the programmer. Use this to control your code and to mark intentionally empty variables.

Input/output. In many programs, you want the user to input some information and let the program react to it. In JavaScript alone, you're limited to the console window or alert/prompt boxes. More commonly, the input/output is passed to a webpage by updating HTML. To write to the console, use the log method of the console.

```
console.log("Hello there");
console.log(myName);    //if myName was defined previously
```

You can also pop up a dialogue box with information using the `alert()` function.

```
alert("Hello again!");
alert(myName);
```

To get text input from a user, use the `prompt` command. Typically, you assign this to a variable, so you can run tests on the answer.

```
var yourAnswer = prompt("What is your favorite color?");
```

You can also supply a default answer.

```
var yourOtherAnswer =
    prompt("What is your name?", "Steve");
```

A `confirm()` box lets the user click OK (`true`) or Cancel (`false`).

```
var playAgain = confirm("One more game?");
```

There are different methods for altering HTML using JavaScript and they all look scary at first. The top priority is to have a unique `id` for each element you want to access, then you call the element through the HTML document. You can do this to retrieve info or to update it.

To get information from a user from a tag that has `"answer"` for its `id`.

```
var yourAnswer = document.getElementById("answer").value;
```

To post information to a tag with an `id` of "response".

```
document.getElementById("response").innerHTML =
    "That's a good answer.";
```

Concatenation. Strings are concatenated (joined together) with use of the `+` sign. `"Hi"` + `"there"` would give `"Hithere"`. Notice that the browser does not automatically add a space between words. You have to do that yourself.

Operators. There are several operators. Math operators are great for numbers (+, -, *, /, %). Modulo (%) returns the remainder after division, so `20 % 3` is equal to `2`, because 3 goes in 6 times to get 18, and `2` is left over.

Operations on variables don't work like regular algebra. If you have a variable (x) and you want to increase its value by five (5), use this.

```
x = x + 5; //adds 5 to value of x, then reassigns to x
```

In algebra, this wouldn't make sense. If you tried to solve for x, you'd get $0 = 5$, which is crazy. Instead, the computer evaluates the expression on the right side of the equals sign (`x + 5` in this case) and when it has the answer, it then replaces the value on the left side (`x` in this case) with the answer.

Operator shorthand. If you are using one of the basic math operators on a variable and assigning the new value back to the same variable, you can use shorthand notation.

```
x += 5;   //same as x = x + 5;
```

Increment and decrement. The notation `++` increases the value of a number by 1, and `--` decreases the value by 1.

```
numberOfCookies++;      //one more cookie
slicesOfPizza--;        //one less slice of pizza
```

Functions. A function is a set of code used to complete a single or small task. It can be called as needed over and over. It is possible to pass parameters into a function and it is possible to return values from the function. Declare a function with the keyword `function`.

```
function calculateArea(w, h)
{
  return w * h;
}
```

Call the function: `calculateArea(4, 7);` This would return a value of `28`. The value can also be stored in a variable.

```
var area = calculateArea(10, 22);
```

However, functions do not need to return any variables. They can just carry out actions.

```
function sayHello(name)
{
  console.log("Hello, " + name + "!");
}
```

They also don't need any parameters, so they're very flexible based on your needs.

```
function sayGoodbye()
{
  alert("Bye-bye!");
}
```

You can even have anonymous functions that don't have names. These are useful in a number of places, such as assigning them to object properties.

```
var beingSocial =
{
  sayBye: function (name)
  {
    return "Have a nice day, " + name + "!";
  }
}

beingSocial.sayBye("Kevin");     //Have a nice day, Kevin!
```

Conditional: if/else. Computers need ways of making decisions. An `if` statement tests for a condition. If it is `true`, then a certain code block will run. You can also set up an `else` statement that activates if the condition is `false`. Conditions can be comparisons, such as if one number is greater than another, or it can test if a Boolean is `true`.

```
if (x > 5)
{
   console.log("x is greater than 5.");
}
else
{
   console.log("x is not greater than 5.");
}
```

The `else` statement is not required, but it is a good way for controlling code. It is also possible to chain several `if` statements together to make a logic chain. When one part of the chain is activated, the program steps out of the conditionals and runs the rest of the code after the logic chain.

```
if (y < 0)
{
   console.log("y is negative");
}
else if (y > 0)
{
   console.log("y is positive");
}
else
{
   console.log("y is equal to zero");
}
```

Logical operators. It is also possible to test for two (or more) conditions at once. Let's say you want to decide if you should wear a jacket. You'll need to know if it is cold or if it is raining. Use the OR operator `||` if only one condition needs to be `true`. If all conditions need to be `true`, then use the AND operator `&&`. You can also use the not operator (`!`) to negate a condition: `!sunny` is read as "not sunny."

```
//this reads as:
//"If it's less than 50 degrees or if it's raining..."
if (temp < 50 || itIsRaining)
{
  putOn("jacket");
}
```

```
//this reads as:
//"If it is greater than 70 degrees and it is sunny..."
if (temp > 70 && itIsSunny)
{
  remove("jacket");
}
```

Conditional: switch. When you have a lot of conditions to test against a single variable, you could use a whole set of `if/else` statements, but a `switch` statement is a cleaner way to go. A `switch` can be used for strings or numbers. Set up all the cases to test, and it is prudent to also include a `default` at the end. Each `case` needs a `break` statement. If two cases give the same result, it is possible to have one case drop through to the next.

```
switch (day)
{
  case "Monday":
    console.log("Wake up early!");
    break;

  case "Saturday": //this case falls through to "Sunday"
  case "Sunday":
    console.log("You can sleep in!");
    break;

  default:
    console.log("Check your calendar.");
}
```

Comparisons. When comparing two values, it is possible to test if two values are equal. To do so, use a double equal `==` to see if the *values* are the same. However, there are some things going on behind the scenes, so you may get some unexpected results.

For example, if you compare a number and a string, JavaScript automatically tries to convert the string into a number for you. Likewise, when comparing a Boolean, it converts `true` to `1` and `false` to `0`. While this may make some comparisons seem easier, unless you're aware of what the rules are, you'll get some unexpected results.

JavaScript also allows you to test if two things are the same value *and* the same type. For this, use a triple equals sign `===`. Because variables in JavaScript are dynamic, it is *always* a good idea to use the triple equals for all comparisons. It is otherwise possible for two different variables to test as equal.

```
//true: the values are the same
"2" == 2;

//false: first value is a string and second is a number
"2" === 2;
```

You can also test for "greater than" `>`, "less than" `<`, "less than or equal to" `<=`, or "greater than or equal to" `>=`.

You may also need to test if something is *not true*. For this, use `!` at the front of the comparison operator, such as `!==` for "not strictly equal to". Examples: `x !== 7;` and `!snowingOutside;`

Loops. A loop is useful when you need to repeat a block of code a certain number of times. It wouldn't be good to write the same code over and over. It is better to use a loop.

There are two types of loops, a `for` loop and a `while` loop. Use a `for` loop when you know how many times you need to run the code. Use a `while` loop when you don't know how many times to run the loop.

```
while (itIsRaining)
{
  wipeOffWindshield();
  isItRaining = CheckForRain(); //this checks to see if
     it is still raining
}
```

There is a variation of the `while` loop called a `do while` loop. The difference is that the code in the block always runs at least once, whereas in a while loop, it is possible for the loop to be skipped entirely if the condition started as `false`.

```
do
{
  washYourHands();
}
while (handsAreDirty);
```

A `for` loop is set up differently. It has three main parts: an initializer that sets a starting counter (`var i = 0`), a condition that keeps the loop running as long as the condition is true (`i < 10`), and the incrementer for the loop (`i++`). You can use any variable name, but `i` is often used as an abbreviation for "iteration" or "index". The incrementer can go up or down and it can do other than count by 1. To count by three, use `i += 3` instead of `i++`.

```
for (var i = 0; i < 10; i++)
{
  console.log(i);
}
```

A loop can also be controlled from within using the keywords `break;` and `continue;`. A `break;` command will exit the loop and move on outside the loop. A `continue;` command is used to jump to the top of the loop and keep going without finishing the code in the loop below the continue.

A `for...in` loop is a special loop used for looping through the properties of an object.

```
for (var oneProperty in myObject)
{
  console.log("Property name: " + oneProperty);
  console.log("Property value: "+ myObject[oneProperty]);
}
```

Arrays. An array is a variable that holds a list of information. Think of a shopping list or a set of test scores. Arrays are set up with square brackets `[]`. Individual items are separated by *commas*. Elements in an array can be added or removed so programs can be flexible. Also, it is possible to access individual items in an array using the index of items on the list. Index numbers start at zero.

```
var scores = [75, 88, 95, 82];
var foodList = ["lettuce", "loaf of bread", "cheese"];
```

Access items in the array using the index. Remember, indexes start at zero. `scores[0]` would be `75` and `foodList[2]` would be `"cheese"`. You can set new items into an array using the index number, too. `foodList[3] = "milk";`

You can also use array methods to alter the list. Use the name of the array, a dot, and the name of the method you want to use.

```
scores.push(83); //adds 83 to the end of the array list
scores.pop(); //removes the last item from the list,
     which can be saved to a variable: var last =
     scores.pop();
scores.shift(); //removes the first element and shifts
     the other elements; can be saved to a variable
scores.unshift(91); //inserts a new value at the start of
     the list
scores.sort(); //alphabetizes or sorts the items on the
     list
scores.splice(2, 1, 77, 78) //at index 2, remove 1 item,
     then insert 77 and 78
scores.concat(moreScores) //add the contents of one array
     to another; this returns a new array
```

Objects. An object is like a super-variable. It holds several pieces of information related to a single object. It can hold variables, arrays, functions, and other objects. Each variable is considered a property and is accessed using a *dot operator*. Properties can be set up when the object is created (*object literal*), but JavaScript lets you create properties on the fly. As convenient as that can be, it can lead to debugging problems and inconsistency in the code.

To understand an object, think of a car. A car has a make and model, a year, a color, cruise control, etc.

```
var myCar = {
    make: "Subaru",
    year: 2015,
    cruiseControl: true,
    drive: function()
        {
            alert("Zoom!");
        },
    registrationDue: this.year + 1;
};
```

You access the information using the dot modifiers: `myCar.year;` You can also access the information using array notation: `myCar["year"]`

Properties can also be reassigned in this way.
`myCar.cruiseControl = false;`

You can make new properties at any time by assigning them:
`myCar.color = "blue";`

If needed, you can also delete properties completely.
`delete myCar.color;`

If your object has functions inside, they're called *methods* to distinguish them as belonging to an object. They're just regular functions, but you call them with the dot operator. `myCar.drive();`

There's a lot more complexity possible, too. The `this` keyword lets the object reference itself so it is possible to perform operations or methods within the object on the object itself. It is advanced stuff and takes some getting used to.

Scope. Variables and functions can only be accessed through your program if they are in an accessible scope. Scope is determined by functions. Something in the *global* scope is available to all parts of your programs. A variable (or function) created inside a function is only available within that function; it has *local* scope. Avoid global scope wherever you can, as it allows other functions to overwrite values.

```javascript
var numberOfSandwiches = 5; //this is a global variable

function makeASandwich()
{
   var slicesOfBread = numberOfSandwiches * 2;
   console.log(numberOfSandwiches); // shows: 5
   console.log(slicesOfBread); // shows: 10
}

console.log(numberOfSandwiches); // shows: 5

console.log(slicesOfBread);
// shows: Reference Error: slicesOfBread is not defined

//slicesOfBread was defined inside the function so it
     doesn't exist outside of it
```

8.1 JavaScript Quick Syntax Reference

Punctuation
Case Sensitivity: HI, hi, Hi, and hI: all different!

Function and Variable names must be one word
camelCase = used for variables and functions
PascalCase = used for naming constructors

Underscores can be used in names: Like_This
Numbers can be used, but not first: thisIsOk2

Use a **semicolon** at end of every code statement;
JS can work without, but use them anyway. This
improves accessibility, use, and readability.

Brackets
() Used for functions to pass info in/out
{} Used to open and close code blocks
[] Used to denote arrays (variables with lists)
' ' or " " quote marks are used for strings
Every OPEN bracket needs a CLOSING bracket

Whitespace
JS ignores whitespace. Put spaces between names
and operators to make the code easier to read.
var h=1; → var h = 1;

Comparisons. Use === (not ==) to compare
equality. === tests for value *and* type → safer code

Comments add notes to code; ignored by CPU
//this is a comment and gets ignored
//put two slashes at line's beginning

Comment Block multi-line; disable code
/* opens comment block; ignores
code; you have to close it with */

Basic Math	Addition +	Subtraction –	Multiplication *	Division /	Modulo % (remainder)
Example	4 + 3 → **7**	4 – 9 → **-5**	2.3 * 4 → **9.2**	4 / 5 → **0.8**	5 % 2 → **1**
Other	x = x + 7; inc x by 7 *It's not the same as algebra!*		Increment: x++; inc x by 1 Decrement: x--; dec x by 1		
			NOT operator: ! if (!hungry) ← read "if ***not*** hungry"		

Variables Store info. Declare with **var** keyword. Reassign as needed.

Type	undeclared	number***	string	boolean
Syntax	var x;	var x = 33.3;	var x = "ok go!";	var x = true;
Description	no value/type	integer or decimal	words/text, need "" or ' '	true/false switch

*** may need to use **parseInt(x)**; or **parseFloat(x)**; to make sure a variable is treated as a number

Complex variables These hold multiple pieces of information in a single variable.

Type	Array [ ]	Object { }
Syntax	*Elements* can be any variable type, separated by commas, all inside square brackets [ ]	*Properties* obey variable-naming rules, followed by a colon, the value. Properties separated by commas, all inside squiggly braces { }
Sample Syntax	var x = ["a", "b", "c"];	var x = { hair:"blond", age:42 };
Description	Refer to elements by their index #. Indexes start at 0. x[0] → "a"	Access properties: dot operator: x.hair → "blond" array notation: x["age"] → 42

Communicate with the user Send information to or receive information from someone.

Log info to console	Display info as popup	Ask for OK/Cancel	Ask for open text answer
`console.log(x);`	`alert(x);`	`var y = confirm(x);`	`var y = prompt(x);`

x = information to display to user (can be numbers or strings); **y** = variable that stores user's response

Loops When you need the computer to do a task repeatedly, use a loop. There are two main types.

Loop type	`while` Loop	`for` Loop
When to use	don't know how many times to loop	when you *do* know how many times to loop

Syntax	`while (trueTest)`
	`{`
	  `//code block here`
	`}`
		`for (var i = 0; i < 10; i++)`
		`{`
		  `//code block here`
		`}`

Explanation	`trueTest` keeps the loop running as long as it is true. This can be a boolean variable or a conditional test.	`var i = 0;` ← starts a counter from 0 `i < 10;` ← tests if loop continues `i++` ← increase the counter by 1

Example	`while (x <= 25)`
	`{`
	  `x = prompt("# over 25?");`
	`}`
		`for (var i = 0; i < 10; i++)`
		`{`
		  `console.log(i);`
		`}`

Variation	`do { //code`
	    `block } while (test);`
	makes loop run at least once
		`for (var prop in object)`
		`{ //code block }`
		loop through object's properties

In code blocks: `continue;` returns to top of code block   `break;` exits the code block

Conditional Statement Allow computer to make decisions.

`if` statement	One Condition	Multiple Conditions	Logic Operators

Test to see if you're cold and if the temp is under 70 degrees. If so, put on a jacket.
 	
Note: `else` statements are not required.
	`if (youAreCold)`
	`{`
	  `putOn(jacket);`
	`}`
	`else if (temp < 70)`
	`{`
	  `putOn(jacket);`
	`}`
	`else`
	`{`
	  `putOn(shades);`
	`}`
		`if (youAreCold || temp < 70)`
		`{`
		  `putOn(jacket);`
		`}`
		
		`if (!youAreCold && temp > 70)`
		`{`
		  `dontPutOn(jacket);`
		`}`
			`||` means "or". If *either* condition is true, then is true.
			
			`&&` means "and". *Both* conditions must be `true`.
			
			`!` means "not". `true` ↔ `false`

Functions Reusable code. Pass in *arguments* to use as *parameters*. Use `return` to send back values.

Function	Popup "hi"	Calculate Volume (version 1)	Calculate Volume (version 2)

Syntax	`function sayHi()`
	`{`
	  `alert("hi");`
	`}`
		`function calcVol(l, w, h)`
		`{`
		  `return l * w * h;`
		`}`
			`function calcVol(l, w, h)`
			`{`
			  `var vol = l * w * h;`
			  `return vol;`
			`}`

How to Call (use)	`sayHi();` *no arguments in ()*	`var v = calcVol(2,3,4);` *l → 2, w → 3, h → 4 passed in*	`var v = calcVol(2,3,4);` *Use `alert(v);` to display*

Array Methods `var x=["r","g","b"];`	`x[1]→"g"`	Math Methods `var x = 36.7;`	
Get # elements	`x.length;` → 3	up to integer	`Math.ceil(x); → 37`
Add to end	`x.push("y");` →"r","g","b","y"	down to integer	`Math.floor(x); → 36`
Remove last	`x.pop();` →"r","g"	nearest integer	`Math.round(x); → 37`
Add first element	`x.unshift("r");` →"r","g","b"	square root of x	`Math.sqrt(x); → 6.06`
Remove first	`x.shift();` →"g","b"	cube root of x	`Math.cbrt(x); → 3.32`
Sort array	`x.sort();` →"b","g","r"	minimum value	`Math.min(x, y, …);`
Reverses order	`x.reverse();` →"b","g","r"	maximum value	`Math.max(x, y, …);`
Returns index of y	`x.indexOf(y);`	get value of pi π	`Math.PI; → 3.14159…`
if y is "r" → 0 if y is "g" → 1 if y is "b" → 2		value from 0 to 1	`Math.random(); → 0.88`

Use `Math.floor(Math.random() * 10) + 1` to get a whole number from **1** to **10**.

303

Chapter 9

Room Adventure Game Code

The entire code set for the game created throughout this book is contained here.

You can also find this code at http://coding.stephenjwolf.com.

9.1 Room Adventure — Version 1 (Text)

This is the code from the end of the initial text version of the project, without any of the added features.

```
"use strict";
var rooms;
var player;
startGame();

function startGame()
{
    //reset the global rooms and player objects
    rooms = getRooms();
    player = getPlayer();

    var text = "Welcome to the Room Adventure!";
    text += " You are " + player.name;
    text += " and you are in a house";
    text += " where many things are broken.";
    text += " Go from room to room";
    text += " to find the items you need";
    text += " to fix what's broken.";
    text += " Earn points for fixing things.";
    text += " There are " + player.itemsLeftToFix;
    text += " things that need to be fixed.";
    text += " You start in the ";
    text += player.currentRoom.name + ".";
    text += " Good luck!";
    alert(text);

    moveToRoom(); //move the player into their current room and start game
}

function getPlayer()
{
    var player =
        {
            name: "Lica",
            score: 0,
            currentRoom: rooms["living room"],
            inventory: [],
            itemsLeftToFix: 10
        };
    return player;
}
```

```javascript
function moveToRoom()
{
  textRoomDescription();
  isThereAnItem();
  fixBrokenThing();
  showScore();
  showInventory();

  if (checkGameOver()) //watch the parentheses
  {
    alertGameWon();
    checkPlayAgain();
  }
  else      //ask for a direction
  {
    var direction = getDirection();
    if (direction)
    {
      player.currentRoom = rooms[direction];
      moveToRoom();
    }
  }
}

function textRoomDescription()
{
  var text = "";
  text += "You are in the ";
  text += player.currentRoom.name + ". ";
  text += player.currentRoom.description;
  alert(text);
}

function isThereAnItem()
{
  var item = player.currentRoom.itemFound;
  if (item)
  {
    alert("You found the " + item + "!");
    player.inventory.push(item);
    player.currentRoom.itemFound = null;
  }
}
```

```
function fixBrokenThing()
{
  //helper variables to make the code easier to read
  var brokenThing = player.currentRoom.brokenThing;
  var fixWith = player.currentRoom.fixWith;

  //test: Is there a broken thing?
  if (brokenThing)
  {
    //get ready to announce there's a broken thing
    var text = "There is a broken ";
    text += brokenThing + " in this room. ";

    //helper variable
    var index = player.inventory.indexOf(fixWith);

    //test: if fixWith is NOT in inventory
    if (index === -1)
    {
      text += "You need the " + fixWith;
      text += " to fix it.";
    }
    else //the item IS in the inventory
    {
      text += "You fixed the " + brokenThing;
      text += " with the " + fixWith + "!";
      text += " You earn ";
      text += player.currentRoom.points;
      text += " points.";

      player.currentRoom.brokenThing = null;
      player.score += player.currentRoom.points;
      player.itemsLeftToFix--;
      player.inventory.splice(index, 1);
    }
    alert(text);
  }
}

function showScore()
{
  player.score = Math.max(0, player.score);
  alert("Score: " + player.score);
}


function showInventory()
{
  var text = "Inventory: ";

  var length = player.inventory.length;

  for (var i = 0; i < length; i++)
  {
    text += "[";
    text += player.inventory[i];
    text += "] ";
  }

  alert(text);
}

function checkGameOver()
{
  return player.itemsLeftToFix === 0;
}
```

```
function alertGameWon()
{
  var text = "Congratulations, " + player.name +"! ";
  text += "You fixed everything in the house! ";
  text += "You should be proud of yourself! ";
  text += "You finished the game with a score of ";
  text += player.score + " points! ";
  text += "Play again soon!";
  alert(text);
}

function checkPlayAgain()
{
  var text = "Would you like to play again? ";
  text += "Click OK to replay. ";
  text += "Click CANCEL to end. ";

  var again = confirm(text);
  if (again)
  {
    startGame();
  }
}
```

```javascript
function getDirection()
{
  var text = "Which way do you want to go? ";
  var direction;
  while (!direction)
  {
    text += "There are exits: ";
    var north = player.currentRoom["north"];
    if (rooms[north])
    {
      text += " north ";
    }
    var south = player.currentRoom["south"];
    if (rooms[south])
    {
      text += " south ";
    }
    var east = player.currentRoom["east"];
    if (rooms[east])
    {
      text += " east ";
    }
    var west = player.currentRoom["west"];
    if (rooms[west])
    {
      text += " west ";
    }
    var northeast = player.currentRoom["northeast"];
    if (rooms[northeast])
    {
      text += " northeast ";
    }
    var southeast = player.currentRoom["southeast"];
    if (rooms[southeast])
    {
      text += " southeast ";
    }
    var northwest = player.currentRoom["northwest"];
    if (rooms[northwest])
    {
      text += " northwest ";
    }
    var southwest = player.currentRoom["southwest"];
    if (rooms[southwest])
    {
      text += " southwest ";
    }
    direction = prompt(text);
    direction = direction.toLowerCase();
    if (direction === "name")
    {
      continue;
    }
    var exitTo = player.currentRoom[direction];
    if (rooms[exitTo])
    {
      return exitTo;      //we CAN go this way, send back the exitTo
    }
    else if (direction === "quit")
    {
      break;
    }
    text = "You can't go " + direction + ". ";
    text += "Please try again. ";
    text += "Use compass points like north.";
    direction = null;
  }
}
```

```
function getRooms()
{
  var livingRoom =
    {
      name: "living room",
      brokenThing: "fireplace screen",
      description: "A cozy room with a fireplace.",
      fixWith: "new wire",
      points: 25,
      itemFound: "batteries",
      north: "dining room",
      south: null,
      east: "hallway",
      west: null
    };

  var diningRoom =
    {
      name: "dining room",
      description: "A great place to enjoy a meal.",
      brokenThing: "chandelier",
      fixWith: "light bulb",
      points: 15,
      itemFound: "new wire",
      north: null,
      south: "living room",
      east: "kitchen",
      west: null
    };

  var kitchen =
    {
      name: "kitchen",
      description: "It needs a little attention, but the kitchen has
                    everything you need to have a snack or host a
                    huge party.",
      brokenThing: "faucet",
      fixWith: "wrench",
      points: 35,
      itemFound: "package with color ink",
      north: null,
      south: "hallway",
      east: "pantry",
      west: "dining room"
    };

  var hallway =
    {
      name: "hallway",
      description: "The hallway helps make the house feel grand, though
                    the old carpet curls up and it's easy to trip over.",
      brokenThing: "rug",
      fixWith: "special carpet tape",
      points: 45,
      itemFound: "light bulb",
      north: "kitchen",
      south: "basement",
      east: "office",
      west: "living room",
      northeast: "bathroom",
      southeast: "den"
    };
```

//function getRooms() continues on the next page

311

```
//function getRooms() continued from the previous page

  var bathroom =
    {
      name: "bathroom",
      description: "You take pride in your pristine bathroom. It's a
                      relaxing place to take care of necessities.",
      brokenThing: "mirror",
      fixWith: "new mirror",
      points: 20,
      itemFound: "screwdriver",
      north: null,
      south: null,
      east: null,
      west: null,
      southwest: "hallway"
    };

  var office =
    {
      name: "office",
      description: "This place is a mess. It's a wonder you ever get any
                      work done in here.",
      brokenThing: "color printer",
      fixWith: "package with color ink",
      points: 40,
      itemFound: "garbage bag",
      north: null,
      south: null,
      east: null,
      west: "hallway"
    };

  var basement =
    {
      name: "basement",
      description: "You hide your eyes behind your hands so you don't have
                      to see everything that's out of place down here.",
      brokenThing: "door hinge",
      fixWith: "screwdriver",
      points: 30,
      itemFound: "catnip",
      north: "hallway",
      south: null,
      east: null,
      west: null
    };

  var den =
    {
      name: "den",
      description: "The den is a comfortable spot to watch TV and catch
                      up on the latest movies.",
      brokenThing: "TV remote",
      fixWith: "batteries",
      points: 10,
      itemFound: "wrench",
      northwest: "hallway",
      north: null,
      south: "cat den",
      east: null,
      west: null
    };

//function getRooms() continues on the next page
```

```
//function getRooms() continued from the previous page

  var catDen =
    {
      name: "cat den",
      description: "An offshoot of another room, the cat den is a place
                    the cats come to play, nap, and meow merrily.",
      brokenThing: "cat toy",
      fixWith: "catnip",
      points: 100,
      itemFound: "new mirror",
      north: "den",
      south: null,
      east: null,
      west: null
    };

  var pantry =
    {
      name: "pantry",
      description: "You have all shelves organized so you can find the
                    food supplies you need.",
      brokenThing: "box of spaghetti",
      fixWith: "garbage bag",
      points: 15,
      itemFound: "special carpet tape",
      north: null,
      south: null,
      east: null,
      west: "kitchen"
    };

  //create an empty rooms object
  var rooms = {};

  //add each room to the rooms object
  rooms[livingRoom.name] = livingRoom;
  rooms[diningRoom.name] = diningRoom;
  rooms[kitchen.name] = kitchen;
  rooms[hallway.name] = hallway;
  rooms[bathroom.name] = bathroom;
  rooms[office.name] = office;
  rooms[basement.name] = basement;
  rooms[den.name] = den;
  rooms[catDen.name] = catDen;
  rooms[pantry.name] = pantry;

  return rooms;
}
```

9.2 Room Adventure — Version 2 (HTML)

This section contains the code for the entire game with all added features given throughout this book. This version contains HTML, CSS, and JavaScript. Each has its own file. The JavaScript file has been split up into five separate files. You can, however, keep all of the JavaScript code in one file.

JavaScript File: main.js

```javascript
"use strict";
var rooms;
var player;
var display = getDisplay();
var passcode = {};
var houseImages =
  {
    outside:
      {
        src: "http://coding.stephenjwolf.com/roomadventure/
                    roomimages/house.jpg",
        caption: "Photo by Rowan Heuvel",
        link: "https://unsplash.com/photos/bjej8BY1JYQ",
        linkInfo: "Courtesy: unsplash.com"
      },
    exitSign:
      {
        src: "http://coding.stephenjwolf.com/roomadventure/
                    roomimages/exit.jpg",
        caption: "Photo by Elliott Stallion",
        link: "https://unsplash.com/photos/wweHSdXdAgA",
        linkInfo: "Courtesy: unsplash.com"
      }
  };
startGame();

function startGame()
{
  //reset the global rooms and player objects
  rooms = getRooms();
  player = getPlayer();
  rooms = randomizeRoomLayout(rooms);     //optional feature
  rooms = randomizeBrokenThings(rooms);   //optional (requires randomizeItems)
  randomizePlayerStart(rooms);            //optional feature
  randomizeItems(rooms);                  //optional feature
  randomizePoints(rooms);                 //optional feature
  passcode = getPasscode(rooms);          //optional feature
  randomizeExits(rooms);                  //optional (part of passcode feature)

  //This explains the game to a new player
  var text = "<h3>Welcome to the Room Adventure!</h3>";
  text += "You are " + player.name;
  text += " and you are in a house";
  text += " where many things are broken.";
  text += "<p>Go from room to room";
  text += " to find the items you need";
  text += " to fix what's broken.</p>";
  text += "<p>Earn points for fixing things.";
  text += " There are " + player.itemsLeftToFix;
  text += " things that need to be fixed.</p>";
  text += "<p>Along the way, you will find pieces";
  text += " of a passcode. Find the exit, and";
  text += " enter the correct passcode to win!</p>";
  text += "<span style='color: slateblue;'>";
  text += "You start in the ";
  text += player.currentRoom.name + ".</span>";
  text += "<h3>Good luck!</h3>";

  display.clear();
  display.info(text);

  var button = "<button id='start' onclick='moveToRoom()'>
                    Start Game</button>";
  display.navigation(button);
  display.image(houseImages.outside);
}
```

```
function getPlayer()
{
  var player =
    {
      name: "Lica",
      score: 0,
      currentRoom: rooms["living room"],
      inventory: [],
      itemsLeftToFix: 13,
      maxScore: 0,
      pathTaken: []
    };
  return player;
}

function movePlayer(direction)
{
  var exits = player.currentRoom.exits;
  var roomName = exits[direction];
  var roomToGoTo = rooms[roomName];
  player.currentRoom = roomToGoTo;
  moveToRoom();
}

function moveToRoom()
{
  display.clear();
  display.image(player.currentRoom.image);
  player.pathTaken.push(player.currentRoom);
  createNavigationButtons(player);
  display.description(player.currentRoom);
  showItemInRoom();
  showBrokenThing();
  display.score();
  showInventory();
}

function isThereAnItem()
{
  var item = player.currentRoom.itemFound;
  if (item)
  {
    display.found("You found the " + item + "!");
    player.inventory.push(item);
    player.currentRoom.itemFound = null;
  }
  else
  {
    display.found("There's nothing to take. You lose 5 points.");
    player.score -= 5;
  }

  showInventory();
}
```

```javascript
function fixBrokenThing(fixWith)
{
  var index = player.inventory.indexOf(fixWith);
  var brokenThing = player.currentRoom.brokenThing;
  var text = "";

  if (!brokenThing)
  {
    text += "There's nothing to fix in here! ";
    text += "You lose 10 points. ";
    player.score -= 10;
  }

  //test: if fixWith is NOT in inventory
  else if (index === -1)
  {
    text += "You're not carrying a " + fixWith + ". ";
    text += "You lose 5 points.";
    player.score -= 5;
  }
  else if (fixWith !== player.currentRoom.fixWith)
  {
    text += "The " + fixWith + " won't fix ";
    text += "the " + brokenThing + ". ";
    text += "You lose 15 points.";
    player.score -= 15;
  }
  else //the item IS in the inventory
  {
    if (playerIsTired()) //optional feature
    {
      text += "You try to fix the " + brokenThing;
      text += " but you feel fatigued and couldn't.";
      text += " You lose 5 points. Try again. ";
      player.score -= 5;
    }
    else
    {
      text += "You fixed the " + brokenThing;
      text += " with the " + fixWith + "!";
      text += " You earn ";
      text += player.currentRoom.points;
      text += " points.";

      player.currentRoom.brokenThing = null;

      //Feature: Getting More Descriptive
      if (player.currentRoom.altDescription)
      {
        player.currentRoom.description = player.currentRoom.altDescription;
        display.description(player.currentRoom);
      }
      player.score += player.currentRoom.points;
      player.itemsLeftToFix--;
      player.inventory.splice(index, 1);
      if (player.currentRoom.passcodeHint)
      {
        text += "<p>You found a piece of the passcode!</p>";
        text += player.currentRoom.passcodeHint;
        player.inventory.push(player.currentRoom.passcodeHint);
      }
    }
  }
  display.broken(text);
  display.score();
  showInventory();
}
```

317

```
//Feature: Making the Player Tired
function playerIsTired()
{
  var items = player.inventory.length;
  var fixes = player.itemsLeftToFix;
  var steps = 0;

  if (player.pathTaken)
  {
    steps = player.pathTaken.length;
  }
  var tiredness = items + steps - fixes;
  var effort = Math.min(tiredness, 25);
  var threshold = Math.floor(Math.random() * effort);

  return threshold > 15;
}


function alertGameWon()
{
  var text = "<h3>Congratulations, " + player.name + "!</h3>";
  text += player.name + ", you entered the correct passcode ";
  text += "and escaped the house! ";

  text += "<p>You earn " + passcode.reward + " points!</p>";
  player.score += passcode.reward;

  text += "You finished the game with a score of ";
  text += player.score + " points! ";
  text += "Play again soon!";
  display.info(text);

  var path = "<h3>Here's how you traversed the house</h3>";
  var steps = player.pathTaken.length;
  for (var i = 0; i < steps; i++)
  {
    var room = player.pathTaken[i];
    path += room.name;
    if (i < steps - 1)
    {
      path += " &rarr; ";      // HTML right arrow →
    }
  }
  display.broken(path);
  display.found("");
  display.image(houseImages.outside);
}


function checkPlayAgain()
{
  //create the replay button
  var buttons = "<button id='replay' onclick='startGame()'>
                     Replay Game</button>";

  //optional: add a second 'leave game' button
  var url = "http://coding.stephenjwolf.com";
  buttons += "<a href='" + url + "' target='_blank'>
                     <button id='leave'>Learn to Code</button></a>";

  display.navigation(buttons);
}
```

JavaScript File: display.js

```javascript
"use strict";
function showItemInRoom()
{
  if (player.currentRoom.itemFound)
  {
    var button = "<button class='item' onclick='isThereAnItem()'>
                    You see something useful in here.</button>";
    display.found(button);
  }
}

function showBrokenThing()
{
  //helper variables to make the code easier to read
  var brokenThing = player.currentRoom.brokenThing;

  //test: Is there a broken thing?
  if (brokenThing)
  {
    //get ready to announce there's a broken thing
    var text = "There is a broken ";
    text += brokenThing + " in this room. ";
    display.broken(text);
  }
}

function showInventory(disable)
{
  var text = "<h3>Inventory</h3>";
  var length = player.inventory.length;
  for (var i = 0; i < length; i++)
  {
    text += "<button class='inventory' ";

    if (!disable)
    {
      //pay very close attention to punctuation here
      //watch the single and double quotes!
      text += "onclick='fixBrokenThing(\"";
      text += player.inventory[i] + "\")'";
    }
    text += ">";
    text += player.inventory[i];
    text += "</button>";
  }
  display.inventory(text);
}
```

319

```
function createNavigationButtons(player)
{
  var buttons = "<h3>Navigation</h3>";
  var toggle = false;

  for (var exit in player.currentRoom.exits)
  {
    var button = "<button id='" + exit + "' ";

    if (toggle)   //add 'even' or 'odd' class to every other button
    {
      button += "class='even' ";
    }
    else
    {
      button += "class='odd' ";
    }
    toggle = !toggle;   //flip the toggle switch

    button += "onclick='movePlayer(this.id)'>";

    var exits = player.currentRoom.exits;
    var roomName = exits[exit];
    var room = rooms[roomName];

    //show room names only if player has visited before
    //and if we're tracking the player
    if (player.pathTaken && player.pathTaken.indexOf(room) !== -1)
    {
      button += room.name + "<br>(" + exit + ")";
    }
    else
    {
      button += exit;
    }

    button += "</button>";
    buttons += button;  //add each button to the buttons string
  }

  if (player.currentRoom.exitHouse)
  {
    //this is all on one line from var to </p>";
    var button = "<p><button id='exit' onclick='enterPasscode();'>
                  Exit House</button></p>";
    buttons += button;
  }

  display.navigation(buttons);
}
```

```
function getDisplay()
{
  var display =
    {
      info: function (text)
      {
        var element = document.getElementById("info");
        element.innerHTML = text;
      },

      found: function (text)     //it's a lot like the last one
      {
        var element = document.getElementById("found");
        element.innerHTML = text;
      },

      broken: function (text)    //Do you see a pattern yet?
      {
        var element = document.getElementById("broken");
        element.innerHTML = text;
      },

      navigation: function (text)
      {
        var element = document.getElementById("navigation");
        element.innerHTML = text;
      },

      gameTitle: function (text)
      {
        var element = document.getElementById("gameTitle");
        element.innerHTML = text;
      },

      inventory: function (text)
      {
        var element = document.getElementById("inventory");
        element.innerHTML = text;
      },

      score: function (clear)     //this is a little different
      {
        var element = document.getElementById("score");

        if (clear)     //lets us clear the box
        {
          element.innerHTML = "";
          return;
        }

        player.score = Math.max(0, player.score);

        element.innerHTML = "Score: " + player.score;

        //if there is a maxScore tally, then show the max
        if (player.maxScore > 0)
        {
          element.innerHTML += " / Max: " + player.maxScore;
        }
      },
```

//function getDisplay() continues on the next page

```
//function getDisplay() continued from the previous page

    description: function (room)
    {
      var element = document.getElementById("description");

      if (!room)
      {
        element.innerHTML = "";
        return;
      }

      var innerHTML = "<h3>You are in the ";
      innerHTML += room.name + ".</h3>";
      innerHTML += "<p>" + room.description + "</p>";
      element.innerHTML = innerHTML;
    },

    image: function (source)
    {
      //if no image exists, set up a blank one
      if (!source)
      {
        source =
          {
            src: "",
            caption: ""
          };
      }

      document.getElementById("image").src = source.src;

      //set up the caption
      var cap = source.caption;

      //if image has a link, include it with the caption
      if (source.link)
      {
        cap += "<br><a target='_blank' ";      //in a new tab
        cap += "href='" + source.link + "'>";
        cap += source.linkInfo + "</a>";
      }

      document.getElementById("caption").innerHTML = cap;
    },

    clear: function ()
    {
      this.info("");
      this.found("");
      this.broken("");
      this.navigation("");
      this.inventory("");
      this.image();
      this.description();
      this.score(true);
    }
  };
  return display;
}
```

JavaScript File: randomizers.js

```javascript
"use strict";

//Feature: Randomizing the Player's Start Room
function randomizePlayerStart(availableRooms)
{
  //create an array of available rooms
  var roomsArray = [];       //this starts empty
  for (var roomName in availableRooms)
  {
    var roomToAdd = availableRooms[roomName];
    roomsArray.push(roomToAdd);
  }
  //randomly pick one room and assign the player to it
  var length = roomsArray.length;
  var index = Math.floor(Math.random() * length);
  player.currentRoom = roomsArray[index];
}


//Feature: Randomizing the Item Locations
function randomizeItems(availableRooms)
{
  player.itemsLeftToFix = 0;  //reset this now and we'll count as we go

  //we need to make a list of fixWith items, start empty
  var items = [];

  for (var roomName in availableRooms)
  {
    //helper variable for code clarity
    var room = availableRooms[roomName];

    //if you ever set a room without something broken
    //then skip the code and jump to the top of the loop
    if (!room.brokenThing)
    {
      room.fixWith = null; //make sure there's no fixWith item
      continue;
    }
    player.itemsLeftToFix++; //now we know there's an item, so let's count it

    //add fixWith item from each room to new items array
    items.push(room.fixWith);
  }

  //now loop again through the available rooms
  for (var roomName in availableRooms)
  {
    //if no items are left, clear other default items
    if (items.length === 0)
    {
      availableRooms[roomName].itemFound = null;
      continue;
    }
    //pick a random fixWith item from the items array
    var index = Math.floor(Math.random() * items.length);

    //set the random item to the current room the loop is in
    availableRooms[roomName].itemFound = items[index];

    //remove fixWith item from items array so we don't put it in two places
    items.splice(index, 1);
  }
}
```

```
//Feature: Randomizing the Point Values
function randomizePoints(availableRooms)
{
  //we need to tally the total point value
  var maxScore = 0;

  //loop through all the rooms that are available
  for (var roomName in availableRooms)
  {
    //helper variable for code clarity
    var room = availableRooms[roomName];

    //helper variable that gets the point value for item
    var base = room.points;

    //get a random number from 0 to base point value
    //add that to the base point value
    var value = Math.floor(Math.random() * base) + base;

    //set the room's point value to the new value
    room.points = value;

    //add these new points to the total point tally
    maxScore += value;
  }

  //let the player carry the total point value
  //just like the player carries the score
  player.maxScore = maxScore;

  return availableRooms;
}
```

```
//Feature: Randomizing Exits for Passcode
function randomizeExits(availableRooms)
{
  //needed variables for the function
  //rooms we do and do not want to have exits
  var roomsToInclude = ["living room"];
  var roomsToExclude = ["bathroom", "hallway", "den"];
  var exits = 2;

  //convert the rooms object into an array
  var roomsArray = [];
  for (var roomName in availableRooms)
  {
    roomsArray.push(availableRooms[roomName]);
  }

  //make sure we have enough rooms for exits desired
  var roomsPossible = roomsArray.length - roomsToExclude.length;
  var numberOfExits = Math.min(exits, roomsPossible);

  //make sure the rooms we want exits for have them
  for (var i = 0; i < roomsToInclude.length; i++)
  {
    for (var j = 0; j < roomsArray.length; j++)
    {
      if (roomsArray[j].name === roomsToInclude[i])
      {
        roomsArray[j].exitHouse = true;
        numberOfExits--;
        break;
      }
    }
  }

  //if we have exits left to add, add them
  while (numberOfExits > 0)
  {
    var index = Math.floor(Math.random() * roomsArray.length);
    var checkExclude = roomsArray[index].name;

    //if the room is on the exclude list, skip it
    if (roomsToExclude.indexOf(checkExclude) !== -1)
    {
      continue;
    }

    roomsArray[index].exitHouse = true;
    roomsArray.splice(index, 1);
    numberOfExits--;
  }
}
```

```
//Feature: Randomizing Broken Things
function randomizeBrokenThings(availableRooms)
{
  for (var roomName in availableRooms)
  {
    var room = availableRooms[roomName];

    //helper object: make sure default set can be used
    var original =
      {
        brokenThing: room.brokenThing,
        fixWith: room.fixWith,
        points: room.points,
        altDescription: room.altDescription
      };

    var brokenThings = [original]; //put default on list

    if (room.brokenArray)
    {
      brokenThings = brokenThings.concat(room.brokenArray);
    }

    var brokenLength = brokenThings.length;

    //pick a random thing
    var index = Math.floor(Math.random() * brokenLength);
    var chosenThing = brokenThings[index];

    room.brokenThing = chosenThing.brokenThing;
    room.fixWith = chosenThing.fixWith;
    room.points = chosenThing.points;
    room.altDescription = chosenThing.altDescription;
  }
  return availableRooms;
}

//Feature: Randomizing the Room Layout
function randomizeRoomLayout(availableRooms)
{
  //optional: randomly return the original layout
  if (Math.random() < 0.05) //5% chance
  {
    return availableRooms;
  }

  //create the roomsArray
  var roomsArray = [];
  for (var roomName in availableRooms)
  {
    //optional: randomly drop a room
    if (Math.random() < 0.05) //5% chance
    {
      continue;
    }

    roomsArray.push(availableRooms[roomName]);
  }
```

//function **randomizeRoomLayout()** continues on the next page

326

```
//function randomizeRoomLayout() continued from the previous page

  //determine the number of rooms per row
  var minimum = 3;
  var maximum = 6;
  var range = Math.abs(maximum - minimum) + 1;
  var roomsPerRow = Math.floor(Math.random() * range) + minimum;

  //determine the number of rows of rooms
  var totalRooms = roomsArray.length;
  var numberRows = Math.floor(totalRooms / roomsPerRow);
  numberRows = Math.max(numberRows, 2);

  //initialize two-dimensional 'rows' array
  var rows = [];
  for (var i = 0; i < numberRows; i++)
  {
    rows[i] = [];   //creates an empty array on each row
  }

  //shuffle rooms into the rows
  for (var i = 0; i < totalRooms; i++)
  {
    var r = Math.floor(Math.random() * roomsArray.length);
    var row = i % numberRows;   //alternate between rows

    rows[row].push(roomsArray[r]); //add room to row
    roomsArray[r].exits = {};       //erase existing exits
    roomsArray.splice(r, 1);    //remove room from list
  }

  //minimum number of rooms per row is needed to figure
  //out how many north/south connections to make later
  var minRoomsPerRow = totalRooms;

  //connect rooms east-through-west across each row
  for (var i = 0; i < rows.length; i++) // pick a row
  {
    var row = rows[i]; //select current row in the loop

    //only keep the smallest number of rooms per row
    minRoomsPerRow = Math.min(minRoomsPerRow, row.length);

    for (var j = 0; j < row.length; j++) // pick a room
    {
      if (j === 0)      //west wall of house: no west exit
      {
        //row[j] is current room;
        //row[j + 1] is room to the right
        row[j].exits.east = row[j + 1].name;
      }
      else if (j === row.length - 1) //east wall of house
      {
        //row[j - 1] is room to the left
        row[j].exits.west = row[j - 1].name;
      }
      else      //room is an inner room
      {
        //add neighboring room to the left and right
        row[j].exits.west = row[j - 1].name; //left room
        row[j].exits.east = row[j + 1].name; //right room
      }         //close else block
    }         //close j loop
  }         //close i loop


//function randomizeRoomLayout() continues on the next page
```

```
//function randomizeRoomLayout() continued from the previous page

  //choose number of north/south connections
  //use Math.ceil() to ensure at least 1 connection
  var connections = Math.ceil(minRoomsPerRow / 2);

  //connect north and south at random along each row pair
  for (var i = 0; i < rows.length - 1; i++)
  {
    for (var j = 0; j < connections; j++)
    {
      var index = Math.floor(Math.random() * minRoomsPerRow);

      //rows[i] is top room, rows[i + 1] is bottom room
      rows[i][index].exits.south = rows[i + 1][index].name;

      rows[i + 1][index].exits.north = rows[i][index].name;
    }
  }

  //create new 'rooms' object to return
  var newRoomLayout = {};
  for (var i = 0; i < rows.length; i++)   //loop the rows
  {
    var row = rows[i];
    for (var j = 0; j < row.length; j++) //loop the rooms
    {
      var room = row[j];
      newRoomLayout[room.name] = room;
    }
  }
  return newRoomLayout;
}
```

JavaScript File: passcode.js

```javascript
"use strict";
//Feature: Create Passcode Ending
function getPasscode(availableRooms)
{
  var passcode =
    {
      reward: 100,
      penalty: 25,
      exitCode: "",
      codes: [],
      rooms: [],
    };

  var numberOfCodes = 3;
  var digitsPerCode = 3;

  //create a set of hints
  var clues = ["apples", "berries", "cherries", "dragon fruits",
                "emu berries", "forest strawberries",
                "golden apples", "honeydews", "ilamas", "junglesop",
                "kumquats", "lemons", "mandarins", "nectarines",
                "olives", "papaya", "quince", "rangpurs",
                "strawberries", "tomato", "vanilla", "watermelon",
                "youngberry", "zucchini"];
  var hints = [];
  for (var i = 0; i < numberOfCodes; i++)
  {
    var index = Math.floor(Math.random() * clues.length);
    hints.push(clues[index]);
    clues.splice(index, 1);
  }
  hints.sort();      //alphabetize the list

  //get the codes we need
  for (var i = 0; i < numberOfCodes; i++)
  {
    var code = "";
    for (var j = 0; j < digitsPerCode; j++)
    {
      code += Math.floor(Math.random() * 10).toString();
    }
    var hint = "{ " + code + " " + hints[i] + " }";
    passcode.codes.push(hint);
    passcode.exitCode += code;
  }

  //create an array of available rooms
  var roomsArray = [];
  for (var roomName in availableRooms)
  {
    var roomToAdd = availableRooms[roomName];
    if (roomToAdd.brokenThing)
    {
      roomsArray.push(roomToAdd);
    }
  }

  //put codes into rooms
  for (var i = 0; i < passcode.codes.length; i++)
  {
    var index = Math.floor(Math.random() * roomsArray.length);
    roomsArray[index].passcodeHint = passcode.codes[i];
    passcode.rooms. push(roomsArray[index]);
    roomsArray.splice(index, 1);
  }
  return passcode;
}
```

329

```
function enterPasscode()
{
  display.clear();
  var text = "Enter the correct passcode to exit the house.";
  display.broken(text);
  showInventory(true);        //true disables item usage

  player.guessPasscode = "";
  //make passcode buttons
  var buttons = "";
  var digits = [7, 8, 9, 4, 5, 6, 1, 2, 3, 0];
  var toggle = false;

  for (var i = 0; i < digits.length; i++)
  {
    buttons += "<button ";

    if (toggle)
    {
      buttons += "class='even' ";
    }
    else
    {
      buttons += "class='odd' ";
    }
    toggle = !toggle;

    buttons += "onclick='addToPasscode(" + digits[i] + ")'>" +
                   digits[i] + "</button>";

    if (i % 3 === 2) //insert a line break after 3 buttons
    {
      buttons += "<br>";
    }
  }
  buttons += "<br><button id='passcode' onclick='checkPasscode()'>
                   Try Passcode</button>";
  display.navigation(buttons);
  display.image(houseImages.exitSign);
}

function addToPasscode(digit)
{
  player.guessPasscode += digit.toString();
  display.found("<strong>Passcode:</strong> " + player.guessPasscode);
}

function checkPasscode()
{
  var text = "";
  if (player.guessPasscode === passcode.exitCode)
  {
    alertGameWon();
    checkPlayAgain();
  }
  else
  {
    var penalty = 25;
    text += "<h3>The door does not open. ";
    text += "You lose " + passcode.penalty + " points.</h3>";
    player.score -= passcode.penalty;
    display.clear();
    display.broken(text);

    var button = "<button class='text' onclick='moveToRoom()'>OK</button>";

    display.navigation(button);
    display.image(houseImages.exitSign);
  }
}
```

330

JavaScript File: rooms.js

```javascript
"use strict";

function getRooms()
{
  var livingRoom =
    {
      name: "living room",
      brokenThing: "fireplace screen",
      description: "The leather sofa and fireplace make this a great room
                    for entertaining guests without the distractions of
                    major electronics.",
      altDescription: "A cozy room. The new fireplace screen keeps the
                    ashes from ruining the floor and burning your guests.",
      fixWith: "new wire",
      points: 25,
      itemFound: "batteries",
      exits:
        {
          north: "dining room",
          east: "hallway",
          up: "staircase"
        },
      brokenArray:
        [
          {
            brokenThing: "sofa",
            fixWith: "repair kit",
            points: 30,
            altDescription: "The fireplace is great to watch now that you
                    can sit comfortably on the sofa again."
          },
          {
            brokenThing: "lamp",
            fixWith: "light bulb",
            points: 15,
            altDescription: "The room feels so much brighter with the lamp
                    fixed, even without the fireplace aglow."
          }
        ],
      image:
        {
          src: "http://coding.stephenjwolf.com/roomadventure/
                    roomimages/livingroom.jpg",
          caption: "Photo by Outsite Co",
          link: "https://unsplash.com/photos/R-LK3sqLiBw",
          linkInfo: "Courtesy: unsplash.com"
        }
    };
// ** function getRooms
    continues on the
    next page **
```

```
// ** function getRooms continues from the previous page **


  var diningRoom =
  {
    name: "dining room",
    description: "With an expandable table that seats up to ten people, this
                  room is calling out for a party.",
    altDescription: "It's a lot brighter in here now that the chandelier is
                     lit. Let's eat!",
    brokenThing: "chandelier",
    fixWith: "light bulb",
    points: 15,
    itemFound: "new wire",
    exits:
      {
        south: "living room",
        east: "kitchen"
      },
    brokenArray:
      [
        {
          brokenThing: "plate",
          fixWith: "new plate",
          points: 5,
          altDescription: "The room is a great place to gather for meals,
                           especially with a good set of plates."
        },
        {
          brokenThing: "chair",
          fixWith: "folding chair",
          points: 25,
          altDescription: "Though not as comfortable as a regular chair, the
                           folding chair lets you sit with family and friends
                           instead of standing for your meals."
        }
      ],
    image:
      {
        src: "http://coding.stephenjwolf.com/roomadventure/
               roomimages/diningroom.jpg",
        caption: "Photo by Erick Lee Hodge",
        link: "https://unsplash.com/photos/el_V6z_h5nA",
        linkInfo: "Courtesy: unsplash.com"
      }
  };

// ** function getRooms continues on the next page **
```

```
// ** function getRooms continues from the previous page **


var kitchen =
{
  name: "kitchen",
  description: "It needs a little attention, but the kitchen has everything
               you need to have a snack or host a huge party.",
  altDescription: "With the faucet fixed, this kitchen is begging to be
                  cooked in.",
  brokenThing: "faucet",
  fixWith: "wrench",
  points: 35,
  itemFound: "package with color ink",
  exits:
    {
      south: "hallway",
      west: "dining room",
      east: "pantry"
    },
  brokenArray:
    [
      {
        brokenThing: "cabinet",
        fixWith: "cabinet handle",
        points: 20,
        altDescription: "The beautiful kitchen is begging for a great chef
                        to get to work, now that the cabinet is fixed and you
                        can reach the mixing bowls."
      },
      {
        brokenThing: "refrigerator's ice maker",
        fixWith: "water filter",
        points: 35,
        altDescription: "The refrigerator is the perfect accent to the
                        kitchen. With the new water filter, the ice maker no
                        longer jams and the cubes don't have that funky flavor
                        anymore."
      }
    ],
  image:
    {
      src: "http://coding.stephenjwolf.com/roomadventure/
           roomimages/kitchen.jpg",
      caption: "Photo by Paul",
      link: "https://unsplash.com/photos/w2DsS-ZAP4U",
      linkInfo: "Courtesy: unsplash.com"
    }
};

// ** function getRooms
   continues on the
   next page **
```

```
// ** function getRooms continues from the previous page **


var hallway =
  {
    name: "hallway",
    description: "The hallway helps make the house feel grand, though the old
                  carpet curls up and it's easy to trip over.",
    altDescription: "With the carpet fixed, you no long trip as you walk this
                     corridor.",
    brokenThing: "rug",
    fixWith: "special carpet tape",
    points: 45,
    itemFound: "light bulb",
    exits:
      {
        north: "kitchen",
        east: "office",
        south: "basement",
        west: "living room",
        northeast: "bathroom",
        southeast: "den"
      },
    brokenArray:
      [
        {
          brokenThing: "light switch",
          fixWith: "screwdriver",
          points: 10,
          altDescription: "Now that the light switch is reattached to the
                           wall, it's a lot easier to walk the hallway without
                           stumbling."
        },
        {
          brokenThing: "fire alarm",
          fixWith: "batteries",
          points: 35,
          altDescription: "The hallway feels much more serene now that the
                           fire alarm is working again. There's nothing quite like
                           peace of mind."
        }
      ],
    image:
      {
        src: "http://coding.stephenjwolf.com/roomadventure/
              roomimages/hallway.jpg",
        caption: "Photo by runnyrem",
        link: "https://unsplash.com/photos/LfqmND-hym8",
        linkInfo: "Courtesy: unsplash.com"
      }
  };
```

// ** function getRooms
continues on the next
page **

```
// ** function getRooms continues from the previous page **


var bathroom =
  {
    name: "bathroom",
    description: "You take pride in your pristine bathroom. It's a relaxing
                 place to take care of necessities.",
    altDescription: "Though you miss the fun house effect, the bathroom is
                    much more serene with the new mirror.",
    brokenThing: "mirror",
    fixWith: "new mirror",
    points: 20,
    itemFound: "screwdriver",
    exits:
      {
        southwest: "hallway"
      },
    brokenArray:
      [
        {
          brokenThing: "toothbrush",
          fixWith: "new toothbrush",
          points: 10,
          altDescription: "The bathroom feels cleaner now that you can brush
                          your teeth properly again. Don't forget to floss!"
        },
        {
          brokenThing: "soap dispenser",
          fixWith: "new soap dispenser",
          points: 20,
          altDescription: "The gleaming bathroom is even nicer now that you
                          can properly wash your hands again."
        }
      ],
    image:
      {
        src: "http://coding.stephenjwolf.com/roomadventure/
              roomimages/bathroom.jpg",
        caption: "Photo by Logan Ripley",
        link: "https://unsplash.com/photos/w8UQkjQ_bS4",
        linkInfo: "Courtesy: unsplash.com"
      }
  };

// ** function getRooms continues on the next page **
```

```
// ** function getRooms continues from the previous page **


var office =
  {
    name: "office",
    description: "This place is a mess. It's a wonder you ever get any work
                  done in here.",
    altDescription: "The messy desk is still a mess, but at least you can
                     print up more color pictures of your cats.",
    brokenThing: "color printer",
    fixWith: "package with color ink",
    points: 40,
    itemFound: "garbage bag",
    exits:
      {
        west: "hallway"
      },
    brokenArray:
      [
        {
          brokenThing: "ceiling fan light",
          fixWith: "light bulb",
          points: 25,
          altDescription: "The room may still be a mess but with the light
                           fixed, at least you see everything again."
        },
        {
          brokenThing: "air conditioner",
          fixWith: "clean air filter",
          points: 20,
          altDescription: "Winter, Spring, Summer, or Fall, you do your best
                           work when the air conditioner filters the air. Ahh,
                           it's great in here."
        }
      ],
    image:
      {
        src: "http://coding.stephenjwolf.com/roomadventure/
              roomimages/office.jpg",
        caption: "Photo by Annie Spratt",
        link: "https://unsplash.com/photos/FSFfEQkd1sc",
        linkInfo: "Courtesy: unsplash.com"
      }
  };

// ** function getRooms continues on the next page **
```

```
// ** function getRooms continues from the previous page **


var basement =
   {
     name: "basement",
     description: "You hide your eyes behind your hands so you don't have to
                    see everything that's out of place down here.",
     altDescription: "It's hard to see amidst the clutter, but at least the
                       door isn't squeaky and creepy any more.",
     brokenThing: "door hinge",
     fixWith: "screwdriver",
     points: 30,
     itemFound: "catnip",
     exits:
        {
          north: "hallway"
        },
     brokenArray:
        [
           {
             brokenThing: "bicycle tire",
             fixWith: "repair kit",
             points: 30,
             altDescription: "The fireplace is great to watch now that you can
                              sit comfortably on the sofa again."
           },
           {
             brokenThing: "shelving unit",
             fixWith: "nut and bolt",
             points: 35,
             altDescription: "The basement feels more organized now that the
                              shelving unit is fixed and some of the stuff on the
                              floor has been put away."
           }
        ],
     image:
        {
          src: "http://coding.stephenjwolf.com/roomadventure/
                roomimages/basement.jpg",
          caption: "Photo by S W",
          link: "https://unsplash.com/photos/mNWsZDYUCFs",
          linkInfo: "Courtesy: unsplash.com"
        }
   };

// ** function getRooms continues on the next page **
```

```
// ** function getRooms continues from the previous page **


var den =
  {
    name: "den",
    description: "The den is a comfortable spot to watch TV and catch up on
                  the latest movies.",
    altDescription: "The TV and surround sound are much more enjoyable now
                     that the remote control is working.",
    brokenThing: "TV remote",
    fixWith: "batteries",
    points: 10,
    itemFound: "wrench",
    exits:
      {
        northwest: "hallway",
        south: "cat den"
      },
    brokenArray:
      [
        {
          brokenThing: "window",
          fixWith: "pane of glass",
          points: 30,
          altDescription: "The den is comfortable now that the window is
                           fixed and you can control the temperature again."
        },
        {
          brokenThing: "massage chair",
          fixWith: "extension cord",
          points: 20,
          altDescription: "The den is a haven where you can watch movies in
                           style, eating popcorn, and enjoying a massage with the
                           Massage-o-Matic 9000."
        }
      ],
    image:
      {
        src: "http://coding.stephenjwolf.com/roomadventure/
              roomimages/den.jpg",
        caption: "Photo by Daniel Barnes",
        link: "https://unsplash.com/photos/z0VlomRXxE8",
        linkInfo: "Courtesy: unsplash.com"
      }
  };


// ** function getRooms continues on the next page **
```

```
// ** function getRooms continues from the previous page **


var catDen =
   {
     name: "cat den",
     description: "An offshoot of another room, the cat den is a place the
                   cats come to play, nap, and meow merrily.",
     altDescription: "The cats are rolling around with the catnip one minute,
                      then crashing in a napping heap the next. This spot is
                      a little place of heaven.",
     brokenThing: "cat toy",
     fixWith: "catnip",
     points: 100,
     itemFound: "new mirror",
     exits:
       {
         north: "den"
       },
     brokenArray:
       [
         {
           brokenThing: "cat tower",
           fixWith: "sisal",
           points: 50,
           altDescription: "The cats love this room and claw at the sisal
                            every time they walk past it. So much better than
                            ruining the furniture."
         },
         {
           brokenThing: "treat dispenser",
           fixWith: "plastic tray",
           points: 15,
           altDescription: "Happy cats mean happy houses. The automatic treat
                            dispenser works again and Merlin, Monty, and Shadow can
                            get a little snack throughout the day again when
                            needed."
         }
       ],
     image:
       {
         src: "http://coding.stephenjwolf.com/roomadventure/
                    roomimages/catden.jpg",
         caption: "Photo by Jonathan Fink",
         link: "https://unsplash.com/photos/Sa1z1pEzjPI",
         linkInfo: "Courtesy: unsplash.com"
       }
   };

// ** function getRooms continues on the next page **
```

```
// ** function getRooms continues from the previous page **


var pantry =
  {
    name: "pantry",
    description: "You have all shelves organized so you can find the food
                  supplies you need.",
    altDescription: "With the spaghetti cleaned up, the shelves look perfect
                  once again.",
    brokenThing: "box of spaghetti",
    fixWith: "garbage bag",
    points: 15,
    itemFound: "special carpet tape",
    exits:
      {
        west: "kitchen"
      },
    brokenArray:
      [
        {
          brokenThing: "jar of sauce",
          fixWith: "soap and sponge",
          points: 30,
          altDescription: "The pantry is clean again and there's no evidence
                  of the spilled sauce on the shelves."
        },
        {
          brokenThing: "spice rack",
          fixWith: "new spice rack",
          points: 20,
          altDescription: "The new spice rack sits perfectly among the boxes
                  of pasta, the mason jars of sauce, and the 25 pound bag
                  of rice."
        }
      ],
    image:
      {
        src: "http://coding.stephenjwolf.com/roomadventure/
                  roomimages/pantry.jpg",
        caption: "Photo by Annie Spratt",
        link: "https://unsplash.com/photos/SvBnIWiLbcQ",
        linkInfo: "Courtesy: unsplash.com"
      }
  };
```

```
// ** function getRooms continues on the next page **
```

```
// ** function getRooms continues from the previous page **


var smallHall =
    {
      name: "small hall",
      description: "It's a small landing that helps keep the other rooms
                     separated.",
      altDescription: "You nailed down the loose plank and now it's quiet as
                        ever.",
      brokenThing: "creaky floor",
      fixWith: "hammer and nail",
      points: 45,
      itemFound: "drawer handle",
      exits:
        {
          west: "bedroom",
          east: "exercise room",
          down: "staircase"
        },
      brokenArray:
        [
          {
            brokenThing: "shoelace",
            fixWith: "new laces",
            points: 10,
            altDescription: "With your laces fixed, the landing looks a little
                             neater."
          },
          {
            brokenThing: "stool leg",
            fixWith: "glue",
            points: 25,
            altDescription: "The glue really secured the stool leg. Now it
                             doesn't wobble when you tie your shoes."
          }
        ],
      image:
        {
          src: "http://coding.stephenjwolf.com/roomadventure/
                 roomimages/smallhall.jpg",
          caption: "Photo by Christopher Burns",
          link: "https://unsplash.com/photos/56tCOHi5OzA",
          linkInfo: "Courtesy: unsplash.com"
        }
    };


// ** function getRooms continues on the next page **
```

341

```
var exercise =
  {
    name: "exercise room",
    description: "It's a great place to work up a sweat and stay in shape.",
    altDescription: "With the spaghetti cleaned up, the shelves look perfect
                     once again.",
    brokenThing: "scent in the air",
    fixWith: "air freshener",
    points: 35,
    itemFound: "hammer and nail",
    exits:
      {
        west: "small hall"
      },
    brokenArray:
      [
        {
          brokenThing: "exercise mat",
          fixWith: "sheet of foam",
          points: 20,
          altDescription: "The sheet of foam not only cushions your feet, it
                           also reduces some of the noise."
        },
        {
          brokenThing: "rowing machine",
          fixWith: "pull cord",
          points: 50,
          altDescription: "The rowing machine works again, thanks to the new
                           cord. You''ve got to get ready for crew!"
        }
      ],
    image:
      {
        src: "http://coding.stephenjwolf.com/roomadventure/
              roomimages/exercise.jpg",
        caption: "Photo by Jesper Aggergaard",
        link: "https://unsplash.com/photos/A97SnfANLeY",
        linkInfo: "Courtesy: unsplash.com"
      }
  };


// ** function getRooms continues on the next page **
```

```
// ** function getRooms continues from the previous page **


var bedroom =
   {
     name: "bedroom",
     description: "It's the most relaxing place you can imagine. And it's
                    almost perfect.",
     altDescription: "Once you pull the covers, you drift off to the most
                    wondrous of places now that the room is perfect.",
     brokenThing: "dresser drawer",
     fixWith: "drawer handle",
     points: 25,
     itemFound: "air freshener",
     exits:
        {
          east: "small hall"
        },
     brokenArray:
        [
           {
             brokenThing: "pillow",
             fixWith: "needle and thread",
             points: 20,
             altDescription: "The pillow is fixed and ready for you to rest your
                         head and drift off to sleep."
           },
           {
             brokenThing: "curtain",
             fixWith: "curtain rod",
             points: 35,
             altDescription: "Now you can pull the curtains closed easily and
                         block out the street light so you can sleep deeply."
           }
        ],
     image:
        {
          src: "http://coding.stephenjwolf.com/roomadventure/
                         roomimages/bedroom.jpg",
          caption: "Photo by Michael D Beckwith",
          link: "https://unsplash.com/photos/XgOr3b5OOpc ",
          linkInfo: "Courtesy: unsplash.com"
        }
   };


// ** function getRooms continues on the next page **
```

```
// ** function getRooms continues from the previous page **


var staircase =
  {
    name: "staircase",
    description: "It's your favorite place to sit with a glass of iced tea.
                  It's also convenient for getting up and downstairs.",
    altDescription: null,
    brokenThing: null,
    fixWith: null,
    points: 0,
    itemFound: null,
    exits:
      {
        down: "living room",
        up: "small hall",
      },
    brokenArray: [],
    image:
      {
        src: "http://coding.stephenjwolf.com/roomadventure/
                  roomimages/staircase.jpg",
        caption: "Photo by Won Young Park",
        link: "https://unsplash.com/photos/zn7rpVRDjIY",
        linkInfo: "Courtesy: unsplash.com"
      }
  };


// ** function getRooms continues on the next page **
```

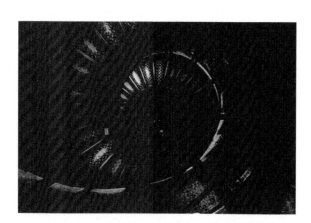

```
// ** function getRooms continues from the previous page **


    //*******************************
    //finish the getRooms() function
    //*******************************

    var rooms = {};
    rooms[livingRoom.name] = livingRoom;
    rooms[diningRoom.name] = diningRoom;
    rooms[kitchen.name] = kitchen;
    rooms[hallway.name] = hallway;
    rooms[bathroom.name] = bathroom;
    rooms[office.name] = office;
    rooms[basement.name] = basement;
    rooms[den.name] = den;
    rooms[catDen.name] = catDen;
    rooms[pantry.name] = pantry;
    rooms[smallHall.name] = smallHall;
    rooms[bedroom.name] = bedroom;
    rooms[exercise.name] = exercise;
    rooms[staircase.name] = staircase;

    return rooms;
}
```

HTML File: index.html

```html
<!DOCTYPE html>
<html>
  <head>
    <meta charset="utf-8">
    <meta name="viewport" content="width=device-width">
    <title>The Room Adventure</title>
    <link href="htmlFeaturesStyle.css" rel="stylesheet" type="text/css"/>
  </head>
  <body>
    <div id="interface">
      <h1 id="gameTitle">The Room Adventure</h1>
      <div id="info"></div>
      <table>
        <tr>
          <td class="text" id="description"></td>
          <td rowspan=4>
            <div id="imagewrapper">
              <img id="image" src=""/>
            </div>
            <div id="caption"></div></td>
        </tr>
        <tr>
          <td class="text" id="broken"></td>
        </tr>
        <tr>
          <td class="text" id="found"></td>
        </tr>
        <tr>
          <td class="text" id="score"></td>
        </tr>
        <tr>
          <td class="text" id="navigation"></td>
          <td class="text" id="inventory"></td>
        </tr>
      </table>
    </div>
    <script src="display.js"></script>
    <script src="rooms.js"></script>
    <script src="randomizers.js"></script>
    <script src="passcode.js"></script>
    <script src="main.js"></script>
  </body>
</html>
```

CSS File: index.css

```css
body {
  font-family: Arial, Helvetica,
               sans-serif;
  font-weight: bold;
}

#interface {
  border: solid 5px black;
  background-color: black;
  padding: 15px;
}

table {
  border: solid;
  border-collapse: collapse;
  width: 100%;
}

td {
  border-right: solid black;
  width: 50%;
  text-align: center;
  vertical-align: middle;
  background-color: black;
  height: 50px;
}

h1 {
  text-align: center;
  font-family: "Lucida Console",
               Monaco, monospace;
  color: orange;
}

h3 {
  color: black;
}

#info {
  color: rgb(255, 248, 220);
  background-color: orange;
}

.text {
  padding: 0 10px;
  background-color: cornsilk;
  color: slateblue;
}

img {
  width: 100%;
}

#imagewrapper
{
  max-height: 300px;
  overflow-y: auto;
}

#caption {
  color: silver;
  font-size: 0.9em;
  font-style: italic;
}

#caption a {
  color: silver;
  font-size: 0.8em;
  font-style: normal;
}
```

```css
button {
  background-color: slateblue;
  color: white;
  padding: 15px;
}

.item {
  font-size: 1.1em;
}

.inventory {
  border-radius: 15px;
  background-color: slateblue;
  color: white;
}

#inventory {
  background-color: orange;
}

#navigation {
  padding-bottom: 10px;
}

#navigation button {
  background-color: slateblue;
  color: white;
  height: 80px;
  width: 80px;
  border-radius: 100%;
  font-size: 0.8em;
  vertical-align: top;
  padding: 0;
}

#navigation .even {
  background-color: orange;
  color: black;
}

#navigation #start,
#navigation #replay {
  background-color: slateblue;
  color: white;
  font-size: 1.2em;
  height: 150px;
  width: 150px;
}

#navigation #leave {
  background-color: orange;
  color: black;
  font-size: 0.8em;
  height: 70px;
  width: 70px;
  border-radius: 5px;
}

#navigation #exit,
#navigation #passcode {
  background-color: #2f2475;
  /* dark slateblue */
  color: white;
  font-size: 1.2em;
  padding: 10px;
  width: 75%;
  border-radius: 0;
}
```

Figure 23. You win!

Remember to check out more ideas and features!

coding.stephenjwolf.com

Did you enjoy the book? Consider giving it a review!

tinyurl.com/roomadventure

Thanks for joining the adventure!

Other Books by Stephen J. Wolf

If you like fantasy, check out my Red Jade series.
Red-Jade.com

Journeys in Kallisor
tinyurl.com/kallisor

The Shattered Shards
tinyurl.com/shatteredshards

The Assembly
tinyurl.com/rjassembly

The Forgotten Tribe
tinyurl.com/forgottentribe

Delminor's Trials
tinyurl.com/delminor

A Shocking Journey

Learn about electricity
through analogies.

tinyurl.com/shockingjourney

Coding for Kids
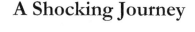
Learn JavaScript:
Build the Room Adventure Game

Learn JavaScript while creating a
text adventure game.

tinyurl.com/roomadventure

Coding for Kids

Learn JavaScript:
Build Mini Apps

Learn JavaScript while creating
several mini apps

tinyurl.com/cfkminiapps

Garinor's Adventure

A Choose-Your-Own-Adventure
Novel

Guide Garinor through the land
as he pursues his destiny.
Can you guide him safely?

tinyurl.com/garinor

Printed in Great Britain
by Amazon